The Hoarder's Wife

A Novel

DEBORAH S. GREENHUT

The Hoarder's Wife

A Novel

DEBORAH S. GREENHUT

woodhall press

Woodhall Press
Norwalk, CT

woodhall press

Woodhall Press, 81 Old Saugatuck Road, Norwalk, CT 06855
WoodhallPress.com

Cover design: Asha Hossain
Layout artist: LJ Mucci

Library of Congress Cataloging-in-Publication Data available

ISBN 978-1-949116-63-2 (paper: alk paper)
ISBN 978-1-949116-64-9 (electronic)

First Edition

Distributed by Independent Publishers Group
(800) 888-4741

Printed in the United States of America

You never know what is enough until you know what is more than enough.

—William Blake, *The Marriage of Heaven and Hell*

Contents

Prelude

"Fear Death by Water"

Monday afternoon, April 4, 2016

"S-s-sorry, Missus," the cab driver stammers.

I half-hear but ignore him as he tries to hand back my credit card with the terminal. My fingers are still tapping out the first movement of a Bach cello suite on the seat next to me, an old, self-soothing habit borne of an anxious childhood spent studying to be a concert pianist.

I have been talking on the phone to my sons since I gave directions to the driver at the airport. The last short stretch from the turnpike to this address is the first moment of quiet I've allowed myself, but it's about to end.

We've arrived at *the house*. This is what my sons and I have called it ever since it ceased to command the meaning of *home* following my divorce from Ludwig Berg four years ago. From the moment Luddy took sole possession, the rotting accumulation of belongings and garbage had drowned out even the metaphor of family.

"Missus? I'm sorry!" I hear the driver try again. This time, he adds a little wave.

"Oh! Right!"

I sign for the ride, leave a nice tip, and then fumble the card back into my purse as I hand him the machine. I want to say something so he won't think I'm crazy, but what? I land on this: "No, *I* should be the one apologizing, for making you listen to those phone calls!"

As if we were in the middle of a conversation.

Hat in hand as he exits the cab, the driver bows his head, waves away my concern, and quickly retrieves my suitcase from the trunk. He rolls it to me gently. I see that he wants to show his understanding, but from a safe distance.

I imagine that his wife—their wedding photo sits on the dashboard just under the hanging cross—is superstitious, and he doesn't want to come too close to my tragedy. He's afraid, I guess, that he might bring it home with him like a virus. He'll have to tell his wife this story. He doesn't want her to panic from the scent of death he might carry from this encounter. Many riders are uninteresting, but I fancy I'm now in his top five most fascinating ever.

At least I've achieved something today.

He couldn't have heard everything, but he must have heard enough to know that he's transported me to a horror show. His furtive glances in the rearview mirror as I spoke of death told me he was on to my story.

I watch as the driver makes a slow U-turn down the block to avoid the ambulance and police cars cluttering the front of the house, glancing over at the driveway where I stand, waiting to embrace my son Simon.

❧

I'm grateful the cabbie agreed to pick me up at the airport. I know I looked like a wild thing—the rider from hell—in front of the dispatcher. Although I was crazed with adrenaline, I still saw myself in slow motion. My flailing hands precipitated the shrinking away of the crowds around me, as if the ocean had parted. People let me cut the line! That never happens at Newark Liberty. I could have been carrying a weapon. I could have been nuts.

My driver risked it. I saw him roll forward, looking apprehensively out the window to take my fare. We both knew that if he passed on it, he'd have to drive back to the end of the queue or head back into Newark. *Que será!*

I guess he figured classical music would calm things down, so he switched on WQXR, keeping the volume low. I saw him cross himself.

"Where to?" he asked, trying to sound nonchalant.

I was headed to a town in the middle of the state with a British-legacy name despite the Revolutionary War, reflecting the largesse of a king, a prince, or a duke as opposed to a more plebeian mill. Many of these mills dot the Delaware and Raritan Rivers, now defunct or serving a random boutique purpose, if only to preserve the property value in each community. I told him that most of the trip would be on the turnpike, so he wouldn't have to think too hard about the GPS until the end.

He nodded with great seriousness.

"I'll give you directions from the exit," was all I said after naming my town. I must have sounded rational enough; he relaxed a little as he pulled out of the queue, heading toward the smallish house on a riverbank facing a wood in a small town in the middle of the state.

The house where we were going to live forever. A little small for four people, but perfect for when we retired.

Within seconds, my phone rang.

"I'm sorry, Simon! I'm so, so sorry!" I blurted between bursts coming from the other end of the line. I had the speakerphone on at first, so the driver probably heard Simon's deep voice, but not the whole conversation. I noticed that he lowered the radio volume in small increments. He would have heard my first question: "What happened?"

Simon's reply: "He's dead, Mom!"

My confusion: "Are you sure? . . . The police are there? . . . Are you all right?"

In between, the words *death* and *suicide* would have snaked through my concerned questions.

Around Exit 9, I told Simon I'd call back because Jake was on the other line.

As if in a round, the same themes were repeated in this conversation with my younger son, only slightly edgier, more rapid-fire: "He could have waited to push Dad's buttons about the doctor's appointment until I came home, Mom!"

I took the phone off speaker again.

"I don't think it would have made a difference to Dad."

Jake was having difficulty getting a flight back from London, where he was presenting a seminar on supply chain management that week.

11

"Near Gatwick? Whenever you can—as soon as you can!"

Poor family, the driver was probably thinking. *Poor broken family*. He might have glanced at the picture of his wife and blown her a small kiss. *There but for the grace of God.*

We had given up believing we were normal long ago. Even so, I knew that each of my sons had tried swimming back toward the ordinary in his own way, as often as Luddy and I had drifted away from it, and each other.

༂

The cabbie had let me off at the end of the driveway, near the lilac bush where my water had broken nearly thirty-five years ago, on the morning of Jake's birth. Each spring, the persistence of that lilac had affirmed everything that was good in our lives.

I notice the bush is still playing dead. Because it's early April, the annual gentian blooms won't appear for a few more weeks yet, until around Jake's birthday, in May. The current absence of scent seems appropriate somehow, given the loss I'm about to confront.

I wonder if anyone here today knows that lilacs were often planted near graves to cover the smell of death.

I square my shoulders as I roll my suitcase up the driveway, past Simon's car, toward the metallic certainty of police cars and ambulances. I walk toward my son, but not quite all the way to my ex-husband's vehicle. The policemen give us a respectful minute to embrace, to cry, to express our wordless feelings. We know the invasive questions will begin soon, albeit with apologies for their necessity.

I learn from Simon that suicide is still a crime in New Jersey, meaning the house I fled four years earlier is now considered a crime scene. Add to this the fact that murder will need to be ruled out, given the dishevelment of the house. I hear the word *carnage*. We two, mother and son, seem closest to the situation. The police already know that Jake was far away in Europe at the time of death, which they estimate occurred this morning, sometime before noon.

It's nearing 1:30 p.m. I know this because I should be boarding a plane at this very moment. When Simon called, I had been on my way to DC to take up a position leading a children's summer orchestra, finally resuming my professional life after four long years of rebuilding following the divorce.

First things first.

Luddy's agenda.

After I make the phone call to withdraw from my position with the orchestra, I will be the one to find a rabbi to help the kids plan the funeral. I know the drill, having buried both my own parents when I was forty-five, nearly twenty years ago. While Simon and Jake are perfectly competent, I won't let them shoulder this alone.

I know there are some rabbis who will have nothing to do with us because of the way Luddy died. As a rearview-mirror Jew, Luddy embraced his ethnicity but was not observant. He had refused to pay the membership dues required to join a temple after our sons had celebrated their bar mitzvahs. Nonetheless, he certainly knew that suicide was forbidden in our religion and that there would be consequences. Professor Ludwig Berg was nothing if not a Distinguished Professor of Everything.

Except.

I know that time will have no conceptual value in the days ahead, despite the organizing rituals of human grief. It's going to be awkward for our family, given the situation Ludwig has created by taking his own life. I'm angry and sad, with these feelings alternating like an out-of-control metronome. And I haven't even spoken with the police yet.

All of this is pounding in my head as the detective introduces himself.

"Detective Robert Brinkman, ma'am. I'm sorry for your loss."

He holds out his hand, and I take it.

As I look at his face, uncertain what to expect from this encounter, I have a moment of recognition. I've seen him before. I have a vague feeling that we were standing on this driveway then too.

Before I can say anything, Simon chimes in with a connection. "Bobby played football with me at Brunswick High, Mom—he was a year ahead of me." *True, but that's not it. Let it go.*

"Right," I nod and manage a smile, thinking, *Relax. You're among friends.* Football moms were near the top of the adult hierarchy in their high school, where dads reigned supreme and the coach was king.

"Mrs. Berg," he says, sounding friendly—warm, even. "I'm so sorry for your loss," he says again. "I remember the Professor made the best omelets."

Smile, Grace. It's awkward for him too. What do you say to a woman whose ex has just drowned himself in the bathtub? I'm just grateful he doesn't bring up the last time we met.

"Thank you," I reply, squeezing Bobby's hand with both of mine. Under the circumstances, a hug might seem out of place.

"I'm afraid I have to ask you some questions," Bobby says. "Please don't worry. We're pretty sure we know what happened here. We don't think you, or Simon . . . you didn't . . . sometimes the family . . . but not you. We just have to ask. It's required. Okay?"

As if he needs our permission.

"Of course. I understand."

Liar. I am way past understanding Luddy.

"Your full name?"

"Grace Berg."

"Address?"

Bobby seems surprised to learn that I still live in town, in a fifty-five-plus community not far away from the house.

Simon walks away while Bobby asks his questions, saying he's going to wait for the coroner. I can see that the burden of responsibility rests heavy on his heart.

෧ඐ

We cannot enter the house today. That's the law. Even if Simon is the one who found the body and called 9-1-1. Even if I hadn't been in the house in four years.

Even if! Even if! A bird mocks us from high in the shade tree while Bobby explains the rules. There's no "if" about Luddy's life anymore. We had clung to "if" for all these years, but it's given way to "when," which is "now."

I look around the yard, noticing that the spiky seedpods from the sixty-year-old sweetgum tree had done their work last winter to over-take the rutted lawn, as if helping form a thorny barrier to defend the hoard inside. Mowing had been abandoned long ago. The house had become my ex-husband's tomb; the bathtub, his casket. The grimy interior with his glorified pyramid of treasures is where Luddy wanted it all to end.

Simon had told me the basic sequence of events—how he had talked to his father, urging him to seek medical attention. How Luddy had bargained with Simon for another weekend before the long-overdue doctor visit, saying to Simon, "I'll go on Monday. I want to be with my things for a bit longer." *My kingdom for a hoard.*

It was an old procrastinator's trick, and Luddy had played it frequently on all of us. Or was it a coded message? Who could tell?

Funny thing is, the time that Luddy bought with this ruse usually resulted in inaction, like the long-ago summer when he'd broken his promise to sand the floors in our house if he could just stay home from a family vacation.

I had driven the kids to Vermont for a week to visit my family. He hadn't answered the phone from Sunday to Friday, and when I'd finally reached him on Saturday, he'd said the sander must have been very loud, and he was trying to finish. Could we stay away a few more days? This was years after his original promise to refinish the floors had landed on a heap with all the others, never to be kept.

We had stayed in Vermont the extra days, and when we got home, Luddy hadn't even started to work on the floors. He had returned the unused rented sander, and we'd never spoken of it again.

On this particular morning, however, Luddy had not procrastinated. For once, he'd taken an unexpected and decisive action—actually, a series of them—that would comprise his last scene on Earth. He would never disappoint anyone's expectations again.

I know the outlines of Simon's story from our phone call, but there's a great deal more to be learned from the bewildered police, who could not immediately confirm that the house was not actually a crime scene. To the uninitiated, it looked like someone had ransacked every room.

"Was he always like this?"

I tell Bobby about my failure to stop the hoarding. *Sorry.*

And how Luddy's anger had become too difficult to live with. *So sorry.*

And how I'd finally had to leave and file for divorce when my fear of his hoarding—and his anger—had driven me out. *So very sorry.*

Finally, all I can produce are tears. There is an epidemic of "sorry" in our future. This is only the beginning.

"Take a few minutes," Bobby offers. "I know it's hard. I can wait for you. Since it's raining, would you like to sit in the police car for a while?"

"No. I need some air."

I'd rather have this conversation outside.

Bobby already knows from Simon that I had been on my way to the airport when all of this must have happened. *This.* We don't want to name it. *This* is the uninvited culmination of our lives here.

Or maybe it was what we'd always wanted.

No. It was not.

After the round of questioning, I look around. I recognize one of the paramedics—Ted, a classmate of Simon's. Football, too.

I imagine, with sudden silliness—you know, the person who can't stop laughing at a funeral?—the entire team gathering, all suited up, forming a minyan in the front yard to sit shiva for Professor Berg.

I had seen Ted since Simon's graduation. He had been working in the ER as a volunteer paramedic the morning I'd come in ten, maybe fifteen years ago, after I had lacerated the back of my head in a fall. *No point in thinking about that now.*

I wave to Ted, who comes over to give me a hug as if I were simply a football mom, revered for my food but not otherwise remarkable. Certainly not a "person of interest."

"I'm sorry, Mrs. B."

"Give your mom my love," I say, trying to make it seem like a normal day.

I wonder if anything will ever be normal again.

⚜

After a long wait, the medical examiner rolls up to the house, radio blaring the Beach Boys' song "Wouldn't It Be Nice?" too loudly, '80s boombox style. Although it's April, it's warm enough to go down the shore even if it is raining. I might have been considering that very thing myself had it been an ordinary day.

The ME lowers the volume after she overshoots the driveway and must turn around. She and her companion are still laughing about something as they step onto the front lawn, but, like mimes swiftly changing expressions, they transform their affects to somber as they approach the driveway. The ME introduces herself as Dr. Patricia Gray and her assistant as Jane.

After they head inside to do their investigation, Bobby moves away to take a call, leaving Simon and me standing together, feeling the old shame of living there.

Our old dialogue of regretful, unanswerable, if-only questions swims up.
Why couldn't he just?
I wish I had . . . but I couldn't . . .

I try to imagine what Jake would say if he were here. Most likely that his brother could have waited—could have forced the issue about the doctor visit at another time, maybe given Luddy another chapter.

I am sure the outcome would have been the same, no matter when they had pressed their father to seek treatment. Ludwig Berg wasn't good at team sports. He always chose the solo—and more challenging—route.

❧

After an hour, the ME emerges with more questions for Simon.

"Tell me about the 9-1-1 call."

"I told the operator he was under the water in the tub. She said, 'Try to lift him out. You can try CPR.' I didn't think I could. He was soaked. Heavy. She said to open the drain."

"Was there blood in the water, or was it clear?" she asks. "While the cuts were inconsequential, knowing how much blood there was might help us establish the time of death."

"Clear. I think it was clear," he says.

"And then what did you do?"

"He was gone. I was sure he was gone. I tried to do CPR. I tried so hard!"

As Simon describes how he lifted his father from the tub at the operator's suggestion, I watch how he unconsciously re-creates the motions of his desperate attempts, a pantomime almost more compelling than his words.

I hold my breath.

The messy interior comes up again—the putative ransacking of the house.

"When was the last time you two were here?" Dr. Gray asks.

I describe once again the last time I'd been in the house after the divorce, how I'd moved to a condo not far away to keep a hometown base for my children. *I knew they would need help when Luddy died. I didn't want to leave them alone.*

Simon describes the agreement he thought he'd made with his father last Friday—to take him to the doctor on Monday. How he'd waited until noon, as promised.

"Did your father ever speak about any intention to . . . umm . . ."

"No." Simon is definite.

"I'm trying to understand how he managed to drown himself, seeing as most people usually fail at this." The doctor looks thoughtful. "We'll know more after I finish the autopsy."

Dr. Gray and Jane go back inside, escorted by two officers.

Simon and I start to follow them, but Bobby holds us back.

"I'm sorry," he whispers. "Police procedure."

After a few minutes, the officers wheel the gurney carrying a body bag down the few steps, bringing it close enough on the driveway for us to touch.

The police go back inside and soon reemerge with various objects in clear plastic bags: a computer, a glass for chemical analysis and DNA testing, and a note, which they hold up so we can read it: . . . *leave everything to my sons. I love you both.*

And, last, a composition book.

"There's a lot of writing in here," one of them says.

"It's my journal," I whisper. "I didn't realize I had left it here."

"We found it on the kitchen table. Funny thing—the space around it was really empty compared to everywhere else. Maybe he wrote something in it. We didn't find any other explanation. I'm sorry, but we'll need to take this with us, just in case."

I nod at the team.

Simon moves toward the gurney. Is he thinking, as I am, about the pending autopsy?

Eight hands reach out to restrain him.

He backs up. "I just wanted—"

"We're sorry, son. Not now. Wait for the ME's report. Once the funeral director takes over, you can work out a time to see him."

Simon complies. He always complies.

"We'll try to wrap up the investigation quickly, so maybe you can come back in the house by the end of the week."

"Thank you," I hear myself murmur, as if someone has just passed the salt.

The black lump on the gurney is going to be one of our last images of Luddy. Although a terrible one, I hope its bleakness will eclipse what Simon saw submerged in his childhood bathtub.

The crime-scene tape on the door has been minimized to two strips so as not to attract mischief, but it's as certain as an armored tank to keep us out.

Repulsion. Attraction.

I want to go back in the house almost as much as I never want to go back in the house.

I don't want to go back in because, now that Luddy is dead, all that remains is a dirty house we will have to clean. Jake will know what to do; he's good at organizing.

Nevertheless, the house that was once my home calls to me again—to Simon too—like an accident on the roadway you have to gawk at in order to comprehend your own safety.

Something in the mind craves restoration. Nothing in the mind loves waste.

I'm not going to let my sons face all of this alone. When I divorced their father, I told them I would continue to help them from the sidelines with anything they needed. I don't know if I did that for them or for me. *Or did I do it for Luddy?*

Indeed, for the past four years I had driven by the house a few times a week—at night, mostly—to see if there were any signs of life. The light from the television remained visible through the kitchen window, and I had checked for it religiously. Sometimes Luddy left a light on in another room, and I would see him sleeping in one of his favorite chairs.

I knew he was stalking me on the internet based on his occasional nasty emails, letting me know he was keeping track of my activities. This made my weekly monitoring seem fair.

❧

Simon and I look past the unkempt lawn to the trees, which over the next few weeks will announce the rebirth of life: now, a snowy dogwood; soon, the buds of deep purple lilacs; and finally, the screaming red Japanese maple. Because Luddy hadn't mowed everything around the trees the way he used to, a few pale violets have bravely appeared.

Awash in memories and suddenly more conscious of the rain, we huddle closer to each other against the garage door.

"You will love the violets," said the woman who'd sold us the house. *I did. I do.*

I am glad, so is Simon, that the police didn't ask us to open the garage. We have no idea what other junk Luddy might have piled in there during these last few years. Clearly it must be a lot, as he'd parked his car outside, on the driveway. Not a good sign as far as I was concerned.

We decide not to take a look today.

All the cars have departed except for Simon's and Luddy's. Feeling the release of legal formality, we walk to each window and look in, like disappointed Halloween visitors, children looking for ghosts in a haunted house.

We speak of nothing for a while after returning to the shelter of the eaves. The aggravating tension of not knowing what Luddy was going to do next, or when, is gone for good, replaced now by the finality of his actions. We stand there in silence, taking in the fresh scent and cleansing sound of rain. I weep more and hug him tight despite his soaked sweater.

"You must be cold," I say. "We've been standing in the rain for hours. Let's go to my house and dry your clothes. You can rest."

My instincts take over, and I hold him even closer, remembering his birth thirty-seven years ago. I'd been his mother for a long time.

All the tributaries of our lives meet here, in this embrace in front of our house.

I think there is no stopping the flood of memory and second-guessing now.

But suddenly I feel myself pulling back. I look up at Simon's face in horror, comprehending that what I'm feeling against my cheek is not just rain soaking Simon's chest, but the water that held Luddy's last breath. When the sob escapes my throat, Simon echoes my cry.

A century passes before we are able to get into his car to drive the long two miles to my clean house.

Tuesday, April 5, 2016

We spent the night at Simon and Angelica's home near Manhattan. We'll go back to Jersey this afternoon, since Jake and Gia caught their flight. Angelica is worried about Simon and me. She worries about everything.

My grandchildren, four-year-old Emma and two-year-old Gabe, want to talk about Luddy. They compete to tell me what they've been told, what they remember, mostly to check it out and to see if it's the truth.

I am grateful that they have both the questions and the answers. My own thoughts are garbled with anger and disappointment, so I revel in their simple explanations.

We discuss the big questions:

"Where is Grandpa now?" Emma begins.

"Wait! I know!" Gabe takes my face in his hands, eager to be the go-to. Like a vaudeville team playing salugi with words, they must have scripted this:

"In *hebben*!"

"In heaven!"

They fight to say it first, right in my face. For once, Gabe is a little faster than Emma, who corrects his pronunciation. I hug them both and nod. *Thank you, Catholic Church or whoever. Probably Angelica.*

The Jewish answer about the afterlife is never helpful. How do you explain to a child about the sins of the fathers? Angelica's religion has the best answer for the questions of tiny souls right now: *Heaven, in all its pastoral beauty*. What happens to us happens to the children, and anxiety is the last thing we need.

Unlike our parents, Luddy and I had never insisted that our sons marry Jewish people. And they hadn't. Among the few things we seemed to agree on was that our sons could love whomever they loved. No conditions.

"What do you think he's doing up there?" Emma, again.

I look to Gabe.

"What do you think, Gabe?"

"Sleeping!"

"I think that's right. He's resting," I offer.

Emma nods her head, "He liked to sleep."

Before we can get into a discussion of why he was always so tired, Angelica and Simon emerge from the kitchen with a breakfast of bagels and fruit. To change the subject, they describe a recent trip to the Bronx Zoo with Luddy.

I admit to myself that I feel a little jealous I wasn't included, but I know it's because they are able to visit me in my new home. Simon would never bring his family into the house where Luddy hoarded, so they had to meet somewhere else.

We chat now about the animals as if yesterday never happened. Soon they will leave for preschool and day care, and Simon, Jake, and I will start making plans for the funeral.

૯૪

I think about my grandmother dying from a stroke, far away in Gibraltar, when I was eleven. My parents may have wished to spare me the truth, but the terrible long-distance phone connections, which necessitated yelling, made that impossible. I knew almost as soon as they did.

My father had to go all the way there to bring back his grief-stricken father along with the body of his mother, embalmed by order of the local government despite their protests for a religious exemption. This was called a *shonda*—a farce. Once everyone thought about it, though, they agreed that flying on a plane with a casket would be less than comfortable without that procedure. My father called the rabbi, and he made an exception for my Grandma Rachel. My grandfather had founded the congregation; what else was the rabbi going to do?

In the end, my parents would not let me attend her funeral, only the gathering at my grandparents' home afterward. My first shiva. After the minyan of men had departed, my uncle became intoxicated and insisted I play a particular song on the piano for him: "Anniversary Waltz." I am sure he did that to hurt my grandfather, judging from the lamentation that followed.

This was the only time I was ever dragged away from a piano.

Having seen more than a few coffins in my life, I think my shiva concert was more traumatic than many funerals I have attended. But, given Luddy's family, I don't know what to expect at his upcoming ceremony. Now that the initial shock is wearing off, I have no idea what I feel about anything. But I do expect to be an outcast among the Bergs.

After Angelica leaves, Simon and I turn to the numerous phone calls that need to be made. He has already spoken with Luddy's sister, Lena, who has demanded that no one tell her mother, Lorelai, about what happened. Although Simon found this awkward, he had no energy to fight it.

First up for me: Find a rabbi. It goes something like this:

"May I speak to the rabbi?"

"May I ask what this is about?"

"Yes, my family has lost a loved one—my former spouse, actually—and we need to have help with the funeral."

There's quiet, then the sound of a deep breath.

"I'm sorry for your loss. I have a few questions, okay?"

"Okay. I'm helping my children because they don't live nearby, and he died at home."

"Oh. Please tell me your name."

"Grace Berg."

"And his?"

"Ludwig Berg."

"Thank you. How did Mr. Berg die?"

"Professor Berg died—well . . . I know this might be a problem, but he appears to have, umm . . . taken his own life."

"I'm sorry, dear. Rabbi So-and-So cannot help in this situation."

Calling me "dear" does not really soften the blow.

"I see. Can you recommend a rabbi who might?"

"Well, you can try the rabbi at the Conservative/Reform—"

"It's just that—well, there's another issue—"

"What other issue?"

"He wanted to be cremated."

"Well, that's probably for the best. Some cemeteries would not allow him to be buried there."

Another wrinkle.

"Thank you. I'll try the other temples."

One mentions the rabbi from the temple we used to attend, but my memory of his strict observances removes his name from my list.

This thankless task takes the better part of the morning.

Seeking relief from the rejections, I turn to mindless Facebook scrolling, and, as luck would have it, I notice a post on the timeline of a childhood friend, Ben, who is both a rabbi and a musician. I send him and his mother a message about what has happened, and he phones me back.

After a few rounds of gee-it's-been-a-long-time remembrances, he offers his condolences and asks me how he can help.

"I don't know if you're free on such short notice, but my family needs to have a funeral for my ex-husband."

"Tell me what happened."

The floodgates open.

The divorce. The suicide. The police. The cremation. The other rabbis.

"Gracie, I am so sorry for what your family is going through right now. First, let me reassure you that there are no prohibitions in Judaism about either suicide or cremation. These customs have grown up over time in certain communities, and there's a lot of confusion. This is not anyone's fault. Your family deserves kindness."

"That's such a relief, Ben. Can you help us?"

"If it's this weekend, Gracie, I regret I cannot because I'm performing a wedding in Vermont. Is it possible to wait?"

"I'll check with my sons and Luddy's family. I'll call you later. Ben, I—"

"Say no more. It's why I'm here."

"Thank you."

"We'll talk soon—either way."

"Soon. Yes."

Simon and Jake prefer to have the funeral this weekend to avoid any more days off from work, especially after Lena screams at Simon that she "has to work, and Mommy has doctors' appointments next week. That will upset her routine."

Mommy is ninety. We understand. This weekend, it is.

I have one more name on my rabbi list. I leave a brief voicemail for Rabbi Jada Goldsmith, including the complications.

Simon finishes up his calls to work, and we get ready to go back to New Jersey, mostly so Simon can retrieve his car and drive it home. The police haven't released Luddy's body to the funeral home, and there won't be much to do until they have him there.

I miss a call from Rabbi Goldsmith. As if she'd had a conversation with Ben, this rabbi confirms everything in her message. "Yes, I can help; yes, even if Ludwig Berg is to be cremated; and I can help you with the funeral this weekend. Can you meet me today or tomorrow?"

I return the call, leaving another message for Rabbi Goldsmith.

I have arranged other family funerals, but this is a new world. Death announcements through Facebook and voicemail for intimate confessions. There is no privacy, but the truth is beginning to come out. Fortunately, Lorelai doesn't know how to use a computer, and Lena and I are not "friends."

Jake calls around two o'clock, and we take an Uber back to New Jersey. Apart from a brief stop to pick him up in Hoboken, the drive is a quiet blur of turnpike scenery.

Jake is either jet-lagged or fuming, I can't tell which, but as we make our way through the turnpike tolls, he announces from the front seat, "This isn't the way I wanted to tell you about our first child, but Gia is pregnant."

Simon and I make a grim effort to be happy for him, which lands like a boulder on the floor of the car.

I'm tapping the seat again. I cannot stop. Pieces of Bach. *Orchestral Suite 3 in D Major.*

෧ৡ

Around the time we arrive at my condo, Simon takes a call from Bobby. He can pick up the computer and the journal.

The police had made short work of exploring Luddy's computer and the other artifacts they had removed from the house. No, they didn't find anything unusual about the suicide. The coroner is apparently disappointed, because she cannot accept that Luddy's strong determination is the only explanation for his "success." Because she couldn't find anything else that would explain his stamina, Luddy will finally be released to the funeral home either late tonight or tomorrow by noon.

Simon drives over to the police department, and I am alone with Jake for a while.

Coffee doesn't help either of us dissolve the fog of grief. We speak in half sentences for a while. *But I knew . . . end this way . . . Aunt Lena. . . Grandma . . . want to know . . . don't like secrets . . . the rabbi . . . why . . . could have waited . . . should have called me . . .* But we conclude nothing.

The baby. We could talk about the baby. But we cannot.

෧ৡ

"I think this belongs to you, Mom."

Ever the diplomat, Simon is stating the obvious, since my name, Grace Feldsher, updated to "Berg" in green ink, appears on the inside cover of my journal. I started keeping it in graduate school as an exercise recommended by Karinna, my harp teacher. She had suggested writing about significant events and using those to create a musical score.

In the beginning, I had made entries frequently, including phrases of music I thought would complement my experiences. As my practice of music had receded and family demands multiplied, I wrote less and less, until Simon had graduated high school and then Jake had followed him out of the nest.

The journal ended with the divorce, and I really hadn't thought about it since I'd left.

Luddy must have read it, though.

I study Simon's face before taking the notebook from him and slipping it into my bag. Had he looked inside? Probably not; that's not his way. He's not talking, so I'm not asking.

I knew that Jake had found my journal and read it as a teenager during Luddy's ill-fated attempt to conquer ADHD and associated disorders. That hadn't been good for either of us. I didn't begrudge him the information, but I was concerned about how the intimacies in my writing might have affected him. I kept the journal better hidden after that.

I have plenty of time to revisit my journal later—if I can bear it. I think I want to read it again, but maybe I don't.

We still cannot go in the house, officially because of paperwork. The crime-scene tape will probably come down tomorrow or the next day. None of us really want to go inside until after the funeral—way after the funeral. Or never. And yet we know we'll have to.

Right now, everything depends on the sequence that won't begin until Luddy's body arrives at the funeral home. He may have crossed the River Styx, but we are in an odd limbo that feels like circling over Newark Liberty Airport without any fresh air.

We lapse into quasi-planning, which is all about expressing intentions but not pinning them down in time. We wonder aloud if certain items we remember are intact and not covered with—the word *crap* comes to mind. Simon tries to prepare us for the level of filth that exists now. I don't mention how Luddy never cleaned a bathroom. Simon cannot bring himself to say "feces" or any other euphemisms, but eventually we get it.

"I was there last month," Jake offers. "It can't be that much more degraded. He wasn't moving around much."

"I can use my imagination," I say.

Neither of them thinks I should go inside at all. With only one parent to care for, they've begun to fear that I will follow their father into the grave, the way they saw my father succumb when my mother died suddenly. My power to reassure them is limited, but I won't be discouraged from going in.

Gia and Angelica want to come too, although Gia probably shouldn't stay inside for long; the air in there won't be good for her.

I decide to face my journal later that night, after Jake leaves with Simon.

Tuesday night, April 5, 2016

When I'd left my marriage, my home, I had decided to put it all behind me and stop trying to figure out my life with Luddy. But now I realize that not confronting my memories would leave me incomplete.

I met Ludwig Berg some forty years ago. I don't really want to tell the story of our time together, but without confronting the shame of it, I will never be free to live my own life.

It wasn't always like this. Four decades ago, my future was filled with promise. Before the house. Before the hoard. Before the breakup.

While our divorce may have removed the hoard from my daily view, the real work of separating from Ludwig Berg has been an ongoing process.

He collected. I recollect. This is our song.

I open the journal and start to read.

First Movement

Salsa son clave. Then, Lamento.

Chapter 1

The Tuning

September 1976

In this Bicentennial year, I, Grace Feldsher, am working my way through grad school as a teaching fellow. Given the job market for liberal arts majors, this makes me one of the lucky ones. Tuition, salary, and health benefits! My parents couldn't believe their ears. These perks are all temporary, of course, but it's a good deal for now. One year at a time. In addition to the coveted job, I also have to complete the requirements for the MFA. And, oh yes, find another job for next year.

"If you want to keep working in academe," my mentors warn me, "it helps to be a generalist." That's Rule Number One. I have kept an obedient foot in both graduate music and writing programs in the increasingly vain hope that I will have the life and job I want when I complete my degree. "The market is terrible," faculty members say to grad students with a shrug. Not their problem. Only a few "special-ists" will advance to the cushy jobs where you teach only advanced classes that pair with your research interests. Many more of us will fall through the upper sieve of higher education into the giant vat of remedial teaching that keeps so many colleges afloat with student loan money but poor graduation rates. I'm a woman who wants to be a conductor. More strikes against me. The revolution has not quite arrived at music's doorstep.

Rule Number Two: "You have to be willing to move away from Mecca"—meaning New York, our culture capital—"if you want to work in higher education." I am not in love with this paradox. I chose this university in New Jersey for its proximity to all the best The City has to offer; and now, to support my habit, I will have to leave the Northeast. And once I do, the question is, will I ever be able to return? If I attain some fame, I might be invited "back East" to teach; but in the middle of the country, where they can't afford to pay for virtuosity, I will be valued only for my teaching. It will be a miracle, friends tell me, if I have time to think about scholarship or performance while teaching twelve credits each semester, plus department responsibilities. Church choirs don't qualify as the concert circuit.

Likewise, states west of the Mississippi don't have time for what they define as "extracurricular" activities. Here's how it goes, I'm told: "It's fine if you want to present concerts, but we really need a music teacher, and preferably someone who speaks another language. We do have a band, but they're pretty much self-directed."

"*There's no place for us,*" my colleagues and I often sing to one another, mocking musicals over a Friday-afternoon beer. This, after reading the miscellaneous requirements on the professional association job postings we must pay to get. No single candidate can possibly possess all those skills. What's worse is that they may already have that person in-house, and they're just posting the job so they can say they've done a "fair" search.

"Be a teacher," my mother has urged me throughout my life. "You'll always have something to fall back on." When I was growing up, there were three main career pathways for women: nurse, secretary, and teacher. My mother, a nurse, nixed her profession as "too difficult a life." Secretary seemed too subservient to both of us, so teacher was the goal. Security would come, she claimed, through marriage rather than a career. During this final year of my education, however, I've felt myself falling further and further behind in the relationship area of my life as I focus on completing my degree and broadening my teaching experience. My parents have noticed this backsliding; this is the era of the biological clock, after all. *Tick. Tick. Spinster.*

I banish these thoughts as I prepare to teach my first class of the day. I'm coaching the State University Salsa Orchestra in an earlier form, the mambo. (Note to self: We've got to come up with a new name. A Filipino student pointed out that the catchy acronym SUSO means "breasts." Diversity has traveled a rocky road.) Mambo is a way into Latin rhythms for them, and for me, a partial fulfillment of my own requirements for the MFA degree in conducting, which includes "demonstrating an in-depth knowledge of three historical periods of music."

What affinity do I, a Jewish girl from New York, have for Cuban music, you might ask?

Among other things, I have studied dance for nearly twenty years, including classes in Spanish and African dance with generous up-and-coming choreographers like Alvin Ailey, Jennifer Muller, and Garth Fagan. I can do a wicked apache tango with the right partner. In college, I had the bruises on my ribs to prove it.

In addition, my grandfather, Sol Feldsher, an attorney who founded an Orthodox Jewish congregation in Yonkers, met Xavier Cugat around the time I was born. As the story goes, Sol was also introduced to Cugie's fiancée, Abbe Lane, née Abigail Lassman from Brooklyn. In the family album, there was a picture of Sol with Cugie. We all became big fans of both, and the mambo became our official family dance. Born the same year as Charo, Cugie's fifth wife, after Abbe, I would often dream of having Abbe's glamorous life with the famous Cuban bandleader. I have discovered this was a popular dream for girls who grew up singing "Babalú" with Lucy and Ricky Ricardo. My Uncle Max took the fantasy one step further, founding a business in Havana. He lived the dream until Fidel Castro took it away. For me, tales of those experiences formed a more personal connection to Caribbean music.

This background surrounds me as I walk into the classroom and set my music on the podium, leaving it closed. Even though this is our first meeting, I want them to appreciate the value of preparation.

My strict piano teacher, Jules Rossi, a Juilliard professor, taught me to play blind, looking at the ceiling rather than the keyboard. He would hold a baton under my chin to keep my head up and me honest. I adapted this tradition when I began to conduct, telling myself that sheet music is for cowards. Is this too much to ask of my students? Perhaps.

I learned even more from Karinna, my harp teacher, who encouraged me to wander off the classical music reservation and fired up in me a love of jazz, even when I didn't practice enough. "Caress the sound with your elbows!" she would whisper when my arms went slack. "Improvise!"

"Good morning, musicians!" I say. "Shall we?" I raise my baton and my eyebrows to indicate the last breath before we play. They will learn my signals. Some fumble to close their music, imitating me, while others search frantically for the right sheet. I don't wait long. I want them to love to come to class. I lead by example but not insistence.

I announce the title of the piece, "*Quizas, Quizas, Quizas*"—"Perhaps," as arranged by Pérez Prado, the Mambo King. This piece was part of their summer assignment to learn for the first class. I signal a measure of rhythm with my baton. I point to the woodwinds to be ready to begin the song. After a nicely executed ascending keyboard *glissando* earns a wink from me, two trombones open the melody, quick on the draw, mirroring each other.

But then the trumpet lags, never to catch up, and the other players must tune it out to keep going. Some hold their instruments too tightly, fearing they will drop them. Others are too casual. All twenty will require some adjustment, whether by intuition or my assistance. Some will figure it out as we play this first piece; others will need support the way I needed Mr. Rossi to press on my shoulder blade or push up the center of my hand. Playing an instrument is physical, involving teacher and student in an intimacy that can sometimes feel confusing.

It's too soon to be quite so familiar, however; I won't touch anyone today. I will simply observe. Like naive lovers, we all need to learn how to speak to each other, and the mambo is a great way to do this. It's all about developing a sense of play, a way of understanding each other. There will be no other intimacy apart from that of our own hands and mouths to our own instruments. Without seduction, there is no salsa.

My baton focuses on keeping time, with light pokes in the air to indicate the entry of different instruments, and my hips dance a light mambo as a visual aid. Although I am lucky to have a harper this year—she will provide a rich counterpart to the guitars—near the end of the piece, the piano and harp miss each other by a mile. The harp is my favorite instrument, and I will work with the harper as if she is my child. As a harper and pianist, I have learned to conduct in a way that defines and balances the strings against the other tones. Pedals and plucking. It will become a dance like the *clack* and echo of castanets.

After the sound of plucking leaves the air, I set down my baton. I briefly notice Paul West, our program chair, lurking at the door of my classroom, but he moves on without coming in.

"Well, we certainly have work to do!" I announce. I try to smile conspiratorially, even though I know some of them are churning inside, dejected. They all have the chance to improve, and by the end of the semester, there will be euphony—hopefully just in time for our January field study in Puerto Rico to learn about salsa.

"This is a mambo. Have any of you ever danced one before?"

Puzzled eyes and a few sideways glances ripple through the room. No one volunteers to answer.

"When you dance the mambo," I say, "you must keep a tight frame on your upper body, because the action is all in your legs. From your shoulder blades up, your aura must be taut, perpendicular." I watch them unconsciously assuming the position. I dance again, saying, "So, when you play, the same thing happens with the melody—it's taut! The rhythm moves back and forth, side to side, above and beneath the song. Where are you in the body when you play it? Think about it!" Their arms, legs, and instruments twitch briefly to find the space. This is what I want them to feel. "Your body will show you where and how to make a sound. Let's try it again."

They shuffle back to the first page of their music. I raise my baton. The piano slide sounds even more authentic this time; the trombones, more subtle; the trumpet keeps pace. We're a long way from ready for the January field study, but I have their hearts, and I will dance with their minds. I have a good feeling as we move through the piece a few times.

Too soon, the hour comes to an end. Most wave shyly with a smile as they leave, but the bassist stays behind as I pack up my music and baton. He doesn't speak, though he seems to have something pressing on his mind. He walks with me to the door of the building. I look at my watch to signal that I must go. I have just twenty minutes to run to the other side of campus to teach a WAC class. Writing Across the Curriculum. *Wordsmith Mr. Hyde, meet well-tuned Dr. Jekyll.*

Some students are clingy. During class, they enter a world they'd never imagined, and saying goodbye to the teacher means being cast out of that world. I'd felt bereft like that myself at times. School was my sanctuary growing up; I'd never loved snow days.

But today I must not linger. If I were a hypnotist, I would snap my fingers to help him. Instead, I reach for my keys and shake them purposefully to break the spell. He has talent and feeling—I know this already. But my WAC class won't wait long. Students are obligated to wait only fifteen minutes if I'm late, so I can't afford to stay for the small talk necessary to soothe his nerves.

Say something! I smile to feign patience.

He opens his mouth. Nothing comes out at first, then—"Thank you, Professor!"

"You're welcome!" I shout warmly as I tear down the steps, heading for the shortcut lane across the quad.

Chapter 2

The List

Fall 1976

"Is it here? Do you have it?"

I belt the title of an old song to Lee—"Our Day Will Come"—before sashaying down the steps like Ruby Nash.

"Stop singing! Where is it?"

"Name the artist and the year," I tease.

"Ruby and the Romantics—1963?"

"Damn! I can't fool you."

"Come on—where is it?" "Okay—wait! Here." Lee is tugging at my blouse like a toddler even though she's my contemporary in grad school. The job search has reduced us to children.

We're sharing a subscription to the "Bible"—the pricey Modern Language Association Job List. You cannot search for a job without paying for this vital resource. Although we're competing for similar generalist positions, the need to economize is dwarfing our need for privacy. We're friends, and we have sworn not to let this job search destroy our relationship.

If there is a goddess, I will find a job that focuses on teaching both music and writing, and Lee will find one that focuses on teaching writing, or, miraculously, literature, the holy grail of the PhD candidate. Finding a listing is only the first step. We are each secretly afraid we're kidding ourselves.

"I haven't opened it yet. Let's go to the office and sit down."

Lee breathes a sigh of relief. We are neck and neck in the race to send out our dossiers. *Early bird. Worm. Umm—job.* All the clichés we would ax with red ink in our students' papers are coming fast and furiously into my mind as we race down the hall to the adjunct room.

That's who we are—add-ons who support the teaching effort in the writing department. We're expendable and cheap, and we teach most of the rudiments of the discipline. "Real faculty don't teach freshmen" is a contractual axiom of most universities. Thank goodness for us, that's the norm, or we would never get enough experience to seek a job anywhere.

While Lee and I had both excelled in our courses, each creating sufficient scholarship to command an interview, the few plum jobs in writing instruction that might be available are usually filled by the old boy network—emphasis on *boy*—before they are posted, and usually by people who have never taught but have attended Ivy League institutions.

I, an interloper from the music department—by special exemption, because they couldn't find enough classes for my load—am only barely tolerated by Lee in this quest. This is because the generalist jobs I am seeking are the ones for a "writing across the curriculum teacher who can also teach piano or harp, or—*Jeez!* [*sic*, expletive mine]—the French horn." I can do two out of three of those instruments, so Lee would not even apply for that offer.

I could also choose to apply for writing-only jobs, and no one would be the wiser unless I got one. I could live with Lee's disapproval, but I'm not going to be able to live without a job.

We tear the list in half to save time.

While my mother believes college is the best route toward a generous engagement ring, I have somehow managed to evade this happily-ever-after through numerous faulty relationships during my college and grad school careers. As Lee and I thumb through our pages, marking *X*'s in different-color pens throughout, I can hear Mom's voice in my head: "No boy will talk to you if you get a PhD." We had compromised on an MFA for me, though the idea of a doctorate was still lurking in the back of my mind. *Someday my prince will come*—and I used the word *prince* advisedly.

"Grace! This one's perfect for you!"

"Where is it? Wyoming?"

That's our standard response for outlandish offers we can't see ourselves taking.

"Actually, yes!"

"You're kidding."

"Read it!"

Generalist Wanted.

Were we criminals? My mother thought so.

Writing Instructor—9 credits of Remedial Composition plus 3 credits of instruction in either piano or harp.

"It's you!" Lee shrieks.

"It's Cody, Wyoming!" I glare at her.

"How many harpers do you suppose there are who have MFAs in music and have taught writing across the curriculum? This has your name all over it!"

"I don't own a horse."

"But you could bring jazz to Wyoming!"

Maybe it could work. I am honor-bound to try. Even if my parents kill me for going so far away. Brought to you by today's earworm: "Don't Fence Me In."

"It says they'll pay your expenses to interview on-site."

That's unusual. What can I lose?

"I'll take a look at it tonight."

"Better get the letter out tomorrow—this probably came by Pony Express."

"Stop laughing! Anything for you in there?"

"I'm still looking. They don't seem to be offering any vegan yoga poetry instructor positions this month."

"That's a shame, given all the kale and hummus you've eaten this past year."

I deserve her light shove on my shoulder.

What would become of us? The faculty had warned us there were no jobs when we'd started three years ago. Nonetheless, our programs had been more than happy to take our money, and we were young enough to believe that anything could happen by the time we'd completed our degrees.

Three years had flown by, but the economy and the hiring process remained stuck in neutral as we approached the completion of our master's projects. I have a teaching license, but Lee doesn't, which gives me a slight edge.

"What does your weekend look like?"

"I'm waiting for a call from that guy—"

"The one your dad set you up with?"

"That one, yes."

"Maybe he'll be . . . *the one!*" Lee jokes, and I smile while rolling my eyes.

My father is a kind and affable family practitioner often compared to TV's Marcus Welby, MD. A great diagnostician and a good judge of people, he usually values our family's privacy, which is why I was so surprised to hear that he had uncharacteristically given out my phone number to one of his patients for the son of her friend, who was, she insisted, "a math professor, age twenty-nine, at the very same university." Contemporary matchmaking. I don't have high hopes, but I'm coming off a weird dating cycle that hasn't even produced a reliable drinking buddy, let alone a fiancé, so why not?

"I wonder if he has a pocket protector?"

"Lee!"

"Kidding."

"You don't have a very open mind."

"I wish you well, kiddo. We both deserve some reward after all this job search pain. Maybe he'll be normal."

"Let me photocopy that Wyoming page. I'll start brushing up on my roping skills tonight."

I make a copy of the listing, skimming for something a little more promising before I return it to her.

"They say all the good jobs get posted in October," I say, to make us both feel better.

"I can't wait," she says dramatically.

"We're going to figure this out."

"How?" she wails.

"I'm not sure yet, but it can't be this way forever. See you Monday if the math professor hasn't swept me off my feet by then."

"You'd better come back. I can't face this alone!" she says, waving the Bible.

"Dinner on Monday?" I offer. "Jazz concert at eight?"

"Where? At that place off College Street?"

"Where else?"

I make a mental note to head to the library to do some research on Cody, home of Buffalo Bill. *Go west, not-so-young musician girl. Cowgirl in the Sand.*

I leave Lee in the adjunct room to pore over the meager list, and scurry back across campus again to pick up my harp from its locker in the music building. I'm looking forward to the next day, which is committed to practice, paper grading, and lesson planning for Wednesday.

As I walk the diagonal paths across the quads, I consider what was missing from this morning's salsa practice. *Duh! Congas!* We were trying to play mambo without percussion. I don't know why I didn't think of it before. First-day jitters, probably. Tunnel vision. I didn't take attendance; I never do on the first day. The percussionist had been absent—a student who had lobbied so hard to be in the orchestra but had already missed a day of practice. Not funny. We can't really play salsa without percussion.

The headache begins. What else did I miss, being so caught up in the moment? I roll it over countless ways in my mind. *Did the students notice? Maybe that's why they were having difficulty. What am I going to do? We are one-deep in all but woodwinds. I don't have time to recruit someone. Damn.* He'd better have a good reason.

By now I'm at Music Hall. Before I pick up the harp, I go to my mailbox; sure enough, there's a phone message taken by Adele, the department secretary: "Robert Joseph, a student in Music 347, is unable to come to class today. He will explain when he returns next week." Partial relief. What should I do? Haven't I ever missed a class? Sure. How am I going to handle this? I hate having to be such a hard ass so early in the semester, but we really can't keep a concert schedule if people don't attend class once a week and practice on their own during the rest of the week. I tuck the rest of my mail in my bag to look at later.

Adele peeks into the mailroom. "I thought I saw you, Grace."

"Hi, Adele. Thanks for the message."

"He didn't say much."

"Suspense is his ace in the hole, I guess."

"Good one!" She laughs. Adele is the music program's chief morale officer and Mama Bear to the graduate students. She can find humor in almost anything.

"By the way," she says, "Dr. West wants you to drop by if you have time this afternoon."

If I have time. No one ignores a summons from the program chair.

"Is he in now?"

"Yes—nothing on the calendar until 4:30. Shall I tell him you're coming in?"

"Of course. Give me two minutes, please?"

As Adele turns to go, I rearrange my belongings. I need a moment to compose myself in case he wants to talk about a student. I'll collect my harp after I see what this is about.

A few moments later, Adele ushers me into Dr. West's office.

He points to the one chair I don't want to sit in—one of those sink-into-oblivion constructions that you cannot get out of without serious awkwardness. I sit.

He's the program chair. He chooses everyone's seat.

"Grace," he intones, as if he's invoking a spirit rather than greeting me. He shuffles a stack of papers in front of him. When he looks up again, I answer.

"Dr. West." I smile, claiming courage for myself, remembering how he lurked outside my classroom door.

"I couldn't help but notice the way you were conducting the salsa orchestra today."

"Umm . . . they're a little rusty from the summer, but there were a lot of dedicated people in the room."

"No doubt. It's you I noticed."

My dry throat prevents me from answering right away.

"I'm not sure how to say this, Grace. . . . Don't you think what you're doing is a tad provocative?"

Nobody really says "tad" anymore, do they?

"Provocative? In what way?"

"Well—dancing in front of young students—mambo, lambada— whatever that was? I don't need any complaints here. Do you understand?"

"Professor West, I'm conducting an orchestra. Many students have never seen a performance of this music. I find that the dance steps help many people to understand the sound. I—I always use my body when I conduct—"

"Sure. Hands, arms, a tilt of your head, your face—but your hips?"

"I can't just erase them!" I laugh a little at the image.

"This is serious. I don't want to have to speak to you again. Restrain yourself!"

"I'll try, but I'm not sure I know another way to make the point about the rhythm—"

"Let me put this another way. You're almost finished with your master's. Don't make any waves that could drown you."

I look down at the floor.

"I understand."

He is quiet for a moment. And then his face brightens.

"You know, there's a way I could . . . protect you."

"From what?"

I play dumb, but I have a pretty good idea of what's coming. There's a reason we call him Paws—a rumor about harassment—which makes this conversation even more hypocritical than our usual exchanges.

"C'mon, honey. We're both adults."

He comes out from behind the desk and sets his well-muscled, six-foot frame next to my tiny five-foot one. He towers over me. He places his hand over mine on the upholstered armchair, pressing it down hard into the paisley embroidery.

I try not to quiver, which he could read as vulnerability. If I confront him, he will deny it.

The discussion about my conducting was a ruse to protect himself ahead of time if I complain.

I start to answer, but he interrupts me.

"Don't give me an answer now. Think about it. It's hard to start a career in conducting. I know people. You will need a great many . . . protectors."

He isn't wrong, but what he is suggesting makes me feel more than uncomfortable.

"Thank you for your concern."

I pull my hand away and stand up to move to the door quickly.

"Stop by next Monday, Grace. We'll chat. I have an interest in you."

I try to run past Adele, but she stops me with some forms.

"Everything okay?"

I roll my eyes. She understands.

"He's a paper tiger. Stand your ground," she says sympathetically.

"Is there any other way?" I half-smile.

"I need these by Friday."

"I'll stop in then."

"Thanks—it's for your benefits. Don't forget!"

I hadn't planned on coming back this week, but Paws never shows up on Friday, his research day, so at least he won't be there to pressure me any further.

Suddenly, this semester seems like it might be a real pain.

Tuesday night, April 5, 2016

I hadn't thought about Paul West for a long time. My professors had been so professional otherwise, and his advances came as a shock. But I stood my ground, and didn't give in.

There would be other challenges that year.

And then there was Luddy.

Chapter 3

The Call

Fall 1976

Davina Weiss. My father called her Ducky. No one ever said "no" to Ducky.

That moment when you give in to an impulse—that's how my relationship with Luddy started. My father did something he would normally never do: He gave my phone number to his patient Davina so her friend Lorelai's son, Ludwig, could call me. Dad was an old-school, house call–making family doctor who agreed to Mrs. Weiss's request.

A blind date. I could have said no, but she was a nice lady. A nice lady who would be obeyed. My parents, Steven and Ginger Feldsher, had known her for years. They were friends—a rare thing, as my mother seldom let Dad's patients cross that Rubicon of familiarity. My mom said, "Doesn't it stand to reason that Ducky would have nice friends whose children were also . . . nice?" My mother is tricky that way—it may sound like a question, but it's really a statement. A command.

Dad must have grown weary of worrying about his daughter in her mid-twenties spending more time on school than on seeking a mate. Or weary of my mother's greater worry about said situation. So the affair started with my parents' blessing. *Did my parents make the requisite Beethoven joke? Can you sing "Matchmaker"? I can hear Ducky saying, "Would it hurt to try? They're at the same university!"*

Luddy was described as twenty-nine (about five years younger than he was) and a professor of math or something at the same university where I was completing my MFA. *You know the drill:* He should be described as a rich scholar—if anyone is really listening, an oxymoron. This general portrait allowed him passage through my father's usually protective filters. He gave out my number. Disarmed by my father's rare enthusiasm, I gave in. Apparently, neither Luddy nor I had high expectations, but we both gambled because parents were involved. And Ducky. Resisting would have been worse.

Luddy called me. We laughed about the awkwardness of our meeting being engineered by Jewish mothers and fathers, and we agreed to make a date. So far, so normal. He offered me the choice of riding in a beat-up Vega or on a BMW motorcycle. The day before our date I was having a cast removed from my leg—a tennis injury—so I picked the Vega, making sure to mention that I would enjoy riding with him on the bike another time.

Note to self: When someone advertises that they drive a messy car, believe that this statement is a synecdoche for the rest of his life. Understand that you may be entering the deep. Open your eyes. There were clues.

When I answered the door that night, I looked up at the silver chain on his chest that was visible through his open shirt. It screamed 1970s. (It was the 1970s.) My eyes continued up higher to see intense blue eyes and curly black-brown hair and a smile that said, "Wow! I'm not disappointed!" So I relaxed a little. Tinted aviators. Not too geeky. True confession: I, too, was dressed as an unbuttoned disco refugee. He told me later that when he came upstairs to meet my roommate, Annie, for the once-over, he thought about backing out because he thought I might be too neat for him. *Sweet blindness.*

Off we went in his paper-cluttered car to an evening of mutually enjoyed Indian food, wine, conversation, sex, and what would turn out to be a lifetime together. I remember we jousted over topics from all branches of knowledge. I didn't hold back, despite my parents' perennial warning that no boy wanted to talk to a smart girl.

"What do you do?" I asked him.

"I'm a failure analyst—I study the bonding of materials at the subatomic structure." He let on that he was internationally recognized.

I giggled, noting the intriguing paradox in being a successful failure analyst.

Sorry, Dad, I'm off to the races.

Fortunately, Luddy thought I was amusing.

"How would you describe what you do, Grace?"

"I study the spaces between the notes."

We bantered about everything we could think of while the wine and curry flowed.

My favorite word for a sixty-fourth note, *hemidemisemiquaver*, was matched by his *Prince Rupert's Tear*, a heat-shocked glass bead. He read everything. We had the same annotated volume of William Blake with the drawings. We compared my Mozart to his Wagner. Beethoven for both and, of all things, Debussy's "Children's Corner Suite." Most of all, Antonio Carlos Jobim, and salsa!

We went back to his apartment, and after he cleaned up his room a little so we could find his bed, our first date lasted into the very early hours of the next morning. The words we could not say fast enough turned to kisses, turned to tumbling into one another, our partial, shadowy images reflected and refracted—"Those are not the same things," he would correct me—all over the room on the smoky mirror tiles that crowned his bed and made a canopy on the ceiling.

A little disorganized? Somewhat-absentminded professor? He copped to both. In my careless vetting, I felt those qualities could be fixed or lived with. I closed my eyes.

He was my soulmate.

❧

The next morning, Luddy's parents were coming to visit with his young nephew, Lena's son, and he wanted me to meet them. I hesitated. We'd only had one date. Was I ready for two? My cushy fellowship at the literary quarterly University Review had ended, and I had just started dual teaching positions in music and English comp. Forty student essays were calling my name from the first week of classes. Not far behind, a long reading list plus performance practice for my comprehensive exams tapped their sadistic feet. And SUSO! Luddy's playful intensity beckoned.

"Come on," Luddy said. "We'll go to the faculty pool for a few hours. You can bring the papers with you if that would make you feel better. It'll be fun!"

I was curious to meet his parents, not to mention having to face Ducky if I declined, so I gave in to his impulse for procrastination. *Just this once. What's a little adrenaline in the life of a grad student?* Plus, we'd clicked. I could still grade papers on Monday.

In fact, I'd had a dream about him during the one hour we'd slept. Upon reflection, I wasn't sure if it signified safety or threat.

In the dream, it's a gloomy day. I'm standing in my front yard, searching the sky for clues. A silver Chevy Vega pulls up, and Luddy yells out the window, "Get in the car!" I don't ask why. He breaks the speed limits on the strangely deserted highway to the university, so in ten minutes we are at the engineering building where he works.

He gets out of the car, and I follow him. As we run down a maze of monotonous concrete hallways, I ask questions he doesn't answer. *Where are we going? Why?*

Eventually he pauses at a door and takes an enormous ring of keys from his belt. He tries a few different ones. When one works, he heaves open a heavy metal door and motions for me to follow him as he sprints down a long flight of stairs. I'm surprised there is a basement in this building.

I try to keep up. It resembles the dark frightening basement of my elementary school, known as "the dungeon," where we would wait out the 1950s vision of nuclear holocaust.

I'm wary of going to the end of the room. He keeps encouraging me until we reach some debris. Luddy groans loudly as he shoves the obstacles away to expose a wall. He locates a handle and tries to slide the door open. At first, it won't budge. He rocks it back and forth a little, tugs, and finally it loosens.

Luddy motions for me to follow him, and once we're inside, he slides the door closed.

"We'll be safe here!" he exclaims.

"What are we doing?"

"There will be radiation. There's enough lead in these walls to give us a fighting chance."

I feel safe here, far from the chaos outside. Security is my main motivation in this world.

I had this same dream most nights during the early days of our relationship—most likely, my subconscious stepping in to corral my fears and doubts. How did I learn how to hold my breath and jump in?

In later years, when the dream returned, I could never be sure if it meant Luddy was my salvation or my prison.

His family.

Lena, Luddy's sister, was on safari in Africa with her husband, Joel Marcus, a zoologist. This worked out well for Luddy's parents, Lorelai and Rudy, and for Luddy.

A made-to-order uncle, Luddy centered his attention on his nephew, Alexander, that day, beginning with a trip to the park before the faculty pool opened. Despite his discomfort on merry-go-rounds, Luddy piloted the whirligig for the little boy until he too wanted the dizziness to stop. Luddy tirelessly explained rocks, trees, birds, and sand to his nephew in grown-up language.

And Rudy and Lorelai? Interested and happy smiles were exchanged among us in a relaxed way at the park. I came to know that Alexander was central to the package. If I liked him, I would be welcome in the family. As the only grandchild, he had assumed the status of archetype. They called him "the boy," with reverence, seldom saying his name.

In this way, our "date" was approved. His parents made it clear that Luddy wasn't getting any younger. "Wouldn't he make a good father?" his mother cooed as he gave her a look.

Impulses.

What did we really know about one another?

At the pool, following water rides on his uncle's broad, powerful shoulders and trusting floats with his guiding hands, Alex's eyes grew big when the relay races began. They widened even more when a large, greased watermelon was tossed into the water for a special competition of "Keep Away." Only the grown men and teenage boys participated in this slimy water brawl, the goal of which was to capture the slick fruit and keep it away from the other team for more than a minute.

As reigning champion of this event—"You watch!" Lorelai emoted to me with great pride, "He will win it again!"—first-draft-pick Luddy made a huge splash entering the pool with a cannonball jump, creating a spray that temporarily confused everyone about the location of the melon. Wearing pro goggles, he recovered first, protecting the melon against his chest with the upper-body strength of a former City College wrestler. He dove into the deep water with the watermelon. A few teens tried to catch him, but he could hold his breath for longer than anyone, so they were not even close to snatching away the prize. He stayed under longer and longer as younger guys surfaced, breathless, regrouping in defeat with their dads.

Luddy remained at the bottom until someone dove in to tell him it was over. He emerged triumphant from the water and hoisted the trophy fruit in the air until the grease finally did its work and the melon escaped his grip. No matter. He had won, and both sides cheered for the hero.

In escaping the limits of oxygen, Luddy showed me the strength I was seeking. This often-repeated feat became the stuff of family legends for decades. I believed I would be safe with him. It was not just a dream. My heart belonged to Luddy.

My feeling of attraction found extra fuel in my mother's *need to be a grandmother now*, and my parents' perhaps well-founded fear that I wasn't meeting the "right people." I was ready to meet *the one*. It didn't hurt that Luddy read more than I did, that his vocabulary was prodigious, or that he also had an annotated copy of *Alice in Wonderland* of the same vintage as mine, in addition to his specialty library focusing on the subatomic structure of metals.

That he was an intellectual challenge meant the world to me. In the beginning, he would talk to me for hours, whispering that I was the best thing that had ever happened to him. Yet he would still tease me about how hard it was to give up the other women. "Don't chase me!" he would say. I did not chase him, but he was being caught, nonetheless. My future children would be safe. We had glass-slipper closure. A match. A catch!

Chapter 4

The Accident

Fall 1976

Come to me.

Saturday. Always Saturday for the first few months. He had given me a choice of Friday, Saturday, or Sunday because he had to keep "the others" satisfied. Luddy was a hardworking, studious man, but he loved his weekend nights with women, even though he found it tough to tear himself away from his lab. Always working, eventually he would appear to pick me up, late, in a car littered with paper and unusual tools scavenged along the way because they were interesting, someone was throwing them away, and someday he would find a use for them. As an experimenter, packrat Luddy had shared a philosophy with the composer John Cage, who counseled people to save everything, just in case.

I subscribed to some ancient social imperative that deems Saturday the "real" date night, so I took it. It fell into a pattern like a mambo. The call on Wednesday then the date Saturday formed a clave, the rhythmic pattern of our relationship—a sound, a sound, a space—a response.

In good weather, his other ride was a pristine, relatively new BMW motorcycle. While it had a full storage container that included receipts, pliers, and other assorted random tools, it was mostly clean. Once my leg had healed sufficiently and I was able to ride on it, he declared me the "best pillion" he'd ever had. I attributed this to learning to ride with an English saddle when I was younger. He said that I wouldn't tip him over, that I shouldn't try to interfere in any way. If we fell, it would not be my fault. This was the role he wanted a woman to fill.

In fact, he often said that he'd never had it so good. No one had made his life so easy before, he said. If I had died young, I think this would have been my epitaph.

So on a particular evening, October 23, to be precise, Luddy was looking into my eyes, confident of my response to his intimate advance as he offered his hand to lead me to his bed. Did he notice how my eyes dropped as I took his hand?

Tuesday night, April 5, 2016

It would be decades before I'd learn that Luddy could not properly interpret facial expressions—that he might not always pick up signals about what I or our children were thinking or feeling. He had no appreciation for other people's conversational tone, especially sarcasm.

After he was tested for learning disabilities at the age of fifty-five, he would be given grade-school worksheets to teach him something about nonverbal communication, but the learned visual expressions he worked on were not so easily felt. His range of emotions was not the nuanced medley expressed by most adults. Happiness, anger, and pity were his touchstones. Sadness was difficult; empathy, elusive.

In those early days, I did not understand that his persistent depression was signaled nearly every day with his catchphrase, "I feel a little bit down today." As his lover, I wanted to make that go away. Stop listening to Wagner, I prayed silently each time I saw him.

October 23, 1976

When I entered his apartment that day, Luddy was standing behind his bar, the most prized piece of furniture in his apartment. I put my hand on his arm to stop him from coming around to hold my shoulder. He relaxed, sensing that something was different. I saw my frightened face reflected in the dozens of black crystal glasses behind him.

"I have some news," I said, carefully reciting the lines I'd rehearsed. The doctor . . . the test . . . yes, it's definite . . . our choices.

He listened in the way a stunned audience hears a new kind of music that does not fit with the old. Inscrutable structure. Unsatisfying, off-key puzzle. Where a constant falls off the edge of the earth.

Shaking his head, he looked down and away from me until he could look up again. Questions formed. Then silence.

I had prepared so well, but the song wasn't playing the way I'd meant it to, and finally it trailed off.

I had worked through the possibilities with a kind doctor two days ago. The gynecologist had met me in the waiting room of the university's health center. While we'd walked back to her office, I felt her arm slip across my back, bracing me for the news she had already seen in my folder. Two weeks ago, she'd been fitting me for birth control, something more effective than I had been using. Today, she had news.

After she'd presented all the options, she pressed me gently. "Tell him. Maybe he wants this too."

I didn't think so, but I let myself consider that thought as I sat by the duck pond near her office. I imagined coming back to the pond with the baby one day to tell him or her, "This is where I decided to keep you." I imagined a daughter; then, looking back at the pond, I saw a son. With a little forced optimism, I imagined how I would tell him. "We are so happy together. A baby might not be the best first step, but I believe we can do this. *I know we can do this!*"

I waited one more day for our Saturday date, to tell him that what I had convinced myself of was good news.

❧

Eventually he came around the bar and walked over to me. The movement buoyed my hope, but then he spoke.

"I might want to have a relationship with you—but not a child. Not right now. I can't do anything to jeopardize my career, my tenure—my future. Can't you see that?"

All the interlocked pieces I had fashioned separated and slid away from me. I had years of training in argument and persuasion. How could I fix this?

"What if it's my last chance? My only chance?"

He was not swayed.

I was stunned by his alienation from the pregnancy. All the red lights had suddenly blinked green in my body, and I wasn't going to just let it go. But he was ready to do just that.

For a moment, an alternative fantasy flashed before my eyes: I would have the baby the following summer, move to that vague place in Wyoming, probably meet someone else, and live to reach my dreams another day.

But the other broken signal kept luring me back. My family is beginning. Here. If Luddy wanted to be with me, wouldn't he someday want to have our baby? Couldn't I make this sensible sacrifice now to hold out for possible fulfillment later? If he really loved me, wouldn't it turn out all right in the end?

Instead of focusing on the terrible bargain in front of me, I resolved that the possibility of a future with Luddy—I was certain it would be our future—was better than being a single mother without tenure in Wyoming. Or, worse, staying on here where competition for academic positions was fierce, meeting my parents' weary, pitying eyes over the soft baby hair of their grandchild while I looked for work and my mother stayed at home with my baby?

Then there was the other thing. I could barely think about the word, let alone say it. I had crusaded for everyone to have a right to choose, but I'd never really thought about what I would do or how I would feel if I were presented with this choice.

Abortion suddenly seemed like a despicable parachute for uncertain love. I was ashamed of myself, and I went from clear thinking to mud that night, betraying everything I believed in for a wisp of an idea about a future with Luddy. I had used birth control, and I hadn't meant for it to fail. Nonetheless, I was the one left to deal with the consequence. He did not want the baby, so now we were faced with the question of what I was going to do about it.

We sat quietly for a long time. I mentally ground through all my beliefs, the hopeful quasi-plans I'd been making, past the duck pond and my hopeful dreams, past my body's clock and into the nothingness of being alone.

Yes, I would call my doctor for that list of names. Luddy would help pay for it and drive me to New York. It. He could do it on Tuesday. No classes, as it was Election Day. Would I let him know? *Of course. Of course.*

After some minutes of funereal silence, Luddy decided to employ the tried and true. He came away from the wall he'd been leaning against and stood behind me to kiss the hollow of my shoulder.

I didn't pull away. I didn't know where to go. I was here; we were touching. My skin was rising to meet him, aching to be embraced again. I hated my skin. Yet our intimacy was the agreement to move forward in our relationship.

He looked at me with tears in his eyes and said, "I didn't know if you would want to make love. I'm so grateful that you did."

Is half a bargain better than none? At that moment, I believed it was—believed I still had some power, and that love would find a way to repair what we were about to destroy. I knew I might be wrong, but I needed someone to hold me. Would anyone else, ever?

That question made me lonely enough to give up one life in exchange for the possibility of living with another. I felt "a little bit down" that day too.

When I drove home the next morning, the radio obliged my ambivalence with Paul Anka's "Having My Baby," followed by John Lennon belting, "Whatever gets you through the night." Such odd musical bookends for the Roe v. Wade era that followed the time of free love.

ॐ

Some things I didn't know before:

I learned how quickly the body can change when it enters the gravid state. The sickness. The swelling. Those clues had begun even before the confirming pregnancy test.

Why didn't I talk to anyone else, especially my parents? They took a liberal point of view about a subject they were both trained in: valuing life. Abortion was a gray zone. It was easy for them to express a conviction one way or the other, or to feel torn about it, until the question arose for their daughter. In our family, tolerance was expressed in hushed tones, and it was clear that ambivalence ruled my parents' thinking too.

In fact, abortion was not merely an abstract idea in our home, as my mother herself had experienced it. She had once hemorrhaged on a hospital bed while trying to convince three male doctors, practicing Catholics all, to let her have an abortion to prevent a miscarrying Rh-positive baby from threatening her own life.

This was a nightmare scenario of genetic inheritance carried from her own birth. My grandmother was Jewish but had converted to Catholicism prior to her marriage. She had been advised not to carry her fourth child, Ginger—my mother—to term. My grandmother died giving birth to my mother, in the name of honoring her adopted religion.

My grieving grandfather kept his first three children, all named for saints, but gave my mother to another couple to raise. Grandpa couldn't handle being a widower and a new father at the same time. Though the foster couple, also Catholic, were kind, my mother converted to Judaism before her marriage to my father.

I didn't want to scratch the scab of her old wound with news of my accidental pregnancy. Born a fighter, my mother was an advocate for choice, but what would she have thought about Luddy's unwillingness to accept this child? I could not risk telling her.

I thought about my father, always interrupting his vacations in the Caribbean in the 1950s and 1960s to fly back to New York every few days to fulfill his promises to women whose babies were due when we were away. When he returned, he would continue his "vacation" by examining the quality of local abortion clinics. He wanted to be able to reassure his white middle-class patients who preferred to travel for this service, either because of their own ironic politics or because it wasn't available in their community. These people wanted to be sure their daughters wouldn't die because of their unfortunate decisions.

Maybe my parents would have been more understanding than I imagined, but it might have been in exchange for control over me, and I was just learning to fly solo. Although I would have to do it with a broken wing, I decided not to tell them at that time.

The loneliness of my decision was something I hadn't anticipated.

It's difficult to describe the aftermath and the flood of feelings I experienced. It may have been legal in some places, but that didn't change everyone's opinion. I didn't tell many of my women friends that I'd had an abortion. A man I knew had a bigger heart, and he remained my friend after I confessed.

If you take such a leap, some doors will close. The door of candor is one. In my experience, some people who crusaded for the right to choose did not want to talk about exercising this right. Everyone has a personal yardstick about what's acceptable when it comes to this choice. Everyone's measure of tolerance is different, and the perceived selfishness of the person who prefers not to disrupt her career or the whole rest of her life just yet is no different in some people's minds than the "selfishness" of someone like my mother, bleeding on the table. I lost friends. For a long while, I lost my heart. And Luddy? He refused to discuss it ever again.

When we make huge decisions like this, do we stop and think about the story we are going to have to tell later? What we'll need to omit or minimize; collect or discard? We position the decision, finally, as our destiny, but we don't realize how it will need to be shaded in our narrative going forward.

The shadowy edges of memories are always there—whether they are guilt or sorrow or madness. Other people may not see them, and we may not talk about them, but they cloud everything all the same. Someone else's happiness would always check me in the sharp moments of deciding what to keep and what to give away. Too many years would pass before I understood what a faulty decision-making strategy this was.

༺✦༻

Luddy fell asleep shortly after his expression of gratitude, and I stared at the moon for a long time. Not looking for my father the way I did as a child, but instead, looking for the faces of my future children, waiting to find their way to being born.

I somehow knew my next two children would be sons, yet for decades I would fantasize about a lost, imaginary daughter, awakening in tears on the November anniversary of her death each year.

No, I don't know whether the baby was a girl, given up too early to know the gender. But I'd still wonder about who she would have become.

The loose bet Luddy and I had made on joining our two hearts together had meant sacrificing a piece of mine. Luddy would decide what to keep, and I would fly along behind, never interfering, ensuring the easier life he needed, the security I desperately wanted.

November 2, 1976

The ride to the abortion clinic in New York City was uneventful, though the usual rush-hour traffic into the city, with all the start-stop traffic on the New Jersey Turnpike, made it difficult to hold a conversation.

I didn't feel like talking anyway, and nothing Luddy could have said would have made it an easier ride. Either he realized that, or he preferred the quiet to concentrate on the road.

I think it was cloudy that morning, though I do remember blinding sun when we emerged from the clinic hours later. That could have been the anesthetic wearing off, or the simple fact that I'd been in a dimly lit room all day.

I wanted to remember every detail of this day.

It was about two weeks before my twenty-fifth birthday. November 2, 1976, Election Day. A win for Jimmy Carter and a loss for me.

This would become a day of tears for me, every year. Four decades later, my body still yanks me back to that experience each November.

We arrived as planned at 8:30 a.m. at the clinic recommended by my doctor and parked in front of an anonymous Upper Manhattan brownstone. During the two-hour wait with more than a dozen other women, we didn't speak much. Luddy dozed off frequently.

I was finally summoned to another room for the intake. I went in alone.

It was a shock to find that I had to identify my parents on the paperwork, but not the father of the baby. I was terrified that the information they were collecting would be released in some public form, finding its way back to my parents by way of some state reporting requirements.

My father read everything, patiently combing through newspapers and other publications, searching for mentions of me and occasionally finding them. This was not like the Phi Beta Kappa key my father had discovered before I received my letter. Would he find out from some random source about the death of his first grandchild? Was I being too emotional? I did not want them to be disappointed in me. I was disappointed enough for all of us.

All hell would break loose. Then what?

After the nurse explained the procedure, she told me that a fetal death certificate would be required, signed by me alone. I was assigned to a dressing room. Gowned. Another long, silent wait, holding my clothes at my side like a prisoner.

I could stop this now. Nothing terrible has happened yet.

"Lie down on the table, dear. Put your clothes next to you. There's a hook on the side. We'll take care of them for you."

I flinched when the nurse came near me.

We'll take care of it.

That's what Luddy had said.

I had so woefully misunderstood what he meant at first. The word *care* is a terrible euphemism. I had made him say the word: abortion.

He didn't change his mind.

❧

My hands were strapped to my sides so that I wouldn't interfere. There was good reason for that. Was the doctor being overly firm while inserting a clamp on my cervix? Was he even a doctor? He didn't seem to like his work very much, muttering occasional passive-aggressive commentary.

Why should he be nice? What did I deserve? Kindness was not in the cards.

As the anesthetic began to affect my thinking, I'm sure I heard him say, "Maybe you're not pregnant."

I know that I panicked then and began to struggle. I believed the clinic was a fake, and I was going to die.

"No! Stop! If I'm not pregnant, then why are you—?"

Sodium pentothal.

"Count backward from one hundred!" a voice commanded from deep water far away.

"Ninety-nine, ninety-eight . . ."

I lost count quickly, cringing from the sound of the music playing loudly from the radio, "A Fifth of Beethoven," by Walter Murphy. Disco. To cover the screams?

I cannot think anymore. Perchance to dream.

Somewhere in the surgical disco my mind flashed back on another time when I could not breathe.

Autumn 1954: Fugue

Bitter smell. Like our kitchen stove at home.

I'm a child, maybe two or three.

"Stop! Mama! No!"

Not our kitchen. Not our home. A strange bed. Hurt. Crying. Rolling away from her.

She hurls herself toward me the way a wolf targets a fawn.

Stuck in the blankets. Angled away from hurt. Strangled. Slammed against the nightstand.

"Mama! Stop!"

Pushing. Scratching. Gas smell. Everywhere. Every light blazing. Where?

I feel my mother's beautiful Elsa Schiaparelli owl pins with the green crystal eyes glowing and the sharp wires scratching their way across my face more harshly than when she'd said "good night" some hours earlier, but on her breast now they heave like stars in a sea storm as she fights to remove me from this bed.

I bat her away because it hurts, and I cannot breathe.

She grabs at me, pulls me in close, and shakes me awake. Why won't she let me breathe?

Crying. Drowsy. Pushing. Coughing. Restrained. Almost hugged but grabbed instead by her hands as I squirm away from her sharp ruby fingernails and the terrifying owls. The warmth she might give is canceled by the pain she delivers.

"How dare you?" Mama shouts.

Freeze.

Me? I did something?

"How dare you almost die? How dare you do this to me?"

The familiar slap of blame stifles whatever I may have wanted to say.

We are both crying and heaving. I am exhausted. I am scared. I finally collapse on her and let the owls sink their metal spokes into my cheek. My blood mixes with her tears. Those brooches were often the leading edge of Mama. Tonight, in her shiny copper evening dress in the blinding yellow light, she is hurting while hugging—

"Why are you doing this to me?" she sobs.

I have no answer.

"We have to get away!"

Mama takes a deep breath and carries me, all sagging and gangly, no fight left, into the cold night outside the mountain cabin. No coat. Struggling again. Cold. Hurt. I try to rub my face. We fall on the path. More crying.

"It was a gas heater—didn't you know that?" she asks.

I just cry.

In the night air of the Catskills, her past skills as a psychiatric nurse—she once carried bedpans for an aging Al Capone—reemerge to take over the scene as emergency workers make a ring around us.

She bows her head to my brow, her tears falling with mine on my face. They taste different, but somehow, we always melt into one. One pulse. One breath. One cry. We'd barely been apart during the two and a half years since my birth, when my father had left for the war in Korea.

We are sprawled on the ground. Mama collects herself first, straightening her head to model perfection, smoothing her dress in a pool of copper around us.

"We are fine. We are fine."

I look up to see a heartbroken Eve, contemplating her strange, ruined garden. We shudder and breathe hard as my hands reach up and then push back, keeping the dangerous owls at bay.

For a long time afterward, breathing did not come easily to either of us.

November 2, 1976

"Is it over? Is it over?"

Panic flooded me with smothering consciousness. I'm sure I heard the cannons of the *1812 Overture* when I came out of the procedure. I remember yelling "Stop!" through the effects of the drugs. Backward in time.

Opening my eyes was painful. Then I remembered. I couldn't move my hands, but the table was moving.

When I finally came to full awareness in the silence of the recovery room, I was surrounded by similarly bereaved women on cots. This was a humbling experience even as it affirmed there was a need for abortion.

Thick-voiced confessions were uttered. Most of the other women had too many children already and no way to care for them. Only one described herself as a free spirit, glad she was rid of "that," as she wiped her hands of it in the air to punctuate her joy. I copped to a mistake and failure of birth control, keeping my feelings of shame to myself.

The grief was instant upon waking.

I asked the nurse to share the news with Luddy, unable to stand up to go talk to him myself.

I wondered what his response would be.

⟡

After an hour or so, they pulled me to my feet to go to the exit interview.

"Are you 'together'?" I remember the nurse quipped in the lingo of the day, to show she was "with it."

I wasn't clear yet. This brutal physical experience had left my mind somewhere in the clouds, invoking the sense of near asphyxiation from that time long ago when I nearly died in my mother's arms, my shame very much with me.

I remember looking around at my body to see if it was there. The nurse repeated her question breezily several times until she realized I wasn't getting it. She stopped being hip long enough to ask me, "Are you all right? Because we can't let you go until you feel all right."

Something clicked over, and I realized my body wanted to be far away from this building. My mind at last collaborated.

"Yes, I'm sorry, I'm fine."

The *sorry* was about something else, but she wasn't interested in my inner thoughts.

They gave me a key chain with the emergency number on it, and Luddy and I left the abortion clinic as quickly as we could in the still messy Vega.

Luddy wanted to return to New Jersey to vote for Carter, though he wasn't sure where his polling place was located.

I was starved.

"Could you eat quickly?"

Not a word about what just happened.

I was too exhausted to care and made him find a coffee shop.

Back in the Vega, hurtling around a ramp to the GW Bridge, Luddy professed his reluctant love for me. He wanted a relationship despite his desire to be free.

Bile rising in my throat, I thought about jumping out of the car, just to get away, but I was afraid I was too shaky and might fall off the ramp into the Hudson. Having given birth to a death, I wasn't going to allow another tragedy that day.

I said nothing. He focused intently on the road.

We drove in silence to central New Jersey, the gut of the state. We visited five different polling places scattered around the county because if he stopped to take me home first, he might not get to the correct one before it closed, and I was all right, wasn't I?

The fifth one was it. Luddy was relieved that Jimmy Carter was now shored up in his presidency.

I was beginning to bleed.

He brought me to my apartment, and although he'd clearly had enough, he knew he shouldn't leave me alone. He collapsed on my couch for a nap while I cooked dinner for him.

I remember putting something in the oven to cook, but whatever it was took a very long time. Something was wrong with the pilot light. I remember bending over the open door and having to catch myself to keep from falling, I was so dizzy.

I woke up Luddy to check the pilot, leaning against the wall as he did so. Once he'd confirmed it was safely working, he returned to his nap.

My roommate, Annie, called to see how I was. She'd thought it better not to be at home when we returned because she was so angry with Luddy.

Was I angry? I was numb and exhausted, memorizing the number on the key chain from the doctor in case I lost it, fingering the ornament like a rosary that held my only hope.

When Annie heard he was with me, she calmed down. I think I omitted telling her about the wild ride around the county's polling places, and I certainly didn't tell her about the bleeding. Time enough for that later, when she got home from her shift.

When Luddy woke up again, he was hungry. We ate together silently. I was scared about the bleeding, but when I called the clinic, they said it was normal.

Normal. I wondered if I'd ever feel that way again.

⧓

Luddy did not stay with me that night. He said he had to prepare for his classes the next day.

I had a day to grieve before I was in a classroom again. Sex was off the table for a couple of weeks. My mind insisted on doing the thinking I might better have done before I became pregnant. Endless questions expanded in my head like a chain of paper dolls. Did he doubt the baby was his? Did I want a relationship? Did he mean it when he'd said "I love you" in the car? Did I care? I would be carrying this overwhelming secret forever. What if he left me? What would I have?

Nothing but red nothingness—the sorrow and regret I would confront in the coming days.

Winter 1976–1977

My mind and body were shawled in misty grief for the next couple of months.

As it turned out, I found I couldn't care about anything. I went where Luddy pointed, content with any show of attention. I lost track of whether I wanted to be with him or not.

The excitable fires of my twenties had been extinguished. I only wanted one thing now: to be a mother.

To hell with combatting the nasty condescension of an undergraduate professor when he presented me with a check for the music award. "You have to share it with three other people, you know. I heard you were going to be a kindergarten teacher." Professor Medford knew I was going to graduate school. I had simply thanked him for the check, let my blood boil, and resolved to be the most intense grad student who ever lived.

Up until the time of the abortion, graduating with a Mrs. Degree had never been my first concern. But now?

Because of the abortion, Luddy's and my divergent purposes had collided on the path laid out by our parents. I believed I might float along in this state for a long time. Perhaps I'd get my wish, perhaps I wouldn't, but the shame I felt now had revamped my priorities and would postpone my academic progress for a long time.

January 1977

"Why don't you get married?" Luddy asked.

"Because no one's asked me," I replied.

Annie had just announced her engagement, saying they'd be getting married in May, so we were planning to end our lease early. I was going to have to move.

When I told Luddy, he'd delivered his version of a wedding proposal, complete with his unique confusion of pronouns, placing responsibility on the other person. But at least he asked.

Uncertain, I chose logic over feeling.

"Well?" he muttered.

"Are you asking me?"

He offered something between a shrug and an affirmative nod.

"Do you mean you want the two of us to get married?"

"Yes!" he said.

I'd finally drawn it out of him.

He wanted to get married, but somehow his involvement in the whole thing was lost in translation.

Tuesday, April 5, 2016

I could have run away from these signs of disorder, a future without clarity or shared purpose. The song "Fifty Ways to Leave Your Lover" was popular that year, after all.

But no.

Reader, I became complicit the day I aborted our baby, jumping into his chaotic world with both feet when I agreed to marry him.

Second Movement

"Yesterday"—Paul McCartney

Chapter 5

Intermezzo

Tuesday, April 5, 2016

"You okay?"

It's Simon, checking in.

"I'm fine."

"I wish you would stay up here with us."

"I'm really okay."

"It's just that—"

"You don't have to worry."

"Did Jake call?"

"Yeah," I fibbed.

"Pants on fire."

"A little."

"I wish he would—"

"People have their own ways of handling this," I say. "There's no map. Batteries not included."

"Yeah, but—"

"He'll figure it out."

"Okay. I'll see you tomorrow. Meet us at the house. We'll take one car."

"Sure. Sleep well. Emma and Gabe need an extra hug. So does Angelica."

"I'll remember. You too."

I'm not ready to sleep.

Perchance to read . . .

May 1977, the premarital interview, Rabbi Feinstein's office

"Are you Jewish?"

I almost laughed out loud at the surprised look on Luddy's face when he heard this nutty question.

Rabbi Feinstein went on to misperceive Luddy's answers about who he was and where he came from: Bronx Science to City College, then Rutgers to Oxford, now a professor in New Jersey. Either the rabbi had missed the geographic hoofbeats of a child from New York's Upper West Side, or he wasn't actually looking at or listening to Luddy, who never would have been mistaken for any other ethnicity.

"What else?" Luddy shrugged, his eyes twinkling.

"Do you live in a dorm?"

"I have my own apartment."

The rabbi's continued line of questioning suggested he truly wasn't registering Luddy's replies.

We were older than the usual couples he encountered, and he had no frame of reference for independent living. That we each had an apartment did not compute. He couldn't shake his assumption that we were both undergraduates, couldn't seem to understand why I wasn't living at home. We slouched awkwardly toward the Promised Land nonetheless, at last coming to the all-important discussion of the marriage ceremony.

It was news to me that I would not be involved in the critical first act of the pageant—an exchange of dowry cattle between my father and the groom. I should have realized I would have no part in the Orthodox ritual. There had been no bat mitzvah for me; I would make no promises during the ceremony.

Once we were together under the chuppah, Rabbi Feinstein told us, Luddy would have an important role to play when he pronounced the Hebrew word for the phrase "to me," which sounds like "lee." It was critical that only Luddy, not the rabbi, utter this word, so that Luddy would become my husband. If the rabbi had to prompt him with it that day, other than the pause and nod he would give, I would find myself married to the rabbi instead.

No pressure.

The rabbi reviewed this information four or five times, Luddy averring with a straight face that he was up to the task, and we promised to practice.

Luddy couldn't read Hebrew, so it was a good thing he had to say only one word. Rudy Berg had refused to spend the money to join a temple, and Luddy had been too busy with national science competitions to pick up the language. His parents had chosen the economy plan for his bar mitzvah, and he had learned his Torah portion by listening to an audio recording.

Luddy was sure he could remember just the one word, especially as it was easy to pronounce.

Near the end of the meeting, so he wouldn't have to discuss it, Rabbi Feinstein handed me a (complimentary!) copy of the time-honored prenuptial classic for Orthodox women, *A Hedge of Roses* by Rabbi Norman Lamm. This precious volume included such powerful solutions for female moods as using lipstick to combat the blues. Key sections focused on abstaining from sex during menstruation and optimizing the fertile days by attending the mikvah, or ritual bath. I remember thinking at the time, *I hope Revlon is ready for me.* Thanks to my peace-and-love days, I hadn't been a customer recently.

Lorelai wanted to do my hair for the ceremony. I remember telling her I was just going to wash it. Many of my early, unintentional errors with the Bergs centered around physical appearance.

Luddy and I laughed hysterically in the car all the way back to my parents' house, where we described the interview as being straight out of *Waiting for Godot.* My mother scolded us for not taking it seriously, while my father appreciated the joke.

This encounter with Rabbi Feinstein had been a mere formality. My father called him afterward to smooth over any rough edges. A check would be in the mail.

"Yes, she will go to the mikvah," my dad promised.

I probably would have done anything for my father.

So the date was set. MFA completed. Arrangements made. We'd be married at my parents' home, a "small wedding," with more than two hundred guests. Conflicts over tablecloths were resolved. We narrowed "our song" down to two Jobim sambas, deciding against

"How Insensitive" and choosing "Desafinado" instead, which means "Off Key." We both enjoyed the poetic tension of the lyrics—a lover's ironic plea about his unmusical heart. This resonated with Luddy, who enjoyed music but couldn't sing or play an instrument himself.

I dreamed of Sonia roses, but the Bergs' florist would, without notice, substitute floribunda at the last minute, even though he knew my preference. Lorelai okayed this without mentioning it to me. Little things.

A month to go.

At my mother's request, and Rabbi Feinstein's ultimatum, I agreed to go to a mikvah for ritual purification before the wedding, because "it was such a spiritual experience when I converted back to Judaism." My mother had placed this demand on herself to make sure the conversion "took." I wasn't converting. I already "was." But once an idea germinated in Ginger's mind, it grew like kudzu, strangling off any part of her brain that offered a competing possibility.

My grandmother Hayes had been Jewish, but Ginger's adoption and baptism by an Irish Catholic family after her mother died in childbirth had thrown all this ethnicity into doubt. Her father had given her away! He'd had three other children to raise without a wife.

My father hadn't cared about Ginger's religion, but his parents, the Feldshers, apparently cared a lot. So, for her sake, I would do as my mother had done before me. *Be quiet and dunk yourself in the water. End of discussion. After all, the conjunctivitis almost cleared up by the wedding day.*

There was just one thing: Luddy had forgotten the date of our wedding and scheduled himself to present at a conference on teaching the day after, at a school in Rhode Island. Maybe more than one thing—our honeymoon would be spent in a dorm, two floors apart. Even *A Hedge of Roses* was not that draconian. I couldn't stop thinking sourly of Freda Payne's song "Band of Gold."

Don't be a baby, I told myself at the time. But *"Be My Baby."*

To salvage the situation, my parents suggested we spend a few days at their house in Sudbury, Vermont, after the conference. It would be Luddy's first time there, and at least I would be on familiar ground, near my alma mater and the place where my parents had honeymooned. Their wedding song was "Moonlight in Vermont."

I forgave him and began to feel grounded again. Vermont had been my family's happy place for nearly fifty years. I'd feel safe there, down by the lake in the cooler part of the summer.

Late May, 1977

"I think it's the beard."

Rudy Berg said this to me at my engagement shower, arranged by Lee, who was my maid of honor. I mentioned the prevalence of beards among the faculty, but Luddy's father wouldn't hear it. He had doubts about Luddy's future.

Two weeks before the wedding, Ludwig Berg was turned down for tenure, and our sky began to fall again. Sources told us that the department review had been prejudicial, claiming that Luddy didn't seem to have completed enough research. Luddy blamed the chair. He claimed the man had "had it in for him since he was a graduate student—his only B+!"

He managed to pull himself together temporarily, having learned of a possible offer of research support and another crack at tenure with help from a different department chair who would help him redo his application and make sure it worked this time. There was an election coming up in his department, and no one liked the current chair.

Thanks to my father's generous purchase of champagne, and Luddy knowing he was wanted somewhere, we enjoyed the wedding. We had the entire summer to figure out a new plan for our lives. Luddy said he believed in equality and a two-career marriage, and I believed him.

June 14, 1977, Rhode Island

I had a lot of time to think on our honeymoon, which began at the teaching conference. There were of course the separate rooms. It turned out that separation would prevail at all our meals too. These fierce male educators needed to bond over breakfast, and they were concerned that an outsider like me would make them stray off topic too easily.

I'm sure I was the only one in the group who had a teaching license and experience teaching secondary school and college. But what could a new bride add to the conversation? I was invited to sit "over there at the table by the window" to prevent corruption of their dialogue.

"Please don't spoil it for me," Luddy said sweetly. "I need to make a lot of connections in case the second round of tenure doesn't pan out."

Little did I know that this week would serve as preparation for a life-time of professional conferences where socially inept scientists would shoo me to the sidelines even when they allowed women scientists to attend—women, who, in fact, were often the greater guardians of the esoteric dialogue. That didn't matter at these conferences, where, like a caryatid for motherhood, I functioned as a boundary between professional and familial topics, often standing awkwardly among scientists, expected to hold my peace until a question about children was posed. How different from humanities meetings, where people might argue with academic spouses, but never outright muzzle them.

As I looked out the window of the university dining room one morning, I thought about our wedding—how my father helped me descend the stairs in my childhood home, escorting me to Luddy's side. Shaking almost as much as I was, he forgot to kiss me.

My mother, sotto voce: *Kiss her! Kiss her!*

Too shy, my father sent me off with his trademark wink and a tiny wave.

Then there was the rabbi, overconfidently storming through the service, not pausing for breath, really, until he came to the word *Li*; then, saying it himself, out loud, before he realized.

Luddy and I had caught each other's gaze. I pulled my roses up in front of my face and we stifled our chuckles. I heard my friend Lee burst out laughing, and my father groaned. My mother kept saying, "What's going on?" I didn't dare turn around to face our guests.

The rabbi had backed up with a roar like a truck, and this time paused and glared at Luddy when he came to the spot for the word. Luddy shouted it out, loud and clear, and I heard my mother's fierce whisper: *He doesn't have much of an inside voice!*

When it came time to break the glass, Luddy went after it with vigor, shaking the house with a stomp, my parents gasping at the sound. More chattering knickknacks and vases. *L'chaim*s bursting forth all around. Challah was torn. Wine was shared. The bride and groom hoisted in the air on chairs. My head spinning with too much champagne.

I stared out the window of that university dining room for hours, wondering, *What have I done?*

June 21, 1977—Return to Westchester

"Get in the front," my father said to me. He could usually find the humor in anything, but he was scowling. His rarely angry eyes made me wish he would yell.

While Dad and Luddy lifted the motorcycle into the huge trunk of the car, tying the lid with extra bungee cords, I slid into the car.

I had called him sheepishly from the Tappan Zee Bridge, on our way back from Vermont, because Luddy had told me his brake cable had given out. My father hadn't wanted us to take the motorcycle in the first place, and I could hear both of my parents' muffled *I told you so*'s before he agreed to pick us up and take Luddy to an auto supply store.

❧

The few days we had spent in Vermont had mostly been a respite. We enjoyed the lake and just relaxed, the pressure of the conference over. For once, I believed I had Luddy all to myself.

Our departure from my parents' house had inspired a series of calamities. Their friends had given us wedding gifts, and Luddy felt pressured to add those to the fully packed BMW motorcycle. I told him to leave them at the house until we could pick them up later in the summer when we came back with the car, but after slamming a few things around and locating two extra bungee cords, he thought he had figured it out.

This was not the first time his passive-aggressive streak had emerged. He took suggestions angrily rather than stopping to talk things through. I hated my reflection as a shrew in these confrontations.

His defensiveness seemed designed to prevent me from asking him to do anything, and I wondered how we would function over time. I bit my tongue.

Regrettably, one of the boxes contained a cut crystal bowl, which came loose from the bike less than a mile from the house. I heard—and saw—it shatter into too many pieces to count. I hadn't even written a thank-you note yet. I felt as if I'd broken it myself by not intervening.

Previously, I had known Luddy to be fascinated by broken things. He had a large stockpile of broken ceramics that we had moved from his apartment to our new house, and he had been very careful of these fragments; they had fractured in a certain way, he told me, and he wanted to study them. I had heard him shout "Save the pieces!" whenever he thought he'd heard breakage.

For some reason, however, he was not interested in this crystal bowl. When we had opened the gift, he'd inspected it with a jeweler's loop and pronounced it "the victim of many flaws." He asked me if we had to keep it. I saw only the love of a family friend, so I insisted on keeping it. For weeks I had sat helplessly while Luddy rejected gift after gift and tasked me with the returns, due to the bubbles or other flaws he found in all manner of crystal and glass. In this case, I'd wanted to keep a gift from someone who reminded me of happy days from my past.

While Luddy watched, I carefully swept up the debris with a piece of cardboard I found on the road and packed everything into a trash bag so no one would be able to spot how careless we had been. I refused to throw it away until we had crossed the border between New York and Vermont. I couldn't bear the thought of it being found by anyone I knew.

"You're overly sensitive, aren't you?" Luddy said.

❧❧

My father dropped me and the motorcycle at home, and my mother and I sat down for coffee, and to laugh about Luddy's mishap, though I saw some worry forming around her tired eyes. I never told her about the crystal bowl. Not telling was a way of keeping myself together as my new identity as Luddy's wife was forming and crazing. The fine cracks in my weakened sense of self were beginning to deepen.

The next morning, my father insisted that Luddy take me back to Jersey in his car. He didn't dare argue. He could fetch the motorcycle next week.

So began my permanent journey away from home. I had moved to a new place every year throughout college and graduate school, but nothing had given me the feeling of disconnection like this ride to New Jersey.

Chapter 6

The Plan

Wednesday, April 6, 2016, 7:00 a.m.

My alarm goes off too early, and too loudly.

No, it's right on time.

There is no right time to plan your ex-husband's funeral, but that's where I'm going today.

A misty hum has taken up residence in my head. I'm sure it has something to do with the journal entries I read before going to bed, which made me toss and turn all night. I will finish reading the journal before the funeral. In a few days, everyone else's story of Ludwig Berg will be revealed, and I want to be sure to hang on to my own. Things happened. I was there. Something had compelled me to compose my *Clean House Concerto* years ago, and I realize it's time to revise that concerto with a better understanding of what I was trying to create.

I drink a few cups of coffee to mute the hum, then don a black outfit as a concession to widow's weeds. *Kidding.* Black slacks and a black T-shirt are my usual uniform. Among my mother's last reminders to me before she died: "Black makes you look thinner."

When I had called Annie in California four years ago to tell her about the divorce, she'd focused on what would come next for me. "Find one who can drive. Then you know they can see." She's never forgiven Luddy for the abortion, so I can predict that when I call her tonight, she will hum "The Merry Widow."

According to an attorney friend, the government has a modern name for what I am: *divorced widow*. While I accept this label, finding a successor to Luddy is the last thing on my mind.

Wednesday, 10:00 a.m., parking lot of the funeral home

"That wasn't too difficult."

Simon, Jake, and I are leaving the funeral director's office, feeling a bit lighter for having completed a step. The director was grateful that we'd brought Luddy's curriculum vitae for the obituary, even though most of the information didn't make its way into the draft, which we outlined while we spoke with him.

It's strange, how this meeting mirrored the one Luddy and I had had with the rabbi long ago, right down to the issue of how Jewish Luddy was—particularly relevant today when it came to the twin sins of suicide and cremation. We decide on a quick summary, hitting the highlights of his early days of public school on the Upper West Side of New York, followed by his long career and distinguished service.

No one needs to know about the political battles he fought with his colleagues, or that his demons took over during the last fifteen years of his life. Our sons and his refugee parents are named, along with his sister's family, the grandchildren specified only by their relationship.

Apart from "Their marriage ended in divorce," I am invisible. I knew that was coming, but it still feels hurtful. This lacuna fails to tell the complete story of his life—*our* life. Moreover, my children and I remain a family, even if some of the others will choose to ignore that. I don't like the prefix "ex," but "former" sounds—well, too formal. After forty years of knowing someone, you don't just disappear.

Keep it to yourself. We never said anything like "until death parts you."

Wednesday, noon, Andy's Luncheonette

We're not due to see the rabbi until one o'clock, so there's time for lunch. Conversation doesn't come easily. It's as though the trip to the funeral home robbed us of some of the protective fantasy we've been able to construct since the first shock.

"When did this place open?" Jake asks me.

"I'm not sure. It was here before—well, before I met your dad."

"I've never noticed it."

I'm surprised, because we are less than a mile from their high school.

"It would have been closer than driving to the university for the food trucks."

"But then we would've missed the thrill of getting back before the late bell!" laughed Simon.

"I don't want to know any more." I smile, hoping we can all relax a little.

"Good times!" toasts Simon, raising a Coke in our direction.

Jake and I return the toast.

"This ain't one of them," Jake says softly. Our sorrow is often drowned in the sarcastic colloquial.

"Listen," I begin. "Please let me know how I can help you both. I withdrew from my conducting project, and I'll stay here until we're done."

I hear "Thanks" and "You don't have to," mumbled by each.

Fortunately, we need to give our orders to the waitress, which fills the awkward moment.

When the waitress leaves, I see their faces morph oddly back and forth between those of determined young professionals and those of their two- and four-year-old selves, who mostly trusted me to keep the world safe for them. I imagine them wearing these tragic expressions because I'd taken them to a restaurant that had just run out of balloons.

Do they know how hard I'm fighting the feeling that I made this happen?

This is not the time to ask.

Wednesday, 1:00 p.m., Rabbi Jada Goldsmith's study

"Your mom has told me about your concerns regarding the funeral. Basically, you can do whatever you want."

The rabbi's conversation starter puts us at ease.

"Jewish funerals are pretty open-ended and brief—the idea is to complete the burial as soon as possible."

She stops short of explaining that this is meant to ensure the body begins to decompose as quickly as possible. Jews believe that after death, the soul remains in limbo, confused, hovering above the body. The sooner the burial takes place, the sooner the process of releasing the soul begins.

Nowadays, people wait for mourners who need to travel to the funeral from far away, but exceptions remain rare. The Sabbath can delay a funeral into the following week, and this is why we are pushing the coroner for Friday.

Jada Goldsmith reads the room well. Jake and Simon are not much younger than the rabbi, and she intuits that neither competitive wisdom nor unpleasant Jewish lore will heal the wounds of this professor's children. She lays out her typical game plan, and we review Luddy's history again, although there's a little more laughter and commentary here than there was with the funeral director.

"Anything you want me to say—or not say?"

We shift uncomfortably. There is Lena's request to not mention Luddy's cause of death—and Lorelai's age—to consider.

Simon finally spills the beans.

"There's no need to explain anything to the mourners," Rabbi Goldsmith offers. "He died. We remember him. We wish him peace. We wish everyone peace. I don't believe this is the time for guilt. As I told your mom, the manner of death is not the issue."

Our collective sigh seals the deal as the pressure of that decision subsides.

"You know," she says, "there is a Japanese custom for repairing broken ceramics by filling the cracks with gold. *Kintsugi*."

"My father would like that," offers Simon. There's a "yes" and a sad smile from Jake.

The rabbi has done her homework.

"I'll mention that, then," she says. "Will anyone else be speaking?"

"I will," says Simon firmly.

"How about you, Jake?"

"I don't think I can."

Everyone looks at me. This is not my time.

The rabbi lets silence do its work. Experience says there might be a change of heart. She will accommodate wherever our feelings lead us. Every family develops its own choreography. Even in shock, the dance describes where we come from. Luddy's outrage was loud, but the rest of us are peaceful people.

"Okay, then. Can one of you pick up the papers from the funeral home tomorrow morning and meet with me briefly to finalize the arrangements?"

"I'll be here," I tell her.

"Get some rest," the rabbi says at the close of our meeting. "Grieving can take a lot out of you."

We thank her and return to the house.

Wednesday, 2:00 p.m., the house

As we pull into the driveway, Simon takes a call from the police. He summarizes: "The tape will come off tonight. They believe it's a suicide. Inquiry closed. Coroner's done. Body to the funeral home tonight. We can go ahead with the service for Friday."

His terseness belies the roiling emotions he must be experiencing.

I can feel the tension building between Jake and Simon. I need a moment, and I hope they will talk to each other, so I walk across the lawn to look inside the windows of the bedrooms where they slept in innocence through their childhoods. It's not easy to see clearly through the screens, but the rooms look like two shipwrecked containers. We will need gloves and masks to dive in. I make a note to shop for those.

I overhear them discussing a division of labor. An argument about how long things will take begins to take shape. Berg arguments can be epic—we all have the graduate training to make them so. I have no interest in taking part.

Simon claims that it makes sense for him to handle probate for the will because he's a lawyer. From Jake: *I know that!*

An industrial engineer, Jake says he'll take charge of the cleanup. Simon wants Jake to wait so he can look through things before they go to the dump. Jake is in a hurry to get back to his life but promises to wait a week before he and the contractor sort out potentially valuable things that may emerge from the rubble.

They don't sound like the sons of a hoarder.

Efficiency means different things to each of them, however. Simon wants to melt into his memories for a while. If he gives in, Jake will make the things go away. Jake is going to have to prevail, because Simon can't afford to take too much time off work.

Luddy's personal difficulties don't surface in this conversation. The boys are too busy arguing with each other for supremacy. For once, I don't jump in.

I left things in the house, but they are not mine anymore. This was a big regret for me—that it would be left to the boys to clean up their father's mess. I hear them talk about protecting me from seeing the inside of the house again, fighting about the overwhelming tasks before them.

I must speak, so I move back across what's left of the lawn.

"I'll come as often as you want—please just tell me what to do. I want to help."

They look at me strangely, as if I'm a talking bird who has flown onto the scene to interrupt their conversation. Both blinking, they recover themselves and remember that I had a role here once upon a time. It feels like our caring thoughts for one another are rapidly separating and weaving together again, like a game of cat's cradle.

Here's another uninvited realignment of our family. I'm alone now, with a million snapshots colliding in my head—how it was . . . how it will never be again.

There's nothing left to resolve right now, so I'm heading back to my house.

Jake and Simon decide to take a walk around the yard to revisit the graves of amphibians and other pets we once cherished. Luddy had always been good at fashioning specialized caskets for frogs, crabs, and fish, and these memories seem to be very important this afternoon.

When they were young, Luddy would tell them he planned to change the locks once they'd both turned eighteen. In the beginning, I thought he must have been kidding. For some reason, they both wanted to live at home forever. They concocted a bold plan to outwit him by parking a trailer in the driveway. One of them would sneak in through a window each night to get cookies and other supplies.

If they'd wanted to stay with us so badly, things couldn't have been too terrible, I thought. *Right?*

Chapter 7

"A Threnody"

Wednesday, April 6, 2016, 7:00 p.m., my living room

I don't know where the last few hours have gone. I didn't think a person could stare out a window for so long without thinking of anything.

I'm not hungry—for food, I mean. My craving for memories has only been enlarged by today's experiences. The idea of Fearless the frog, Hermie the hermit crab, and the unusual Bruce Lee fish, named for Jake's imaginary friend, have whetted my appetite for the journal again. I hope to find some solace there. What has congealed as my current heap of recollections may not be accurate.

To appease my hunger, I start to skim through journal entries, faster and faster . . .

July 1, 1977

Luddy has a new habit of not coming home before one o'clock in the morning. I don't know what to think. Barely a month has passed since our wedding.

I feel so lonely.

July 3, 1977

I asked Luddy if we could go to the faculty picnic at the pool. He "thinks" he can take the day off.

July 4, 1977

We get there too late to enjoy even the watermelon races.

And so on, through the first several weeks of our marriage. There are a great many entries like these. Flipping through, I find that the disappointment I remember is accurate. I don't have to read them all.

In one entry, I mention that Rudy and Lorelai called to complain that we hadn't visited; likewise, my parents. I promise to share their concerns with Luddy.

Nothing changes. There is no other woman. Despite the glimmer of hope he had received from the other department chair, Luddy is fighting off the shame of not getting tenure on the first round, sleeping late in the mornings while I go off to teach a summer school class, gone before I return. It looked like avoidance to me, so I stopped asking him about it.

My friend Lee has moved on to a job in Arizona, and Annie is now a resident in a Los Angeles ER. Luddy doesn't want me to spend money on long-distance calls, so our weekly chats dwindle.

Reading these entries, I understand that Luddy was already fighting depression at this time. I know I was humming "Lonely Teardrops" in the manner of Jackie Wilson singing Berry Gordy's song, alternating with the encouraging "Golden Years" of David Bowie, hoping against hope that he would come around.

My life jangled around his emotional distance like the bouncy rhythm and choreography of the Miracles' version of "Tears of a Clown," counterposed against "Sempre Libera" from *La Traviata*.

Always free. I am always free. I just cannot see it yet.

Chapter 8

Jake's Melody: *Dal Segno*

Thursday, April 7, 2016, just after midnight

"Mom? You still up?"

"I am now."

"Sorry. I know it's late. Go back to sleep."

"I can't."

"How's Gia?"

"She could sleep through a nuclear event."

"Lucky."

"That's just recent, actually, since the pregnancy."

"I'm so happy for you. We'll celebrate next week—"

"Why couldn't he just wait?"

I'm not sure whom Jake means by *he*, Luddy or Simon, so I wait a beat.

"I don't know."

"Remember when Dad fell off the roof with the chain saw and took out the power and the cable? Remember when he nearly burned down the house to keep warm after Superstorm Sandy, after you left?"

I take a chance that we're heading into the lighter ironies of Luddy's life—the black edge of laughter you share after an emergency. To further soften the moment, I dip into our cache of family memories of self-inflicted catastrophes. "Remember my dad, with the lighter fluid?"

A giant sob originates from deep in Jake's body.

"I tried to stop him!" he cries. "I cleaned up everything the last time! It was all organized in drawers, by shape and size. He just ignored it and started new piles. What was *wrong* with him?"

"Jake, we've talked about this before. He couldn't make decisions about all those things. What we did was probably not even helpful. Your dad would have exhausted Gandhi."

"How did you stand it for so long?"

"I had Simon. I had you."

"How did he ever think he was going to get the Nobel Prize?"

My brain throbs with the sound of Mozart's *Don Giovanni* in D minor. How Luddy would recite from *The Sorrows of Young Werther*: "But alas! when we have attained our object, when the distant 'there' becomes the present 'here,' all is changed; we are as poor and circumscribed as ever, and our souls still languish for unattainable happiness."

Was the medical examiner aware of these faulty synapses as she sought the cause of Luddy's death?

"I don't know, Jake. For a long time, the thought of ending it all was the only thing that kept him going."

"We could have put off the doctor's appointment. . . . Simon broke Dad's pattern. Why did he have to force the issue now?"

"We've always said it would end this way."

"I know. But why did Simon have to wait until I was away? I was working with Dad. I knew how to deal with him. You can't—you couldn't just order him around!"

I hadn't wanted to watch him die.

Sometimes I thought I would go first, lost under piles of junk, unable to find Luddy. Just like the Collyer brothers. I think Langley died trying to bring food to Homer. Could anyone call their existence living?

"Why is it that whatever you think you've fixed stays broken?" Jake says. "If only other people would just—I thought I knew where I was going. I thought I knew what I had. Who I am. Who was Dad, really, in the end? Why couldn't he . . . ? I don't know what I'm trying to say."

"I know you tried to help him, Jake."

"I had a different idea about how to handle this."

"We have to help each other."

Jake's sigh tells me he's not ready to accept what's happened. He's fatherless now, just as he's about to become a father. Luddy was there for Simon. It isn't fair.

I'm angry with Ludwig Berg. I don't know if I can ever forgive him for this last act.

"I'm tired now."

"You should rest. Gia needs you. Maybe she shouldn't try to go to the house tomorrow?"

"I'm not going to let her stay in there very long. She shouldn't be breathing that stuff, and I don't want her to touch anything."

"I bought gloves and masks," I say. Then, "Do you know what you're trying to accomplish tomorrow?"

"Yes. Mostly I just want to figure out how many dumpsters we're going to need."

I was happier speaking with his inner engineer. "Plenty of time for that."

"Simon's going to get all sentimental about everything, I'm sure."

"Everyone feels this in their own way."

"I don't have time for that. We've got to get this done and move on."

"Okay. I'll see you tomorrow."

"Good night, Mom. Love you."

"Sleep tight." I say. I don't add *little man*, like I used to.

October 7, 1988, after school, Mrs. Bain's classroom

"How long should a sentence be?" Jake moaned.

"Longer than these!" Mrs. Bain chided him.

"How many words?" he whined.

"Well, I don't know—they're not all the same."

"A number," demanded his eight-year-old self. "I need a number!"

"Seven or eight words, at least!" his teacher emphasized.

From then on, Jake meticulously composed eight-word sentences, except for the last one in each paragraph. That was always seven. Mockery or compulsion? Plenty of both in his genes. Efforts to get him to mix it up a bit were epic failures. He would not, he protested, yield to any additional outrageous demands. Mrs. Bain accepted his effort, and we survived third grade.

Spring 1992

After the episode with Mrs. Bain, Jake remained a sharp critic of his teachers. "They're not teaching!" he would complain.

At twelve, he was the scourge of Hebrew school. Kicked out of class for complaining, he sat with me in Rabbi Stern's office, searching for a solution. Luddy and I had laughed together privately about Jake's seriousness, but we really had to come up with something to make sure he got through his bar mitzvah.

"Why do you keep asking the teacher how to say 'What time is it?' in Hebrew?" the rabbi asked, trying to stay grounded in observable facts.

"Because I'm sick of coloring in pictures of Noah's Ark. We're wasting natural resources here."

"But why that phrase?"

"I want her to be cognizant of how much time is being wasted," Jake said, using Luddy's favorite word. I cringed even as I realized it was Jake's way of touching all the ironic bases.

"Some of the children like to color." A different tack from Rabbi Stern. Was he enjoying this torture from Jake?

"I'm twelve. You're wasting my time, not to mention the burnt sienna for all those arks. You could save a lot of money in the budget."

"Okay, Jake. I see your point."

The rabbi scheduled Jake for weekly private language and Torah sessions to prep for the big day.

Thursday, April 7, 2016, around 1:00 a.m.

You can tell a lot about a child's mind from how he handles his toys. When Jake was around two, we gave him a set of colored blocks comprising all sizes and shapes in four colors. Left alone with the box, he unloaded them and reorganized everything into Escher-like planes by size, shape, and color. He was the Busby Berkeley of blocks. Way before we knew what his future would hold, he was sorting and organizing arrays of data.

For him, Luddy's death just did not compute.

Simon had had the same set of blocks, but his methods were different. His interest was always in how high he could build a tower before it all fell.

☙❧

It's getting late, but I can't stop the thought train at this point.

The boys have always been so different. That's been the case right from the beginning, even with their birth stories.

Despite twenty-four hours of unproductive labor, Simon refused to emerge. Finally, a nurse pressed him out by leaning on the top of the fundus while the doctor pulled from below. Simon was kicking and thrashing as he made his way through the birth canal, and by the time he finally emerged, he was screaming, outraged.

I waited, empty of energy and baby, praying against my superstitions. Having sacrificed his older sibling for the sake of my relationship with Luddy, I could only hope that I would not be punished through this baby.

Was he all right?

Luddy held him first.

As I slid into a half sleep from exhaustion, I remember hoping he was telling Simon how much he was loved.

At last, they laid him next to me. Simon's eyes were bluer than Luddy's, or Lorelai's, or even Lena's. His copper hair gleamed like no one else's. What did he think of my eyes, broken blood vessels and all from the pressure of pushing? He locked onto them and didn't look away for hours, and I was in love like never before.

Simon, my firstborn. Old Blue Eyes. Eventually known to his football buddies as "Mr. Four-O," in a backhanded tribute to his grades. A rock on the offensive line. Exposing the secret of his cello playing to his teammates only when their senior season ended. Steady and cautious. College and law school. Living through 9/11 as a newcomer to New York City. Quietly waiting for the right moment for marriage, for family, for the fair solution.

For this?

❧

I almost lost Jake the morning of his birth.

After my water broke near the lilac bush, we called Simon's babysitter to wait with him while our parents started their trips from New York. Expecting no excitement, I stirred chocolate pudding at the stove with Simon. We thought we knew better now—that lying down for a day must have delayed Simon. This time I was going to stay upright if possible, even if that meant I took my time getting to the hospital.

Shortly after I arrived, they inserted a monitor, which showed that Jake was in distress. Quarts of fluid flooded the bed, and my obstetrician turned it nearly upside down, inserting his arm inside me to hold back the baby for twenty minutes until a delivery room was available.

Baby Berg, at nearly eleven pounds, was hiding behind a prolapsed umbilical cord, and we could lose him if I didn't have a Cesarean section. *O, triggering moment.* Fortunately, I would not know about this near loss until after the anesthesia had worn off.

When I finally met Jake, his nearly black eyes were laughing already. I wept because I had everything I wanted, and we were safe.

In the chaos, Luddy had assisted in the Cesarean because, as luck would have it, he'd been wearing scrubs at the time, his customary leisure outfit, and the doctor had mistaken him for an intern.

He went where most men wouldn't go.

I loved him so much.

Chapter 9

What the House Said

April 7, 2016, midday, the house

I always lived at the margins of my house.

That's because Luddy cut a wide swath, strewing shoulder bags of work he meant to do wherever there was an open corner or counter. I resented my shrinking environment, and over time I found reasons to spend less time there.

I could feel my shoulders tighten whenever I came through the door. If I ever forgot to look down, the obstacle course of junk on the floor could easily cause me to trip and fall. Given the array of sharp objects, two-liter bottles of soda, and wrapped candy that Luddy dropped all over the house, falling was practically inevitable.

The police hadn't known this when they had entered to find Simon with Luddy's body, but today, as my family pushes through the junk at the side entrance, we warn one another to walk slowly.

Jake goes first to try to clear a path for Gia, but the slippery mail on the floor insists on refilling the space.

"Be careful!" Jake says, touching Gia's face. They both look at her tummy.

Angelica looks at Simon. Her widened eyes look away.

House. A word. A place. *Where you keep your belongings, and your heart.*

What if you have so many belongings you cannot find your house anymore?

Where will you keep your heart?

The house does resemble a crime scene.

So much more stuff has accumulated since I left four years ago. The putrid smell of decayed fruit, moldy papers, and God-knows-what-else pervades our senses. We don't want to stay very long.

Everyone talks about the cleaning process and what some of the mystery smears might be, but we soon lose enthusiasm for identifying them.

We stand in the kitchen for a while. The floor appears to have been washed in mud mixed with mail and supermarket circulars. I notice a prayer book there, my father's siddur, which Luddy made me drop one day when I was trying to retrieve some keepsakes. For four years, it's gathered dust on this floor.

There's a sticky outline the size of my journal on the kitchen table where it was found the morning that Luddy . . .

We are still having trouble deciding on a verb. An ellipsis will do.

As Simon lingers in the kitchen, Jake, Gia, and Angelica start wandering around, trying to make sense of what Luddy left behind. The wives, scarves over their faces, press their hands to their cheeks, unspoken horror in their eyes. We try to avoid touching anything.

When I finally concluded that I would be getting a divorce, I had quietly moved what I could into my study—clothing, some important books, my conducting batons, and a few photos of the family. The study was the only room Luddy had not controlled, although he'd often blocked the door with his stuff. When Luddy was away from the house, I would take a few things at a time over to Jake's in the trunk of my car.

If I tried to remove any items in his presence, Luddy would chase me out of the room, shouting "Thief! Whore! Bitch!" (It's no wonder the three months we lived together while the divorce was being finalized made me physically ill.) This included our precious family photo albums, which I'd been forced to leave behind because Luddy had stacked huge piles of wood, old thesis binders, unanswered mail and bills, and winter boots and shoes in front of the shelves that held them.

Spotting the albums now behind the piles, I was seized with a desire to have them again.

I walk over to the top of the stairs that lead down to the basement. Looking at the heap below, I see the frame of my harp sticking out from where Luddy must have thrown it after I left. Yet another belonging I was forced to leave behind.

My harp was heavy, and I could never count on Luddy being away from the house long enough for me to move it safely to my study—and I couldn't come up with a good excuse for why I might be moving it to my car.

The only way I had summoned the strength for my final departure was to understand that I might have to leave everything behind. So that's what I did, hoping that Luddy would calm down and let me come back inside someday to retrieve the rest of my belongings.

My family now flits here and there throughout the house like birds returning to the woods after a long winter to see if their nest might still be available. The windows are filthy. It's difficult to see the river and the trees that drew us here.

The boys go straight to their rooms to look for souvenirs from childhood—a hockey stick, baseball cards, something. But the sheer mass of the hoard has lumped so many things together, they hesitate to remove anything from its particular heap. I see Jake reaching for his baseball card collection on a shelf and Simon pocketing a puck signed by the Devils, their faces red with grief. *What do our belongings mean, anyway?*

My daughters-in-law hold back their unspoken questions. I notice discreet tears. Because Jake and Simon never wanted their wives to see how we lived, this is their first experience of the mess, and I meet their shocked eyes with shame. Even though I haven't lived here for years, I understand that this disaster area is quickly becoming part of their image of me. Will I ever shed the identity of the hoarder's wife? The old humiliation returns like a shawl that chafes my shoulders as we pick our way through the shards of Luddy's life.

After barely twenty minutes of wandering around, failing to reset our mental images to the time when the three of us also lived here, my sons and I must get out. Gia and Angelica make no argument. Each of us peers quickly at the scene of Luddy's death, but we don't speak about the mix of thoughts that collide with our desire to be outside as fast as possible.

Outside, we walk down the driveway, birds decidedly without a nest, forced to search out materials for a new one. I see Jake pocketing a blue pebble; Simon, a red one. I find an unopened pod from the sweetgum tree. Gia and Angelica bob their heads in shock, still reeling from the encounter with Luddy's mess.

When we say our goodbyes near my car, Jake opens the door and tosses his pebble onto the floor in back. My chest tightens as Simon follows suit with his red one. "Yocks," we say in unison—their childhood word for the rocks they made me keep, picked up from every place we went. This remembered ceremony makes me bite my lip to hold back the tears as I put my pod on top.

This is the last time we'll all be in the house together.

❧

After the divorce, I had trouble remembering any happy times with Luddy. While I certainly remembered good moments with Simon and Jake, it was hard for me to see Luddy as anything other than a one-dimensional figure of anger after everything that had happened.

And now I'm the one who is angry—at him, for taking his own life. Over the years I had begged Luddy to think of our role as parents and grandparents. I'm still shocked that this wasn't enough. Our family was the one part of his life he couldn't hold on to, and this hurts me in a way I cannot convey to my boys.

I find myself looking in my journal again for reflections of myself before I knew Luddy. The four years we've been apart since the divorce have only partially restored me to myself.

I think about the remnants of my harp, abandoned in the basement. If I decide to rescue it from the pile, will I somehow be able to miraculously re-create the world as I once thought it was—the beautiful home, the family that loved one another, the scientist who desired the Nobel Prize, the concerto I finally composed? Or will it all fly off the frame into dust . . . as if it never was?

I close the journal, not ready to start reversing that avalanche today.

How did we get so far out of tune, so far from our dreams?

Chapter 10

"The Bee Meeting"—Sylvia Plath

June 23, 1978

That day early in our marriage began as an ordinary day at the supermarket. Last stop, frozen foods, so the items wouldn't thaw before I got home.

I bent over the frozen juice freezer chest to sort through and find a container that had not formed any crystals. Although Luddy studied crystallography, he was no fan of freezer burn in his morning juice, and I was being new-bride careful. I remember I was wearing a navy-blue silk V-neck blouse with delicate, tiny buttons that were difficult to fasten. I was looking at my hand as I rotated the containers, so I didn't notice the bees as they flew out of the freezer and into my shirt.

I stood up, suddenly itching between my breasts. Embarrassed, I didn't want to call attention to myself by putting my hand inside my blouse, but the itch became persistent and compelling. I tried patting myself, and this disturbed the bees even more than their blocked exit from my clothing, so they began to sting me.

"Don't upset them!" Luddy would always say, trying to teach me to be calm when bees came around.

Breathless with pain, I saw my body reflected in a chrome panel gyrating from side to side in a frenzied hula, pulling at my shirt and screaming unintelligibly. People were beginning to look at me as if I were insane. The other shoppers whispered behind their hands and stepped back, afraid to come too close to my Crazyville dance.

As I twisted into different positions, the bees stung me again and again between my breasts. When they could escape, they crawled along my bra straps up onto my shoulders.

"Orange juice!" I remember shouting, or something equally inane. I think I screamed "Bees!" but this seemed unintelligible to the crowd. No one moved to help.

At last, I tore my blouse open.

This was a bridge too far for the employees with brooms who were shaking their heads around me. Think "Sorcerer's Apprentice" crossed with the Valkyries.

I careened around like a wounded deer, no more naked than a swimmer at the community pool, but with my shirt now missing in the wrong venue, this behavior spelled "crisis" to the onlookers until the bees ran out of stingers, fell out of my shirt, and I could speak clearly again.

"Orange j-j-juice! More bees! Drunk—sugar! Freezer! They'll get you!" I stammered, trying to prevent anyone else from stumbling into the same fate. "Don't you understand?"

One man whisked away a dead bee with his broom, and other workers emerged from their stupor. People came closer, and someone finally asked me if I was all right. The thought of liability had probably kicked in, although no one wanted to come too close to me.

"Let's see," ventured the manager tentatively, looking around as if to make sure the people with brooms would be right behind him, ready to swat.

Not much detective work was required. The back door was open, and bees were flying in and out of the market. Now, everyone could see them.

"That's where they came from," exclaimed the brilliant head of produce, a latter-day Inspector Clouseau. He'd been trying to figure out where to look—at the crumpled shirt in my hand or the welts rising between the curves of my breasts—when spotting the open door saved him. There was nothing in the employee handbook for this situation.

I had always been terrified of bee stings, and this incident did nothing to help me manage that fear. If anything, I acquired a new dimension of terror. (Bugs were an early source of conflict in our marriage. If a spider crossed our threshold, Luddy would gently guide it onto a piece of paper and place it outside to thrive, me shrieking in the background all the while.)

When my pounding heart had slowed down a bit, I shook out my shirt. Inspector Clouseau stood a little closer as the broom people formed a dressing area for me, turning their backs discreetly now that they'd confirmed I was probably sane, not a Fury casting a spell on the market.

"Yes, I'm okay," I lied, wanting to get my mortified self out of the building as fast as possible. I paid for my groceries (they couldn't even . . . ?) and loaded them into my car. For no reason I can think of, although home was only a couple blocks away, I drove past my street, across the Raritan River to a pay phone I remembered on the campus where I taught and called Luddy in his office back across the river. (I didn't want to drive there because I thought he would be annoyed that I had frozen food defrosting in the back of the car.)

When he answered, I told him I had been stung several times in the supermarket.

"I don't feel right—I feel confused."

He blew it off.

"Just a few stings? I remember when . . ."

I blanked out as he told some story about when he was the nature counselor back at Camp So-and-So.

I must have interrupted.

"I don't think I can drive—"

"Well, just sit there a while and try to calm down—"

"I'm not sure I can. I feel dizzy."

"I'll hold on."

He made no offer to come and get me, but at least he didn't mention the groceries. I remember how much I wanted to be rescued. I just wanted to be held. I was crying, but I don't think he heard me.

The operator intercepted, requiring more change. I heard Luddy's voice breaking in as I inserted more coins, suggesting we hang up, followed by a frustrated sigh.

"Are you okay now?" he asked.

"I guess."

"When you feel better, you should drive home and try to relax. You're too sensitive. If you would just try to avoid swatting at them—"

"They flew inside my shirt! I didn't see them!"

Silence.

"I guess I'm feeling better," I lied, giving up. "I'll see you later."

Dazed more by our conversation than the bee attack, I sat in my car with the windows closed to prevent the incursion of any more winged invaders. I let the air-conditioning run until the nausea and confusion passed. Too bad about the cost of gasoline.

I found a cookie among the groceries and ate it quickly because I suddenly felt hungry—hungrier than I'd ever been in my life.

Although I was sitting next to a huge haul of food, I couldn't think of any way to feed my soul—to escape my pain.

Chapter 11

"Flight of the Bumblebee"—Nikolai Rimsky-Korsakov

June 25, 1978, morning, at my parents' home

"He's a good man. You need to go right back to him," Ginger said, giving me her this-is-not-negotiable look, the epitome of a female priest, if such a thing were allowed. Kinder. Gentler. That's what I wanted. Being allergic to bee venom herself, I thought she would have been more understanding.

This was the weekend following the bee episode. Luddy was working again, so I'd driven to New York to see my parents.

"Working on a Sunday?" Ginger had wondered when I'd called to tell her I was coming to visit alone.

"Easier to get the microscope to himself, I guess," I hedged, not wanting to explain the real reason for my visit.

Ginger was on to me, though. Although we fought often, we had that intuitive, mother-daughter connection when something was amiss. Or maybe that was always the case, because "What's wrong?" was our customary telephone greeting.

I thought Ginger would understand why Luddy wasn't coming, given my father's twenty-four/seven approach to doctoring. But Luddy wasn't "that kind of doctor," so my mother was suspicious before I arrived.

I'd fallen into her arms at the front door, crying, feeling faint. My mother let me sob awhile before asking questions.

I told her about the bees—about Luddy's lack of concern.

She reminded me about her allergies and how careful she had to be. She said he was trying to build a life for me, and I should be grateful. She reminded me that I was the product of a union of love, and I had accepted the sacrament of marriage. She said to draw comfort from both her religions. My mother commanded me to return to New Jersey and never speak of this again.

"Maybe you're pregnant?" she said, instead of "Goodbye."

Why have you forsaken me?

Someday I mean to write a sonata for Esther, Queen of the Jews.

–––

When I came home that afternoon, Luddy was sitting on a stool behind his favorite piece of furniture, the bar, surrounded by the smoky mirror tiles he had salvaged from his bachelor apartment. He had set out an ice bucket and a bottle of champagne: *Moët & Chandon*. Siegfried's "Forging Song" provided the soundtrack. The room seemed boisterous somehow, grazed by sorcery.

"What's going on?" I was resigned to the next chapter and intrigued that he was not, for once, projecting Werther-like sorrow. No pining for unrequited love; no chagrined face.

"Tenure!" he shouted, releasing the cork. The repackaged résumé and the unqualified praise from one of the hardest-working chairs at the university had done the trick. That, and the death of the cruel department chair. *La forza del destino!*

I hugged him, hoping that maybe the difficult part was over.

Third Movement

Arias. Duets. The Minuet of Détente.

Chapter 12

Da Capo: The House

September 8, 1978, near sunset

"It's a little small," said Cara as she turned the key in the lock. "But since you said you'd like to be on the water, I thought we should take a look."

We were tired. I was exhausted from months of walking through houses. Like Goldilocks, we weren't sure exactly what we were looking for, convinced we'd know it was "just right" when we saw it. Not too helpful to Cara.

Luddy was after the perfect house, even though he couldn't describe what that might look like. At this point, five months into my pregnancy, I simply wanted to avoid stairs.

Dazed from hours of driving around suburban cul-de-sacs and seeing only variations of the same model house, we had come to the decision that we'd buy a piece of land on the water somewhere and design our own place. At least, I thought, we could do that kind of planning while sitting down.

Cara had obligingly located a few waterfront lots, and we had traipsed around them all afternoon. Now we were at an unassuming ranch house—our last stop. Cara hadn't even mentioned it until we had seen all the lots. Clearly, she was tired too; we weren't easy to please.

It was Cara's custom to go into a house first and make sure it was empty, so we waited on the front step until she threw open the door.

My brain began a familiar symphony.

Key in the lock. (Da-da-da-dah)

Open the door. (Repeat)
Key in the lock. Open the door. Enter the house!
Then, suddenly, an unexpected chord . . .
We love this house!
The epic view—
Our search is over!
Key in the lock! Open the door! This is our house!
That was it. Just one look and we were sold!

September light at four in the afternoon warmed the main room
with a gorgeous amber glow. The light reflected from wood trim everywhere—fireplace, moldings, and picture windows—oh, those beautiful
windows! Casements flanking the picture windows opened onto a
private wild wood that revealed glimpses of a sparkling river beyond
the trees.

My thoughts roamed to performing an afternoon concert on the
water. We heard an owl hooting! Mozart would meet Beethoven in
the ivy-covered yard. The view from the living room made us crazy
with desire.

Instantly enamored, we walked around the three-bedroom ranch
only half listening to Cara's details, like butterflies returning frequently
to the blossom of the central living room / dining room. It formed one
long theatrically glowing space, bisected now by the owner's grand
piano. A good omen. Music lived here. This was a place where I would
thrive.

Joyful. Joyful.

Luddy shushed me in a corner when he saw I was about to gush to
Cara. Sotto voce: "Don't let her know how much you want the house!"

We stayed to look out the picture windows for as long as we could,
smiling like children who'd found a treasure, and then Luddy told
Cara we'd give her a call.

"Don't wait too long," she said. "They're looking for a quick sale.
Divorce."

I had noticed an extra lock on the bedroom door. I planned to ask
Luddy to remove it because I couldn't imagine why it was there. It
seemed creepy to me at the time. The thought that the house could
be cursed was only strengthened when Cara told us the owners had

lost a child to cancer. They later divorced. She knew the ex-husband, who was also the real estate agent.

I pressed this knowledge to the furthest edge of my mind like I pressed dough to the edge of the bread board while making challah, but this story was baked in as a warning. Even so, I was confident we would write a different history here.

The house was only three miles from our apartment—over the Raritan and the tributary stream that meandered into the waterway that bordered our home-to-be. We both knew it would happen—that we'd be raking those bountiful leaves from the ready-to-turn forest.

Luddy had determined the lowest bid he could reasonably make: $90,000. I was shocked, sure it was a deal-breaker. I called my parents, gushing about the windows, the fireplace, the three bedrooms. They were excited but shared my concern that Luddy had underbid too far.

Luddy called his father to check his thinking, saying that he was willing to come up a bit—hey, he was willing to pay the whole $99,000! If you don't try, you'll never know. I was afraid the owners wouldn't bargain, but Rudy was in complete agreement. He and Lorelai gave it their blessing. Everyone wanted to come and see the house.

Luddy called Cara that night, beginning one of the longest weeks of my life.

                                                                             ॐ

In the end, the ex-husband half-owner gave up his agent's commission, and his former wife agreed. We took another walk through our dream house with the ghostly ex-wife, whose eyes were vacant. She animated for a moment as we said goodbye on the lawn near the dogwood tree, saying, "Mrs. Berg, you will love the violets in the spring!" Sure enough, when they bloomed the following year, they were unique—the palest shade of violet I'd ever seen.

We closed on Yom Kippur, ignoring our transgression.

The Bergs and the Feldshers visited our new home the next day, to feel the baby kick inside me and take pictures of us in the yard. For that proud moment, life seemed pastoral, a minuet of détente.

Da capo! We began again.

Thursday afternoon, April 7, 2016

I'm going to finish the journal before the funeral tomorrow. While I have mixed feelings about thinking of Ludwig Berg as a complex person, it will help me to feel pity for the unmitigated disaster he became.

I'm safe, I remind myself. The horrifying devastation of our relationship can no longer hurt me.

At least, not in the same way.

Chapter 13

"Lonely Women"—Song by Laura Nyro, 1968

Thursday afternoon, April 7, 2016

I wish I could say that everything continued along this rainbow path in between our move to the house and the birth of Simon, but that's not the way it happened.

December 5, 1978

After we bought the house, we both still had to complete a semester of teaching. Once I'd turned in my grades for a freshman writing class, I thought I would finally be able to relax, put my feet up, and wait for the baby. I hoped that Luddy would take some time to get ready too.

I was set to complete my student conferences yesterday. Most of the meetings had gone very well. After reviewing their grades, my students would wish me happy holidays; many would ask me to let them know about the baby when "it" came. (We had to say "it" because gender knowledge wasn't usually provided after a sonogram. Mine had been ordered at four months to check for the possibility of twins. My obstetrician had looked at the film for me, but said the baby was turned so that no one could be sure of the gender.)

I'd been feeling nervous and tired all day. About two months from my due date, I was relieved to be closing out my teaching schedule. For my last conference, a very tall, athletically built student—I'll call him

Walt—strode in through my open door and sat down abruptly, facing me. He put his final paper on the desk near him with a warning slap, looked me square in the eye, and announced, "This won't do!"

"What won't do?" I asked him.

"This grade!"

We both looked at where his long index finger was pointing on the page. I remember thinking that Walt might have been a strong pianist if he'd wanted to be, which I wasn't due to my small hands. On each student's paper, I had carefully written separate grades for both the final paper and the course grade so they wouldn't have to wait for the registrar's copy in the mail. Sometimes, as in this case, my prompt organization skills backfired when an angry student protested.

I tried to take a deep breath without making a sound, like a flutist between phrases. Although I was looking at the paper, I could feel him glaring at me with the eyes of a predator.

"B-plus is a very good grade," I said.

"Let me explain—I'm pre-med, and I need this to be a solid A."

"Well, when I compare this with writing from other students, although it's very good, it's not quite an A. I would need to see a clearer thesis statement—"

"In case I didn't make myself clear, I'm pre-med."

"I understand why this grade might be important to you, and with a bit more effort, I think you have the potential to earn an A in the second semester of this class, but this is not an A paper. Some students took advantage of the option to rewrite papers to improve their grades. I can't find one instance where you revised a paper."

"I don't know if you're familiar with how demanding it is to study for pre-med."

"As it happens, I am."

"This is not acceptable!"

"I am sorry you're disappointed."

He stood up, towering over me. I also stood to preserve my authority, not thinking about the vast difference in our heights—at least a foot by my belated calculation—and as I stood, he shoved me and my extra fifty pounds of baby weight up against the wall with a thud.

At just that moment my colleague Jason poked his head in the door.

"Everything okay in here?" he said, looking from me to the student, who took his hands off my shoulders and backed away.

"I think it is now," I said. My voice was shaking.

Walt sat down again.

Jason raised his eyebrows and gave me a pointed look. When I waved him away, he said, "Next door if you need me," and walked back to his office.

"Something has to be done," Walt argued.

"What do you suggest?" I asked. I remained standing, determined he wasn't going to intimidate me.

"How can I get this grade changed? You're not going to stop me from going to medical school!"

"You can speak to the program chair about it if you'd like. Students have a right to be heard."

"Are you sure you won't change it?"

"Quite sure. And I think you might reconsider why people go to medical school in the first place. I don't think shoving a pregnant woman up against the wall is part of the curriculum."

He grabbed his paper and ran down the hall toward the stairs.

Jason came back into my office and put his hand on my shoulder. "You okay?"

"I think so." My hand went instinctively to my belly. My mother had had a car accident when she was three months along and had almost lost me. *Please. Not now.*

"That was stupid."

"I know, right?"

"I don't mean him," Jason said gently.

"Huh?"

"I mean you—in your condition."

"I guess you're right. I should have called the chair when Walt started complaining. I wonder if he'll change the grade for him."

"Nah," Jason said. "He knows you're an excellent instructor."

"Come on, Jase—I'll buy you a cup of coffee from the truck. I owe you."

December 6, 1978

The writing program chair phoned me today to say he had changed Walt's grade to an A because he didn't want any, "you know—trouble." One of those moments that makes you doubt your choice of profession, to say nothing of how much I worried for Walt's future patients in the event he subsequently scored well on the MCATs.

When I told Luddy about the grade issue, he commiserated a little and then told me his "hilarious" story about the female engineering student who showed up in hot pants to request a similar grade change. I said I hoped he had at least kept his door open. He said he would do that next time, adding, "No one would dare question my grades!" *My kingdom for a job with tenure.*

Luddy never said a word about the baby, even though he knew I'd just had a prenatal check. *When someone shows you who they are, believe them.*

New Year's Eve, 1978

While my body has focused on learning to be a mother for most of these nine months, my mind is still trying to have it all. Although Luddy and I agreed we would have a two-career marriage, in recent months I have come to understand who will be making the necessary adjustments so it will all work. Career might not be the right word for my share.

"You can do anything you want, as long as I can stay here," Luddy had said as the capstone to our conversations.

By *here*, I realize he means not so much our house as his current university.

I pride myself on creativity and flexibility, but I feel shocked by the finality of this, which lands on me with the force of the crashing chord at the end of the Beatles' "A Day in the Life," without the resolving harmony. I'm not sure what to say.

I'm coming to the end of temporary appointments on the faculty, and I've taken an unpaid leave for the spring semester to get at least one more semester next fall. That's if I can manage to pay for a babysitter—so I can try to guarantee more work to pay for more babysitters in the future. The second career is all on me, and it sounds like descending arpeggios. Luddy, having attained the safety of tenure in one place, cannot fathom starting over in another.

Facing this reality, I adopt the bleak mantra of my women grad school friends: "We are one man away from welfare. We will always be working, always looking for work." In our lives, a job will not always be meaningful work in our fields of study. An unbroken résumé trumps our chosen career as we "branch out" to show how resilient we are.

"Pregnancy brain" has scattered my thinking since the first trimester. I usually try to fight it, but tonight, alone in my home, I let it take over. Facing around eight months of unemployment, I'm thinking about a project I can launch now to work on later, when the baby is sleeping.

Right now, Baby Berg is a night owl, so I slip in a cassette of *Peter and the Wolf* by Sergei Prokofiev, a childhood favorite of mine. There's no harp among the strings of the original score. It's been several months since I could play my harp, as my pregnant belly means I can't quite reach the strings, and Luddy didn't want a piano cluttering up the room. Without an instrument, I have been fantasizing about conducting again. And of course I am thinking about children and the sounds to come. *Laughter in a clean house where love marries knowledge. I imagine competing arpeggios rumbling to rest on a whole note. Someday I will bring it forth in a concerto. I want that.*

I've read that babies respond to music even in the womb, and mine seems to swim enthusiastically when it hears the flutes conveying birdsong in *Peter and the Wolf,* just as Prokofiev intended. (I'm tired of saying "it" when my gut insists the baby is a "he!")

Luddy is in Utah, learning to ski in Park City.

"Don't spoil this for me." That's what he'd said over Thanksgiving weekend when he casually dropped the news that he had committed to going to Utah from December 30 to January 4 to do some consulting for a manufacturer there.

Do they work on New Year's Eve? I had wondered.

"We always celebrate the New Year together at home," I'd said. "Can't this wait until after the baby?" The word *always* may have been a bit of a stretch, but we'd so enjoyed it for the past two years; why was he ready to toss that all away?

"They want to start on New Year's Day, and they offered me a couple of nights in Park City beforehand so we can all socialize."

"I can't go with you."

"I know. But this will lead to more consulting in the future. I know I can solve their problem, and then next time—"

"But what if the baby—"

"Next time we can all go together!"

Not the promise I was looking for.

Experience told me with the definitive sound of a plucked bass string that Luddy would not be dissuaded from a commitment once he'd made it. He was oblivious to "us." I knew the baby wasn't yet real for him, and its arrival would need to be worked around his career like an intrusive refrain from an adjacent rehearsal room, or the unexpected sound of traffic when a backstage Broadway door is left ajar.

Luddy did not handle interruptions well. I remember the near death-match conversation we'd had the night we met, regarding which was the best novel among our favorites. While I argued for either *Pride and Prejudice* or *Ulysses*, he had clung to *Gravity's Rainbow* as the "best ever," annoyingly mispronouncing Pynchon as "Pin-con" no matter what I said. Following a principle that Jane Austen might have lauded, I knew not to try and beat him at this verbal tennis, so I had demurred.

But we were talking about my life now. Didn't I have to be seriously in the game?

❧

I call my parents around dinnertime to say Happy New Year.

My mother reminds me that my dad had served in the Korean War, not just for New Year's Eve but for two years. She'd had to manage without him, taking care of me on her own.

I don't tell my parents what I'm really worried about tonight—the fact that I don't have enough cash to get to the hospital in case I should need to go. Taxi drivers don't take credit cards, and that's if I could even find one. I barely fit behind the wheel of my car now. I must sit much too close to the airbag, so I'm not driving often.

Starting in 1974, women could at last apply for credit cards without a husband's signature—if they had jobs with reasonable salaries. I have tons of "credits," but no "credit." I do have some money saved from fall semester, so I'll be able to hire a babysitter to go back to work part-time in the spring, but tonight I have no general credit card and no access to "our" bank account. Luddy didn't even leave me an emergency check. In the chaos of his departure, I think he forgot.

These may be strange thoughts when you're worried about having a baby, but I am not alone. Most faculty wives have no credit cards of their own, and it was a topic of intense conversation last summer. One day at the faculty pool, we thought we had enough couples gathered to raise the issue—perhaps to shame our husbands into a new approach. Some were swayed, but not Luddy.

Why won't Luddy answer the phone? It's New Year's Eve!

My feelings of abandonment flood into my river of doubt. *What if? What if?* sings a mockingbird in my head. The questions crescendo in my mind: *What if I can't find a ride to the hospital? What if I can't get there in time? What if I lose the baby? What if Luddy is running away from us?*

This recitative makes me wild with fear.

"Why do you do this to me?" I flame at Luddy's empty chair.

I leave my fourth message of the day with the Park City hotel desk clerk and turn back to thinking about my project.

Three of the greatest composers of all time failed at performing music—Sibelius, Schumann, and Handel—but their compositions are among the most beloved masterpieces in performers' repertoires. Though my own repertoire is limited by the size of my hands, I am forever running melodies through my head, and I mostly conduct from memory. Apart from his less-frequent binge evenings of Wagner, Luddy has become more of a TV freak lately, so I am guiltily grateful for these nights of free-ranging concerts.

I imagine Emily Dickinson and Jane Austen composing on small scraps of paper in and around their busy households.

I can still do something creative.

Rummaging around encyclopedias, I learn that in 1936, Natalya Sats, the music director of the Central Children's Theatre in Moscow, commissioned Sergei Prokofiev to compose a musical play for children that would introduce the instruments of the orchestra. Despite the international success of *Peter and the Wolf*, in 1937 Natalya Sats was arrested for being a "traitor by association" when her husband, foreign trade minister Israel Veitser, was arrested. Her refusal to confess earned her five years in a Siberian labor camp and exile in Kazakhstan. Like father, like daughter. Both served time in Siberia, where Natalya was born. She was finally "rehabilitated" by the post-Stalin Soviets in 1958, and even now continues to advance children's theater.

There is no excuse for not continuing to produce.

As Peter and the Wolf concludes—with first the oboe's reminder of the duck and then the resolute last notes of the triumphant ensemble—I find myself sitting awkwardly on one side of the harp, which had been banished to a corner of the room. There, despite my difficulty in reaching the strings, I begin plucking the unembellished melodies of familiar children's songs. Surely there is another composition to be written about an orchestra.

Riffing for a long time, I become fixated on the progression of the "Inchworm" song from *Hans Christian Andersen*—how intricately the words, music, and rests parallel the motion of the insect. The process is hypnotic, and I doze off for a while, thinking "Lullabies with One Hand for the Gravida" would be a good title. In my opus, there would be a harp . . .

I startle awake from a dream about wolves in the mountains around Bromley.

There are no wolves in Vermont.

No matter.

In the dream, I take out my harp to save myself, and suddenly I have wings to fly away.

Cue the French horn for the wolf's entrance.

This reminds me of a recurrent dream from my childhood about a red fox chasing me.

When I was seven, my mother had suffered a miscarriage requiring an abortion, and all the talk of blood seemed to evoke my terrors in the form of that animal. In my dream the fox would always catch me and pull me to the ground. Everything around the fox was red.

Shivering from the memory, I try to shake off this gloomy line of thought with some sixties' oldies. That's how I come to find myself tapping out "Where Did Our Love Go?" while singing simultaneous lead and backup. By the end, I realize why.

Don't think about your love enjoying himself in Utah . . .

I'm remembering a short song about Utah called "The Beehive State" by Randy Newman, when a commotion outside interrupts my free association.

I turn on the lights to assess the noise from our wildlife-filled backyard just in time to see a raccoon, some deer, and a fox on the slate steps leading to our screened-in porch. The light frightens everyone, including me. I'm sorry I illuminated the yard, because they all scatter. I'm not sorry I alarmed the fox.

At last, I am killing the wolf. I am so killing the wolf.

Thursday, late afternoon, April 7, 2016

I lay the journal aside to catch my breath. I remember a feeling like paralysis. I was carrying our child and felt responsible for everything. Luddy never thought to comfort me. I wanted to be held myself.

Through the years, I became someone I did not like very much. I stopped asking for intimacy because it was so difficult for him to give. When he wanted closeness, I could offer the physicality without the emotion, a plant withering for lack of the sun.

But the children! They kept my heart beating.

Luddy finally called me the day he was leaving Utah. He said he couldn't figure out how to work the phone. It seemed so preposterous at the time—that he could be a stunt pilot on a scanning electron microscope but be bested by a mere telephone.

Now I can marvel at how often the two of us were blinded by our own intelligence. I didn't understand about learning disabilities back then. Neither did Luddy.

When he came home from that trip, Luddy strewed a collection of tchotchkes from the couch to the center of the room. It was the first of many such deliberate archipelagos he created. I had to step over it, to honor this extension of him whenever I walked across the room. It served a dual purpose, reminding me of his existence and preventing me from coming too close to him in the last weeks of my pregnancy.

After Simon was born, he had to remove the clutter to allow for visitors, which he did with great resentment. This first experiment proved he could succeed in claiming territory by using this method.

I didn't realize it then, but he was already pushing me out of the house.

Chapter 14

"I'm Only Sleeping"—John Lennon and Paul McCartney, 1966

October 10, 1984, Dr. Marsha Kindlove's office

"But he's not here right now. We need to focus on you," Marsha says.

Four months ago, just short of a doctorate in literacy education, my enthusiasm had cooled for writing up my research on music and learning. I'd decided to see a therapist to try to restart my thesis.

To keep up my résumé, I'd taken a metaphorical page from Luddy's curriculum vitae and signed on for a job as a freshman coordinator—because in academe, when in doubt, add administration to your credentials. At least there was no grading involved. It might not be an ideal position, but it would give me the appearance of job continuity in the wider world if I ever had to leave the ivory tower.

With this job, trying to work on my dissertation, and getting Simon and Jake to kindergarten and nursery school every day, I was exhausted by dinnertime.

And there's something more.

In my sessions, I keep coming back to Luddy and his behavior. And Marsha keeps redirecting me back to myself.

"I think he's bulimic."

"Why do you say that?"

"He throws up after dinner every night."

Marsha doesn't answer right away.

"I hear him retching. If I ask him about it, he denies it. But I can smell his breath. . . . And his mother always talks about vomiting to clear her stomach if she doesn't like what she ate."

Marsha blinks. I'm grateful she doesn't ask how the smell of his breath makes me feel.

She waits for me to say more and, when I don't, asks, "What are you thinking?"

After more silence, willing my mind to reject Lorelai's obsession with remaining thin, I dance toward another precarious thought.

"He sleeps in the living room."

I see Marsha's eyes brighten. At last—we're entering territory she thinks she can help me with. Sex.

"How do you feel about that?"

How does she think I feel? I want to say cheekily, "Sometimes sleeping in the living room is just sleeping. (Beat.) In the living room." But I don't want to experience her disapproval, mirroring, as it does, my mother's own disenchantment with me. I will speak about my mother another time.

I bluster through a few useless, dismissive choruses of *I don't think he's sleeping well* and *He's working too hard* while Marsha nods.

At last, I come to the heart of it: We have no intimate life together. What to do?

I don't give her a chance to say, "And how do you feel about that?" Instead, I jump right to the moment I asked Luddy about it.

Marsha nods approvingly.

I tell her how he put me off with the excuse of his huge workload. What I have witnessed, I tell her, are his terribly inefficient work patterns, making himself accessible to everyone at all hours, an over-commitment that multiplies the number of deadlines he faces and his concurrent memory lapses. He can't seem to finish anything, jumping from one project to another, driving away with boxes of student papers flying from the top of his car. He drops off into a heavy sleep after stuffing himself with all kinds of carbs when he comes home from work at night, without much interaction with me or the boys. He awakens at two or three in the morning, and I hear him turn on the television. He makes it clear he doesn't want to be disturbed by ignoring me if I go in to check on him. Sometimes, I hear Simon trying to convince him he should go to bed.

"We're here to focus on you, Grace. How do you handle all that?"

"I'm just trying to work around it."

"But how do you *feel* about it?"

"I think I just told you!"

My dancing around the issue continues through much of the hour, my emotional pendulum stuck on Luddy's side of the story, which I believe is the cause of my anxiety and frustration. I never talk about myself. I don't know how.

Although I keep talking, I tune out, listing examples on autopilot until Marsha interrupts me. "Why not try something different?"

I look at the clock. Five minutes left. "Like what?"

"Schedule a social activity and invite him to come."

"What if he says no?"

"Just go on your own. And do it again the following week. See what happens. See how you feel."

Thursday afternoon, April 7, 2016

I remember that I took her suggestion and began to live a life mostly without Luddy, revolving around the children's schedules. The morning after each concert I attended—I had to put music back in my life—I experienced a miracle. I found I had enthusiasm for my research again and was even thinking about my concerto.

From September through May, Luddy was too tired to come with me to any of these concerts. In the summer he might revive a bit, and we'd attend performances together at the university. He would sleep in our bed at night, and we might restore our love for each other a few times a week, as long as the children were asleep.

But then late in August, as subtle as the change in temperature, Luddy's enthusiasm would drift back to his lodestar, teaching, and, sure as a late September day without a shawl, I would be shivering outside of his orbit again.

That first summer, though, felt like a revival for us, thanks to Dr. Kindlove.

Emboldened by this success, I used to try to convince Luddy to walk around the neighborhood with me on the weekends. He would decline, his face seeking pity, his voice mumbling excuses: "My feet hurt. . . . I must grade papers. . . . It's time to clean the gutters."

Luddy had taken a walk with me once after Simon was born, but after that, never again. We took walks only when we were on a trip, and only to get from one place to another—never for the emotional satisfaction of traveling through life together.

This realization stings, even after all these years. I know that I missed his touch—craved his embrace—but this part of our relationship was absent for most of the year. He made it clear that my requests for physical intimacy were an imposition. I believed he was working hard for us, so I gave up asking, and waited for June each year with the anxiety of a woman living near the Arctic Circle, hoping for six weeks of sunlight in which to celebrate being human.

But each summer, our efforts were a little less frequent, a little less satisfying, like descending minor scales. For me, with each refusal, the memory of the baby I had destroyed rose to take the place of desire. Every. Single. Time. Finally, my yearning resurfaced only faintly, until the day I realized I could turn it off like a switch in my mind to avoid the fugue of rejection.

I had tried to talk with him about my feelings many times over the years. This is how it always went during the early years of our marriage:

"I don't think we communicate well enough with each other."

"I disagree."

"I think there's a problem here that we can look at—that we can try to solve together."

I'd see his pupils shrink, and his large ears seemed to pin back flat from his red face before he'd shake his finger at me and shout, "I don't have any problems with the way things are. If you have a problem, you go get help!"

"I just want to be your wife! Why can't you tell me what you want me to do?" I would plead.

My husband would mutter unintelligibly and walk away from my tears. He would stay away from the kitchen until my sobs had stopped. Humiliation was my constant companion.

Luddy had no words for discussing his emotions. I never knew what he was feeling. Following the New Age parlance of the '70s, I once asked, "If you were an animal, what animal would you be?"

Without hesitating, he replied, "A turtle!"

This was an answer we both understood.

October 17, 1984, Dr. Marsha Kindlove's office

"Why can't I bring myself to leave him?"

"You have found a mate—you have a family. That's a very powerful connection."

Silence.

"What do you think makes you stay?" Marsha asks.

Still quiet.

"What is it?" Marsha whispers, her voice like a gentle bow across strings.

"Well, I was thinking about a time when I was in college."

"And?"

"Okay . . . His name was Chase. I used to kid him. I'd say, 'Chase, as in the bank?' He'd say 'Kinda,' with a sneaky smile. It turns out that he was a descendant of Salmon Chase, a chief justice of the Supreme Court of the United States, the man for whom the bank was named. Rockefeller owned a major share; Chase did not. But still. Old money. Lots of that at my college.

"Did you know Aaron Burr owned Manhattan Bank, and when they merged, voilà! The full name . . . Salmon Chase himself served in all branches of government. Umm, anyway, Salmon had a daughter named Kate, who married Governor Sprague of Rhode Island. But I digress . . ."

Marsha nods. She looks amused.

"So, about Chase and me . . . He was an aspiring playwright, and I was majoring in music composition and education. Our junior year— seeking some relief from the intensity of reading for our majors— Chase and I met in a production seminar where we had signed on to be the tech team, learning to make sound and light illusions on the stage. It was fun! For five months we designed remote explosions and strung lights from a catwalk and spent our nights together, arguing about Arthur Miller and John Cage, art, our muses. We tested our hypotheses by experimenting with different sexual positions. Did art descend from some creative force on high? Or were you able to make it from the chaos around you? Who was really a creator?"

Marsha smiles.

"We were surrounded nightly by colored lights, new music, and constantly flowing words made flesh by actors. I remember feeling so free then. It was a time when musicians reinterpreted the classics, and we thought we had invented everything. Everything was an experiment worth trying. Now I wonder: Were we free, or unwitting slaves to our times? Ian Anderson—he arranged Bach's lute suite in E minor, 'Bourrée' for jazz flute—have you heard it? Jethro Tull? No? Well, it was something old made fabulously new. He took off the chains of chamber music and made it slightly sinister. Chase used that as an example of the composer as a medium for the divine; I argued that it was an original, bringing the old material out of the chaos and into a liberated context. It didn't matter that we argued. For a slice of time, our passion burned, and our minds were very much a part of it.

"As I look back, my friends and I viewed love as a serial project. As with art, whether we saw it as inspired by some divine muse or seized from the natural world around us, we viewed it as temporary. Passion and love aligned like a superstorm in those days, without room for any gentle, forgiving friendship."

Marsha gives me her *I'm waiting* look.

"One cold night in April," I continue, "we were in a canoe with our parkas and ski pants on, to keep warm. Chase had thoughtfully purloined fishing boots from the costume department so we could avoid soaking our feet in the freezing lake. We both wanted to see the sky from the middle of the lake. A thaw had come early, which left pockets of snow on the shore and tiny icebergs in the water. We had paddled carefully through the floes to the center of the lake, looking for delicious danger. We made explosions! We controlled light! What could go wrong?

"I remember Chase opened a beer for me. Then he chugged half a six-pack and began kissing me so hard that the canoe started rocking.

Capsizing was the only thing on my mind. Could we make love out there? After some uncomfortable clumsy attempts, and because it was too cold to take off our clothes, we mutually abandoned the possibility and faced the moon overhead.

"He called me 'Iceberg,' laughing. I laughed too, because he knew I wasn't frigid. 'Adam and Eve didn't have this much difficulty,' I mourned.

"'A man, a woman, a tree,' he said. 'Life was simpler for Adam and Eve—if only they'd stuck to what they'd been given.'

"'A woman, a man, a boat!' I replied. 'We're free to come and go.'

"'As long as we can cut through the ice!' When he said that, I laughed, but he didn't."

"What do you think he meant, Grace?"

"Something larger was on his mind. In the quiet, he said, 'It's too bad I can't bring you home to meet my parents.' I hadn't given this option much thought, as we'd been so focused on the present—immersed in the play and exploring each other. I struggled to sit up for the rest of the monumental intrusion of reality I feared would come in his next words.

"'What do you mean?' I asked.

"'Well, I can't possibly bring you to the country club. Mummy wouldn't allow it.'

"Confused, I made him say why.

"'Because, Gracie, . . . you're Jewish.'

"'No!' I said in mock horror. But then I looked at his face, and I saw shame.

"In pastoral Vermont, even with the peace, love, rock and roll, and drugs, there was plenty of racism. Had we ever spoken about our parents much beyond the tiny lecture on his ancestors? I couldn't remember, but we had both drawn and ignored inferences. The college gave us a venue to escape the divergent worlds we had both come from in our shared state of New York. We deluded ourselves that everyone was equal here. Yet, more than halfway through our education, the Hamptons and Scarsdale remained as irreconcilable as Mozart and Salieri, the Stones and the Beatles. The truth is, we never would have met had it not been for this college. Despite the intensity of our experience together, I expected we would remain apart.

"'Thanks for not sugarcoating it, Chase,' I said. My father had taught me to blend—to never let them see you cry.

"Chase remained paralyzed with dejection in the bottom of the canoe while I paddled back around the dying ice into the new water of spring, ending our winter idyll. You could take the boy out of the Hamptons, but you couldn't take the Hamptons out of the boy.

"When we were safely back onshore, I yelled stupidly at him, 'I won't let you ruin Vermont for me!' I stumbled out of the canoe, leaving him to get himself out. I didn't care if he floated back into the middle of the lake. That night—the moon—so much ice. My frozen fate. We had started college a week after Woodstock, for God's sake! What was so different about me? I was glad we had only one more week to work together. We could be civil, professional. Everyone would know we weren't together. Too bad about the boy. *End scene.*"

I look up, and Marsha is staring intently at me.

"And?" she says.

"It wasn't the first moment of truth for me. My first college boyfriend, Ulf—which means 'wolf,' you know?—he had rubbed my head vigorously on the night we decided to 'do it.'

"'What are you looking for?' I had kidded him, pushing his hands away.

"'Horns!' he'd exclaimed, with great seriousness.

"'Are you freaking kidding me?' I asked.

"Ulf told me he had heard that Jewish girls 'put out,' but, growing up in the heartland, he had also heard about the horns, and he had to check. And so it went. In America I was always the Other.

"I knew it was time to move on from Ulf, Chase, and their entitled cohorts. I wasn't going to be the Emma Goldman of dating. I felt that there must be someone out there who didn't put religion first, whether he was Jewish or not."

I pause for a moment, reflecting.

"You know, my father spent his summers near my college town at camps run by Jewish families. He had wonderful local friends who lived near the lake house retreat he had built as an adult. He kept these friendships over the years. We even went to church with them at Christmas to sing carols if we were visiting around the holidays.

They would join us for Passover seders when it was warm enough for us to come up in the spring. I developed a deep feeling for Vermont, and it felt like my second home. Maybe even a better home, because my parents were usually relaxed and happy there."

I take a quick breath here because I don't want Marsha to get hung up on my parents.

"As a college student, though, I felt alien. My college may have been in Vermont, which I knew to be a tolerant place, but students brought their values from elsewhere. I never mentioned my religion unless someone else did, and then I tended to minimize its importance in my life."

"How did that work out?"

"To revise an old cliché, one of my best friends was Jewish, but we didn't learn that we shared a common faith until the week before graduation. We were having a celebratory dinner at our professor's house when his wife asked us how we had experienced being Jewish at the college. The look of shock we exchanged with each other conveyed a world of harm. 'Oh, my,' she exclaimed. 'You didn't even know!' Our professor's wife was Jewish, and she had known about us, but we hadn't! My friend and I had blended so well that we'd lost our heritage."

"How does that make you feel?" Marsha asks.

I'm not sure how to answer that.

"Awkward? Sad? Like our lives had been a lie for four years?" I reply. "The situation seemed to demand that we hide. I feel like somehow Luddy and I were fated to find each other and hang on to our traditions, together. We'd been floating out there around the broken-off pieces of our family. I had one Irish grandfather. Our siblings married Catholic spouses, and Lena tried to appease Rudy and Lorelai by promising to have bar mitzvahs for their children. My sister fled to another continent to avoid dealing with them. But Luddy and I stood firm. We didn't have to make promises to the rabbi about how we would raise our children; we simply maintained the rituals as best we could."

I look at Marsha intently. "Why don't I feel closer to Luddy?"

"I don't know. What do you think the reason might be?"

"I have no idea. I know why he won my heart initially—we had Otherness in common. But Judaism was not the whole explanation."

I pause, then say, "When I went to my five-year reunion at the college, I heard that Chase's bride ran through his inheritance in a year."

"You're still angry about Chase, aren't you?"

"Not exactly angry."

"What did you want to make happen back then?"

"I really don't know."

Marsha says quietly, "I think Emily Dickinson said, 'The heart wants what it wants.'"

I nod.

"I see our time is up for today."

Next week, I plan to speak about my parents. I really will.

Thursday, April 7, 2016

In 1991 Chase died of complications related to AIDS. At our next college reunion, we planted a tree in his memory, but I didn't share my remembrance of Chase at the ceremony.

Chapter 15

A Placere, Rubato

October 24, 1984, Dr. Marsha Kindlove's office

"I can't stop eating. Can you help me with that?"

"Why do you think you can't stop eating?"

"I can't seem to find a way to make Luddy happy."

"He's not here. We need to focus on you."

Quiet.

"I just want to be his wife."

"What does that mean to you?"

"Well . . . I want to feel closer to him. Like we're speaking the same language . . . any language, actually."

"Tell me more about that. What would closeness feel like to you?"

I'm stumped. "I don't know."

A look of doubt slithers across Marsha's face.

"You must have a memory of your mother holding you? Comforting you? Everyone does."

This seems a bit pushy and judgmental, but nonetheless, I try to conjure up some good memories of my mother. I think she *wanted* to comfort me, I really do, but the only hug I remember getting from her was after that time she left me alone at age two with the leaky gas heater. Does that count? It certainly wasn't comforting to be cut by her owl pins when she squeezed me so tightly. When I'd told her about my first crush at age eleven, she had put her hand firmly on my shoulder and said, "You can do better."

Marsha lets my nonresponse hang heavy in the air like a towel caught on the clothesline in a thunderstorm.

In the cold silence, I suddenly remember that I had begun cutting myself at age ten.

I'd been so terrified about an upcoming piano recital that I had begged my mother to let me skip it. My teacher and my mother focused on my disappointing behavior and delivered homilies about quitting. Although these hurt me, they didn't work, and the pain sat boulder-like on top of my heart.

I wasn't good enough to be a concert pianist, and I wasn't good enough to love. I cut the staff lines of a measure into one heel, then pricked a drop for the circle of an eighth note's head, drew one perpendicular for the stem and two short curves for the flags. Perfect! The anguish subsided, and I blotted my heel gently to preserve the art. Someday I would lead an entire orchestra, I promised myself. I could focus. I could do anything if I could stop disappointing my mother.

That night, my mother discovered the small bloody cuts on my feet where I thought they'd be hidden. She screamed at me as if I had injured her. It was a delicate balance, but I'd felt driven to let the bad feelings out, and cutting seemed to be the easiest way, so I'd continued. I had never told anyone about my seven years of self-torture, and I didn't feel safe enough with Marsha to start now. Did I have to share everything for this therapy to work?

Marsha seems disappointed, and she doesn't answer when I tell her it was my father who taught me about love and compassion.

When I was afraid of making a mistake at my piano recital, it was my father who'd sat me down to share a story of how early in his career he'd once been afraid to take blood from a patient because he'd thought he might hurt her. His mentor, seeing his reticence, had taken him out in the hall to remind him of how he'd be helping her, and although the patient had winced a little, she had thanked him later when he'd delivered the results.

"Think of the beautiful music of Poldini!" my dad reminded me. "'Poupée Valsante,' 'The Waltzing Doll' is waiting for a pair of lovely hands to set it free." Then, taking my hands in his own, Daddy said he knew just the pair.

I'd gone to the recital and performed for the audience with just one small mistake, and for once, I hadn't felt the need to harm myself that night.

Thursday, April 7, 2016

My parents were not bookends. Like a pair of North Pole magnets, they could repel each other in their handling of me and my sister, Lisa, whom I hadn't seen or heard from in twenty years. At fifteen, she had run away with a jazz guitarist to Paris. She'd left a note on my pillow, and when my mother saw it, she'd said, "Well, she's made her bed now," and tore it into a hundred pieces.

I had to be the one to tell my father. He was the one who cried.

Occasionally, postcards addressed to me showing some Rive Gauche landmark would arrive, signed only with a small heart. My mother would hand them to me without a word, and when she wasn't looking, I would share them with my father.

During college, I had found my liberation in music, and I tried on new personae whenever my own inner drummer suggested them. We music majors all aspired to study with famous composer and conductor Nadia Boulanger, just like Jenny in Erich Segal's *Love Story*. You could count on one hand the number of women leading major orchestras at the time, but they were out there, especially Boulanger, and I was determined to gather enough experience to lead one myself. My constant was music and organizing other people to produce it.

I owed my earliest love of music and conducting to my father. On the weekends he would nap on the couch while I practiced. He would hug me and say, "I love to hear you play!" When I had finished, he would sit on the same bench and produce a few minutes of a Rachmaninoff piano concerto and sigh, "There's nothing like the piano!"

For some reason, Marsha never really wanted me to talk about my father. She would listen patiently for a minute or two and then redirect my meandering back to my mother.

And I would sit, stranded, struck dumb by the memory of the parent who didn't allow anyone else to have feelings.

October 24, 1984, Dr. Marsha Kindlove's office

After yet another attempt to turn the conversation back to my mother, Marsha sits there, assuming her listening face.

I feel so closed off, like I'm back in an encounter with my mother, where I couldn't say a thing.

"I want to talk about my father," I tell Marsha.

I want to tell her how I learned about love and affection from Steven Feldsher. How I missed riding around with him on house calls in the solid, safe car with the incredible sound system. How beloved he was to his patients in Yonkers, where he could safely leave me in the car on any street corner. Some inaudible signal would summon all the mamas in the neighborhood, and they'd come bearing cookies, stories, puppies for me to pet, to pass the time in safety.

Marsha should want to know this stuff—shouldn't she?

About how my father would conduct Gershwin on the radio with one hand while steering his car with the other. Luddy was similarly inattentive to the task at hand, but his intolerant perfectionism produced a different result. Whereas my father would never let spilled milk get in the way of happiness, for Luddy, preventing the milk from spilling in the first place was his happiness.

Instead of sharing all of this with Marsha, I spend the whole session staring out the window.

Wednesday, April 7, 2016

I remember that a few weeks after I'd had the secret abortion, I introduced my father to Ludwig Berg. I asked Dad what he thought of Luddy because I believed we were very serious about each other.

He searched my face, his brown eyes darkening to meet my seriousness.

"I wish you'd finish your degree first" was all he said.

Chapter 16

Adagio, Con Amore

November 8, 1984

Our routine upended because I had to take my car in for service, Luddy met me at the repair shop with the kids in his car. We hustled to get Simon to his school across the river first so he wouldn't be late, even though it was closer to Luddy's office and would have made more sense as our last stop. Panic and traffic contributed to the already thick tension in the car.

I heard Luddy's unspoken accusations. *Of course I had a nine o'clock meeting. You couldn't do your car on another day?*

We had planned out the day ahead of time, but Luddy had overslept. There were no "other days" for two-career parents.

I walked Simon into his classroom where the honeyed tones of "Bluebird, Bluebird" filled the air. Simon put his jacket and lunch in his cubby and settled into his place.

His teacher winked forgiveness at me. I loved her for beginning the day with music, summoning the best of the children's hearts in unison. I wished I could have stayed and sung with them.

I waited five beats in case Simon had second thoughts about staying but realized that he probably found it calmer at school than at home. When I felt it was safe, I hurried back to the car.

Luddy gunned the accelerator, speeding along the highway toward my office.

We were almost there when a loud voice from the back seat caused us to gasp.

"Where's my nursery school?" thundered Jake.

Luddy jammed on the brakes and pulled over to the side of the road. We all took a few deep breaths. How could we have forgotten Jake? Yes, he was the quiet one, but when he spoke, we listened. Even at three, he seemed to know all the routes we traveled frequently, and where they went.

I was relieved to see that this incident was somehow having a calming effect on Luddy.

"I didn't mean to forget you, Jakey."

"It's plain old Jake," he said.

I laughed quietly into my hand, and Luddy shot me a sidewise glance as he turned the car around. This only made me laugh harder.

"I'm sorry, plain old Jake. I won't let it happen again!"

"Jake!" came the annoyed admonition, and he turned to his teddy bear, from whom he knew he would soon be parted.

When we got to his nursery school, Jake ran ahead of me into his classroom without even saying goodbye. I waved to his teacher and left quickly.

"We need help," I said to Luddy when I'd returned to the car.

No answer.

He backed out of the parking space and continued the drive to my workplace, across the highway.

November 15, 1984, Dr. Howard Friedman's office

To help free me of my preoccupation with Luddy during my sessions, Marsha had recommended we consider counseling with Dr. Howard Friedman, a couples and family therapist.

The past few sessions had focused on practicing several scripts to learn how to better communicate with each other. I am finding this therapy more practical than my solo sessions with Marsha. Stories are told, course corrections are suggested, and plans are formulated.

Last week, Ludwig Berg learned how to give me a bouquet, and I learned how to thank him before offering the flowers back to him so he could arrange them to his liking. Luddy has made it clear that I'm not good at it—he worked for a florist after school, for heaven's sake—saying I'm careless and just plop them in jars. *Stilted* is the operative word when it comes to sentimental gestures between us. I feel doubtful. Luddy won't express how he feels.

Although more practical, the sessions feel robotic—Luddy sounds like Young Frankenstein when he offers his lines—but we've agreed to give it some time and practice more at home. Actors need to learn their lines before delivering them in a convincing way, right? We're like an old vaudeville team telling that joke about Carnegie Hall: practice, practice, practice!

Today we're discussing the quality of our fights. Luddy says he can't remember our exact dialogue, but Dr. Friedman allows him to correct my version as I begin.

Example:

Luddy, wanting to bring another table into the living room for paperwork, might say: "You haven't played that harp lately. How about moving it to the basement?"

My retort: "How do you know? You asked me not to play it when you're home."

This is only partly true.

Luddy: "I never said that."

Me: "Well, that's why you don't hear me playing it."

Luddy: "I doubt that. Look at the dust on it!"

Me: "There's dust on everything, since you haven't vacuumed in months!"

Dr. Friedman interjects: "Who does the vacuuming?"

Me: "Luddy. He won't let anyone else do it."

Luddy: "She doesn't do it properly."

I reflect that I've watched Luddy vacuum a nine-inch square of rug for five minutes to make sure it's perfectly free of dust, then turn off the machine to rest. If I say anything or offer to help (our guests might be arriving in a half hour), he will stomp out of the room with the vacuum, saying, "I'm doing it, aren't I?" as if I'm his mother.

I don't have a chance to include this in our role-play narrative.

Dr. Friedman: "Can you describe how 'properly' would look to you, Ludwig?"

Luddy: "Done—as in, no dust!"

I can't fathom the depth of Luddy's understanding of dust or any other substance, probing as he does the subatomic structure of things. My way of looking at dust is to liken it to the subtlety of the pedal's effect on a tone issuing from a harp string. Luddy, intently studying the same image on his scanning electron microscope, looks past it to the bonds between silicon and oxygen. I just couldn't go there with the dust on the harp. While I often find his deliberate, focused work quite beautiful, when it comes to the living room rug, what I need is a timely solution. Our household metronome does not stop. Stalemate.

Dr. Friedman brings up other chores.

"Who does the dishes in your household?"

Me: "I load. He reloads."

Dr. Friedman laughs, and we relax a little too.

Luddy: "She wants to run it before it's full."

Me: "I can't turn it on unless it meets Luddy's definition of full, even if we run out of glasses or silverware. We seem to use a lot of plates for some reason. He's like the National Institute of Standards for household appliances!"

Dr. Friedman: "Okay, okay; a lot of couples fight about this. Usually, one partner takes certain jobs while the other takes something else. Division of labor. Reduction of arguments."

No comment.

Dr. Friedman: "Let's talk about laundry. Who does it?"

Me: "Well, Luddy, but—"

Dr. Friedman can't help himself. "And what do *you* do, exactly?"

I swallow my anger at the apparent sexism of that interpretation.

"It's a little more complicated than that. I gather the clothes and load the washer, and then Luddy reloads it. I think there should be some space for water and soap to move around, to actually clean the clothes—"

Luddy: "She wastes everything! She doesn't fill the machine!"

Me: "*She* doesn't cause it to overflow!"

Dr. Friedman: "I'm sensing a theme here. So, after it runs?"

Me: "I unload it as quickly as I can because Luddy doesn't want his shirts to wrinkle. They must be hung, buttoned, and straightened, all seven or eight of them each week, and then I put the rest of the clothes into the dryer—no time for special treatment of anyone else's! I fold everything on the dining-room table or on a couch if Luddy's papers are spread out, which they usually are. Luddy told me he never wants to see an empty table or surface, waiting to be used. He considers it a waste of space."

Dr. Friedman: "Let's stay on the laundry for now. Who puts the clothes away?"

Me: "I put mine away. Luddy wants to do his own. I've tried, but it's hard to walk on his side of the room. I can't get to his dresser."

Dr. Friedman: "Why not?"

Me: "Shoes, books, papers, stacks of clean laundry on the floor."

Dr. Friedman: "So, it sounds like you do the laundry, Grace."

He pauses, waits for some wisdom to fall from the sky.

How the situation evolved over time:

"All he has to do is throw it on the heap, Mom."

In high school, the boys took over their own laundry, dealing with their sports grime on their own. Pointing emphatically at the heaps in the living room without words as they passed by me with their clean uniforms. Talking about it when Luddy was away on business, not mentioning it when he was home. How we all cringed around his ever-expanding mess.

How none of us could do anything about it.

Dr. Friedman: "How does your morning routine go?"

We laugh and describe what happened recently when we forgot about Jake in the backseat. Dr. Friedman laughs too.

Then: "Do the children find it difficult to get ready in the morning?"

Me: "No."

Luddy: "I find myself asking them if they are cognizant of the time every morning."

Dr. Friedman: "Cognizant? That's an interesting word to use with young children."

Luddy: "I don't see anything wrong with teaching them new words."

Me: "It might go faster if you said 'know' instead."

Luddy: "Why would I say 'no'? I'm not arguing with them—"

Me: "I mean, as in 'Do you *know* what time it is?'"

Luddy: "I guess."

Dr. Friedman: "When in Rome . . ."

Luddy: "Now I have to change my whole way of speaking?"

Dr. Friedman: "A wise person once said, 'I can't change anyone else. If the situation is not working, how can I change myself?' Does that make sense?"

Luddy: "I suppose."

Dr. Friedman: "How did your assignment with the flowers go? Do you have any observations?"

Luddy: "She let me arrange them in a vase."

Dr. Friedman: "Grace, how did that feel?"

Me: "It was nice to get flowers from Luddy."

Luddy: "They looked good."

Dr. Friedman: "Luddy, how did that feel?"

Neither of us seems to have words to offer on the subject of feelings. Dr. Friedman doesn't press; instead, he shifts gears.

"Last week, we were talking about your parents—all four of them. How unsupportive they have mostly been, even when they're not saying much. There's a theory, you know, that in a therapeutic marriage, you choose the mate who most reminds you of the parent you had conflicts with and then try to resolve the original conflict in the marriage. Could either of you talk about a time when you felt that a parent had seriously wounded your feelings?"

When neither of us jumps in, Dr. Friedman volunteers me to go first.

A forgotten moment is bubbling up. Even though it's long repressed and I'm not even sure I want to share it, holding it back is like trying to keep champagne in a bottle once it's been uncorked.

Me: "All right. But this is new territory. I'm not sure I can."

Luddy: "Thank you for going first."

Me: "You're welcome." I start slowly. "From the time I was a little girl, beginning, in fact, shortly after my mother entered me in a beauty contest—Miss Junior Freckle of Miami Beach in 1954—"

Dr. Friedman: "So you were about, what, three years old?"

Me: "Yes. Well, every couple of months after that, for the rest of my life at home, my mother would scrutinize my face and tell me it was dirty—that I couldn't go around unclean and impure. She would prepare a washcloth with soap and water and scrub and scrub until I would cry out from the rawness of my skin. I would insist that it was just my freckles; there couldn't have been any dirt left after all that scrubbing!

"After rinsing my face, she would check again, dubiously. She'd usually say that I still looked dirty, but that it was 'better now.'

"In high school, I was that rare, fortunate teenager who had no acne. I gently cleansed and moisturized my face twice a day, but to my mother I was always a dirty girl, 'not worthy of making my way in the world.' She would shout in my face, 'You are not pure,' and rub harder, disregarding my tears. My sister was never subjected to this ritual, just me.

"In my heart, I didn't believe my mother's accusations, but I wanted her to feel satisfied somehow, so she would stop punishing me. She never did any of this in front of my father.

"When I was seventeen, I finally told her to stop—my face wasn't dirty, and we weren't doing this anymore. She never did it again, but whenever I look at her, even now, my skin feels raw."

I sink down into the couch I'm sharing with Luddy. When I dare to look at him, I see tears in his eyes.

Dr. Friedman: "So your father never knew about any of this?"

Me: "He was always working. . . . Maybe he did know, on some level. He always told me, 'Don't be like your mother, Gracie," which I never understood. I always thought she was beautiful and pure and wise—that I could never hope to be any of those things."

Luddy: "You are beautiful to me, Gracie."

When we both stop crying, Dr. Friedman asks Luddy for an example from his life.

Although he seems to be struggling, he finally manages to speak.

Luddy: "When I was a boy, I never had my own bedroom; I never had any privacy in our apartment—not even a separate place to keep my belongings. I had to continually shift them from one temporary spot to another. My sister, Lena, got the second bedroom because she was a girl. My parents had a small fold-up bed in the dining room for me. At night, I was allowed to keep a few things on the dining-room table after I'd cleared the dinner dishes.

"I had to rearrange my things and put away my bed each morning before everyone came in for breakfast. Even when I hit puberty, I wasn't allowed to control the space for myself, or have any privacy until everyone had retired for the night. The empty table during the day was like my unattainable room. The fact that I wasn't entitled to any space of my own enraged me, but I wasn't allowed to complain about it. They were saving for their future, they told me, and I should be grateful for what I had."

In a flash it becomes clear to me why Luddy covers every surface with his things. I realize with a burst of anger that his parents were currently enjoying their retirement years traveling around the world thanks to the savings they'd accrued from his reluctant sacrifice.

After many weeks of frustration with each other, we share a quiet moment of mutual forgiveness. *Would it be enough to save our marriage?* Scoured to the dry bones of our histories, we are astonished beyond words to discover that we are living in the same emotional cell.

When Dr. Friedman says he's sorry, but our time has ended for the day, neither of us says a word. Luddy stands and holds out his hand to help me up from the couch.

I take it and he leads us out of the building to the parking lot, where we stand by our car for a long time, looking softly at each other, unwilling to let go.

Pianissimo. Lento.

Chapter 17

Con brio. Caesura. Silenzio.

January 2, 1985

Happy New Year.

On Monday I start a new job as an executive assistant for the dean of Fine Arts, Hollace Rollins. I'll be writing speeches and other correspondence for him. Dean Rollins hired me because of my familiarity with music and artists' issues.

That phrase, *familiarity with*, seems to understate things, but as a working mother, I've been told I'm not hirable for jobs that require "expertise" because my home life might compete with the demands of the profession. Never mind that I have worked through two pregnancies. Never mind that men have parental commitments too. Yes, I am familiar with writing and familiar with music. Yes, I am familiar with issues confronting young artists. And, yes, I want to work, so service writing, sometimes pithy, will be my current specialty.

Not content, however, with the challenge of a four-day-per-week, three-year, grant-funded job, which I know will overflow the official number of days, I also plan to launch a musical combo. We'll call ourselves "The Women's Movements."

Yes, the phrase *familiarity with* stuck in my craw, so I need to dust off my rusty expertise—or else I fear I'll be out of the conducting game forever.

January 12, 1985

Our first rehearsal went well. The Women's Movements comprises a string quartet—Jane, a violinist, the wife of a touring pianist; Hermione on viola, a single mother of two; Lilya, our cellist, mother of three, who lives in a commune and plays electric cello with a fledgling rock band; and Al, our bassist (and token male), father of one—his spouse is the tenured academic and he is the homemaker; and yours truly, as conductor. With eight children among us ranging in age from infant to ten years old, we have all done our time on the adjunct teaching trail, peripatetic scholars and musicians all, so we understand one another, and it feels like everyone's commitment to making this a professional endeavor is sincere. We are not young artists anymore. No one knows how long the mid-career phase can last before it turns into no career.

As risk-takers—we don't see ourselves as having much to lose—we've decided to include some wit, so our first performance will include John Cage's *4'33"*, Debussy's *Children's Corner Suite*, and some of Chick Corea's *Children's Songs*. I have rescored these pieces for string instruments. Sure, we chose *4'33"* due to the limited rehearsal time it requires, but The Women's Movements also wants to make a political statement about being silenced and pushed out of the profession due to our gender and parenting responsibilities. The children's music was selected to honor our families, who have so generously accommodated our practice time, which has often cut into their play circles.

We'll have four rehearsals together and then perform in a space we can rent cheap from a local church on February 17, a post–Valentine's Day event.

January 13, 1985

The job.

It's exciting to work with Dean Rollins. He's a builder following an unproductive placeholder. Of course that means a lot of work for me, but I love the material and the dean loves a good metaphor, so the assignment of writing his correspondence is fun. At least I don't have to be a clock-watcher, and I can work from home if the kids are sick.

Germ factories, those preschools and kindergartens. Our society has a long way to go toward supporting working parents.

My income doesn't add a huge amount to the family coffers, and Luddy has been complaining that my working costs us too much in taxes. But I don't see him complaining about how I pay for groceries for everyone and clothes for myself and the kids. If I don't work now, I can't imagine trying to restart fourteen or fifteen years from now when Jake goes to college.

Something has to give.

There is one potential glitch here. Another facet of my job requires me to become a "PC expert" to assist the division's transition to personal computers. The description is pretty sketchy, because no one here really knows what that means. I have asked for training, and they've come up with a small budget—$100!—so I've got to make it work along with teaching myself. I foresee an opportunity here. Scientists are saying this is how we'll make music one day—a further development of Moog. I'm not so big on synthesizers, but it's all fascinating. I'm diving in with both feet.

Learning this material feels like speaking a whole new language—LAN, twisted pair cable, user interface, WYSIWYG. I bought several books to try to understand software, and I asked around. People throughout the university seem to use many different programs for writing. Most of them include "Word" in their titles, but some require a mind for numbers in their commands. After a couple of long nights, I find it's really just different key combinations, like chords; memory is an important tool for this. No one has imposed a standard program here, and different professions also prefer different tools. The programs don't interchange files! From WordPerfect to WordStar is a long journey. Some, like WordStar, are clearly designed for engineers.

Luddy doesn't want me to pay for any resources. He thinks the dean should take care of it all. He might benefit from buying some for himself, as engineers are using the most difficult one—WordStar! He cannot remember all the individual dot commands, and the so-called manual is just a mess of photocopied instructions in no order, without an index. For all their emphasis on efficiency, the developers of WordStar practice jazzy improv without theme or organization. I have a pretty good memory, but this is overwhelming me. I don't think it will succeed with humanities writers.

Meanwhile, I'm scouring the state in my spare time to try to find free courses. There's one in North Jersey at a technology college open to any state education worker—"How to Take Apart and Assemble a Microcomputer." My experience with tools has been limited to that college production seminar and some set-designing experiences at summer camp. I think it's time to brush up, since no one seems to be an expert in all things PC, and there aren't enough people in computing administration to put the whole university online. I already know that I will have to install everything but the wiring.

Although it's demanding, I like the opportunity to blaze a trail. It reminds me of how I feel when I'm conducting, trying to bring dissonant pieces together into a cohesive whole.

That four-day-per-week job has turned into seven days a week if I count all this research—and why shouldn't I? It's a good thing I can cook and read at the same time. All that tuition money well spent.

February 17, 1985

Things fall apart. We probably should have called ourselves "The Mothers of Distraction," with apologies to Frank Zappa.

Last night, Hermione called me around six o'clock to tell me her youngest had scarlet fever. She hadn't realized he had an ear infection, and it wasn't caught in time. Hermione felt so guilty about it that she refused to leave her son until he felt better.

Her sister couldn't get to New Jersey in time to watch the kids during the concert, and I couldn't think of anyone else I could call to sub for her. Hermione was "so very sorry" that she wouldn't be able to make it.

I couldn't stop thinking about Helen Keller and sent everyone's love and concern to Hermione.

Clearly I hadn't prepared for this. We were only one deep in each instrument, with no backups. I left a message with a few faculty members on the off chance a student might be able to fill in for Hermione. We were just going to have to perform without a viola. Our quartet would become a trio—meaning our sound would be a bit thinner—unless a fourth dropped out of the sky. We had each contributed a hundred dollars to the space rental, and no one wanted to forfeit the deposit. We all voted to press on.

I avoided telling Luddy about this wrinkle; he would know soon enough.

I had stayed up late the night before to see if I could compensate by rearranging the score somehow. Not really. Would an empty chair put an even finer point on Cage's piece about silence? How many women's creations have been kneecapped by caring for someone?

While this reality is nobody's fault, I'm frustrated nonetheless. I try to remind myself that Clara Schumann mothered eight children while married to a suicidal husband and maintaining an intense touring concert schedule. I will figure it out.

By our call time, an hour before the three o'clock concert that afternoon, only Al had appeared. No sign of Jane and Lilya.

At 2:45 the minister met me in the lounge with two telephone messages and a sad look. The first message said that Jane's husband had collapsed in London, and she had to catch a flight from JFK that afternoon. She was sorry, but she would not be coming. The other message, from Lilya, explained that she had unexpectedly run out of gas, and with most of her fellow commune residents undertaking an EST retreat in New Hampshire, there was no way for her to get any until they'd returned, later that night. Lilya had forgone the opportunity to play in our concert. "So sorry."

Al and I decided to perform *4'33"* and call it a day. We knew it was a cheesy gesture, but neither of us wanted to go out there and cancel the concert. Peeking into the sanctuary, we saw a scattering of maybe fifteen people, mostly our spouses and friends. We had hoped for twenty-five, so we told ourselves we were more than half successful. What artist hasn't made use of a lie in the making of art?

We wished each other luck in the lounge. I entered the hall first, to warm, mostly familial applause. The high point for me was hearing the booming voice of Simon exclaiming, "That's my mom!" as I approached the podium, followed by Jake shouting "Shhhh! Mom said, 'Be quiet!'"

Al's wife had planned to come with their son if soccer practice did not go too late. Maybe it wouldn't be so bad, I smiled to myself, thinking we might be edging closer to twenty people if they showed up.

I announced the shortened program, heard a few sighs, and saw one or two sympathetic looks.

Then Al entered and took up his bass. More applause. Five minutes later the room was silent, though there had been some audible light amusement during our performance, acknowledging the "air baton" and "air bass" touches that we had added to create some reality and illustrate our notion of the changing modes of silence.

I invited Al to take a bow, and then I joined him in another one. After a short burst of kindly applause, people scurried to the exits. Sunday was a school night, after all.

Al and Luddy helped me empty the heavy coffee urn into the sink when no one stuck around for the doughnuts and coffee I had brought at the last minute. Jake and Simon were thrilled about the leftovers, even though they would have to wait until after dinner to dig in. I half heard a competitive dialogue about who could eat more of the doughnuts. Al's wife had banned sugar, so we were stuck with all of them.

We had meant for the concert to be a "happening," although with no money for colored lights, it was mostly cerebral. Aspirational. Theatrical. That's who we were.

We had decided not to make it a fund-raising event since it was our premier concert, and none of us had time to keep track of ticket sales anyway. Admission was free. Given our family situations, it had been difficult enough to find rehearsal time or space.

What had I been thinking? I felt like Alice in Wonderland obeying the bottle that said, "Drink Me," only to find my life getting smaller each day.

Nonetheless, we made a concert event happen. I have a picture of the empty musicians' chairs that Luddy snapped to prove it. He labeled it with a fat black marker: "The Women's Movements, 1985."

January 21, 1986—Simon's Operetta

Has it been a year already? Work and getting through our days have consumed us all.

Our household has gone off the rails, and Simon seems to be running it in our absence.

After I say good night, he listens for Luddy to rise heavily from his recliner in the living room, where he has eaten dinner between two dead-to-the-world naps. I am aware of Simon's nightly patrols now only because I hear him talking paternally to his father tonight, gently suggesting with the certainty of a near-seven-year-old: "It's better to sleep in your bed, Daddy. I tell you this every night."

"Not right now, Simon." Luddy sounds convinced, but that only makes Simon try harder.

"Are you cognizant of the time, Daddy? You should turn off the TV and go to sleep so you won't be tired tomorrow."

Eventually, Luddy stomps into our bedroom and heads toward the bathroom. I hear the scratchy shuffling of Simon's pajama-covered feet heading toward his room. He stops momentarily at our door, his polished aquamarine eyes reproaching me in the dark.

"Simon, it's okay to go to sleep now."

He doesn't move.

Luddy flings open the bathroom door and trudges over to his side of the bed. He yanks the covers over himself.

"Simon," I whisper.

He puts his blanket to the side of his face and backs away from the doorway, turning toward his room only when he believes Luddy won't rise again.

❧

I'm going to have to do something in the morning. I just don't know what to tackle first.

Luddy has reported dozing off at work, angrily focusing on his colleagues' reactions to these naps rather than his responsibility.

We need to have a discussion about our finances and the distribution of work at home. I'm exhausted from the horror show of watching

Luddy writing checks for hours every Saturday, each one seeming to take forever because the kids are too loud, or I use too much electricity, so the power bill exceeds the amount of funds he'd budgeted.

It seems he never budgets enough. Once he puts money into our savings account, he is loath to take it out no matter how often his estimates of monthly expenses prove to be too low. He is sure it's my fault. He's sure I'm going to put us in the poorhouse. I can't imagine how life would be without my salary going toward clothing, food, and the occasional mortgage payment when he miscalculates. We've never bought anything on credit apart from the house, and we seem to have enough savings for big expenses, so I don't understand his ire. I'm not sure where the disconnect comes from.

I am also growing weary of waiting for Luddy to finally leave for work after four or five return trips back into the house for lost or forgotten items, which often require my help to recover. I usually wait until he turns toward the county road near the end of the block, because it's more than likely he has left his checkbook and the possibly unstamped envelopes with the bills on top of his car. Someone will need to retrieve them from the lawn or driveway, or even the street if it's windy enough.

I have no retirement account; all the money is in Luddy's name. He has a small life insurance policy, but I have learned that I'm not the beneficiary. Years ago, before we got married, Luddy named Lena's children as beneficiaries. As their godfather, he felt this was a logical choice, and he's never made any changes to the paperwork since. I asked him what he thought would happen to me and the kids if something should happen to him, and he replied that I would just need to work more.

This all suggests that a return to Dr. Friedman would be helpful, though I feel less optimistic about couples counseling now. A month after we'd concluded our previous sessions, Luddy told me he was relieved it was over so we could get back to "normal."

"Normal" is just not working for me anymore.

June 17, 1986

We do end up returning to Dr. Friedman for a few more sessions. He suggested that we make some revisions in household management—mainly, that I take over budgeting and bill payments. Luddy is still reluctant to give up control of the checkbook. He did agree to a joint account, but he doesn't want me to write in the checkbook because he says my entries will just confuse him. He cannot comprehend why I write in the amount that I will deduct in order to subtract correctly. He does it in his head, and says my "extra" entries confuse him.

We decide that I will keep my own checkbook and he will add my entries to his checkbook on a weekly basis. He swears he can do better with the bill payment. Luddy's system seems overly elaborate, even to Dr. Friedman, but it's a start.

We don't address the items he leaves on top of the car.

October 21, 1986

The checkbook scheme has been officially abandoned. Luddy experienced it as a loss of control rather than the delegation of an annoying task.

Dr. Friedman had tried to build him up: "Luddy, you think the big thoughts. Let Grace handle the mundane. You know, many people find it difficult to focus on high-level research while dealing with nitty-gritty details. Give yourself a break!"

Nice try, Dr. F.

I can't say I was 100 percent happy having the minutiae dumped on me, but I had been willing to do it to smooth out our days.

Wine has reentered my life.

Fantasies of Hollace Rollins have begun to invade my thoughts.

I would never. Would I?

February 14, 1987

Valentine's Day.

This morning, Luddy left some roses on the counter along with a box of my favorite cookies—a little joke we share about an amusing

TV ad in which the husband brings his wife flowers, but she exclaims something like, "What? Did you forget my cookies?"

Simon drew a large red heart and signed his name, and Jake contributed a picture of Luddy and me holding hands, with Jake standing between us. We are near the house, where Simon waves from a window. We're standing somewhat apart from Jake, our arms stretched a little too far but our hands holding his, as if he still feels the connection between us. I'd say Jake's appraisal was quite astute.

Chapter 18

Fantasia. Fuga.

May 30, 1988

There comes a moment of reckoning in the life of a faculty spouse where the quest for tenure has to combine with a major change in discipline or disable itself. The tenured academic may face a path of challenges, but running out of a profession or a job is usually not one of them.

Having reinvented myself two or three times already, I realized I was at the disabling point. Yeats described it when speaking of something more cosmic: "The center cannot hold." I don't think I'm being melodramatic in borrowing that phrase. This will be a huge change for me. It's an admission of failure that I will need to overcome. I can only imagine how Luddy would handle a similar situation.

Looking around, I could see that our culture offered only a contrapuntal misunderstanding of my situation: I heard Bobby McFerrin soothing everyone with "Don't Worry, Be Happy," but then Michael Jackson was urging self-assessment in "The Man in the Mirror." I may have had some music in me, but I couldn't deny the obvious about my career path any longer. The band would have to play on without me.

My moment of truth: I had run out of a job. As a faculty spouse clinging to a grant-funded position, I had known this was coming; I just hadn't known when. There was no more funding for my position. Yes, I'd done great work, they told me, but there was a budget freeze due to football. Was I aware of that? There was simply no money available for a self-trained computer expert, no matter how much they'd depended on me in the past. There were other priorities. Paper was important too, even in this cyber age.

The answer was so lopsided, I needed to stop asking the question.

I had also run out of adjunct possibilities within a twenty-five-mile range. New York City wasn't calling. The glut of MFAs competing for so few opportunities made it laughable to even try.

I had gotten an offer from a college in Michigan to run a program, but Luddy had dragged his feet about looking around to see if he could move his research or get a spousal accommodation. When the deadline came for my decision, he said that I could do anything I wanted but that he needed to stay here, in this job, and the children would stay here too. There's that old story about the wisdom of Solomon. I was not going to try to divide my children.

I chose to keep the family together.

I also chose to continue working.

August 4, 1988

I don't like to sound like a cliché, but here goes: One door closed, and another has flung open with an opportunity. Yes, those frantic computer years have paid off. An international training company needs experts to develop and teach courses throughout the United States, Canada, and Western Europe. I had taken one of their courses two years ago and kept a copy of their brochure recruiting trainers. I took a deep breath and applied last month after I got tired of brooding.

They want me! I've scheduled an interview at their New York City headquarters next week, which they say is just a formality. It's one of the oldest adult education companies in the United States. I won't have to commute to New York every day, and I'll be working ... *everywhere!*

How many weeks per month could I give them?

I offered three or four—I'll be home on the weekends unless it makes sense not to fly back from the coast. Let's see how it goes. It's all contracting work, so I can stop anytime.

Maybe I'll like it. Maybe it will work.

But Jake. Simon. I'll call every day—as often as they want to talk.

And Luddy.

Caesura. I see a notation of parallel diagonals, like railroad tracks. // For a moment, I freeze as I think of this turning point in our journey.

Who will wait for him to pull out of the garage in the morning to chase after whatever he left on the roof as it falls to the ground?

Maybe a bit of separation will save our marriage.

September 23, 1988, circling San Francisco

I'm completing my third week on the road this month. I have begun to acclimate to the thin-line existence of the road warrior. I pack very little in a small suitcase and carry a heavy laptop and projector.

This week I've allowed myself the luxury of checking a bigger suitcase because I'll be traveling for two weeks, including this weekend, so will need more than the two paired outfits I usually bring for shorter trips.

I have lived with the terror of lost luggage for the past several days. It's almost not worth it, but I haven't seen Annie or Lee in nearly eight years, so I'm taking this opportunity to squeeze in some fun this weekend before I fly to Vancouver on Sunday night.

This job is exhilarating, although the night flights make you grind your teeth. I have needed a break, and Luddy was kind about it. Jake and Simon were another story, but I'll have a week off when I finally go home next week, and I'll make it up to them then.

I'm not sure how Luddy is handling it all. He doesn't dare complain after taking such a drastic stand about staying put in New Jersey. The boys have been disappointed with his limited repertoire of kid-oriented meals, so this time I cooked all weekend before I left so they could have their favorites. Jake wouldn't come to the phone twice when I called. Simon just kept asking, "What day are you coming home?"

"They'll get used to it," Luddy said, trying to sound brave.

I closed my eyes to the other possibilities.

Tomorrow is Saturday. I'll spend the day with Lee and her little girl in Golden Gate Park. After I see her apartment near the zoo, I'll head over to Annie's neighborhood for a long-overdue glass of wine.

These first weeks have gone well. I whisper a thank-you to my former boss, Hollace Rollins, for making this new chapter possible by naming me technology officer. I feel so confident explaining software to everyone. They don't have computers, but I do. I'm also grateful that I decided not to mess up my life with an affair.

My teaching style mirrors my conducting. I move around the projection screen like a dancer, encouraging people to put their hands in the air and practice "air computer" in the manner of air guitar. Learning, I tell them, is a full-body activity, emphasizing the fun.

My evaluations have tracked well—two 4s ("excellent") for every 3 ("good") on a four-point scale, with occasional 1s ("poor") or 2s ("below average") from people who didn't read the directions. I can tell they didn't read, because their glowing comments do not agree with their number selections. Occasional negative comments are left by people who did not read the brochure and simply assumed they had signed up for an advanced class on the days when I taught the beginners' version.

My only learning curve has been figuring out how to maneuver through the airport late at night with my baggage. That, and missing everyone at home.

As we begin our descent, I mouth a prayer that my suitcase has traveled with me.

A soft bump for the landing. Multicolored lights on the taxiway. The endless ride to the gate. The wait for a bridge. The whoosh of air before we are set free. Goodnight to the crew. Dragging my tired legs to baggage claim where my suitcase is first to appear on the carousel.

Amen.

September 24, 1988

It was so great to see Lee! Her daughter, Jenny, is bright and funny and seems to know all the plants in Golden Gate Park, the way Jake and Simon used to know all the dinosaurs by name. (I'm not sure they still remember all of them, as they've started to replace those conversations with football stats.)

Of course being with Lee and Jenny made me miss my children even more. Lee marveled at how Luddy let me take on this job, and we agreed that it had something to do with his desperate desire for stasis. In any case, she was happy to see me so joyful about my work.

It was almost a perfect day.

Then Annie called me just before we were supposed to meet in my hotel lobby to say she had to work an emergency shift at the hospital and probably wouldn't get off until midnight.

I empathized about the long day and night she was having.

"You probably won't want to try for breakfast at 6:00 a.m. tomorrow before I head to the airport, would you?"

Annie groaned, and I groaned back.

I was actually grateful that it didn't work out. I knew I'd need a good night's sleep in order to be a live wire on Monday.

On my next flight I asked a flight attendant what she thought was the most valuable thing in her suitcase.

"Moisturizer," she said. "Nothing else matters!"

She was right. It's all about battling dehydration.

September 26, 1988

So, I begin two days in Vancouver teaching the beginner and advanced WordStar classes in sequence. Wednesday's class in Toronto was canceled because Tuesday's flight to Toronto was canceled. Apparently, this happens often. While I lose my fee for the day, I don't have to fly home and back. It's a blessing in disguise based on the three-hour time difference from Vancouver to Toronto. Any delay would rob me of valuable sleep. I need to have a chat with the agent who booked me from west to east.

Late Thursday night, April 7, 2016

I remember I worked in thirty states and three cities in Canada during my first three months on the job. I must have had reflections at the time more worthy of recording than merely my arrivals and departures from hotels and airports?

I know I did a lot of thinking on those night flights, absorbing the incredible immenseness of the country, skimming the air above earthly formations I would have preferred to explore on foot. Sunsets and moons populated my nightscapes, random thoughts flying off into space.

Fall 1988

What are the bones of a piece of music?

I return to Ian Anderson, listening to a recording of Bach's "Bourrée" for lute—the fifth movement of the *Suite in E Minor for Lute*, but adding the breath from a flute in his head. He reinvents the piece and, Pied Piper–like, leads hippies in worship, waiting for the hard drums and guitar to return but, stoned on song and breath, waiting patiently for the crashing return, and loving the pipe in spite of their hunger for percussion.

I know how to do this. Why am I not doing this?

I spend all these hours in twilight sleep, collapsing after the twelve-hour day spent serving other people. I come to teach, and people ask me for cream for their coffee. My dream of making my own music is benched apart from these night-flight rhapsodies in my head.

When I return to earth and Jersey Central, I set these dreams aside. It is the children's time. Luddy escapes to his lab to catch up on his work.

What are the bones of love?

Our relationship is arthritic, seeking relief. Is that true of everyone in middle age? I know couples who are not stuck. Why are we?

I think back to the summer of Mimi, last year. How a shy girl moved forward.

I'd allowed myself to teach that year, and it was glorious. I worked with a class of conductors, all girls, including Mimi. We spent all summer looking at how we understand a piece. We discussed our sense impressions of it, then we took it apart. Played it in a different key. Changed time; changed mode; rearranged it for an unconventional instrument. How else would a tuba get so much airtime? Is it right the way it is? Why? Why not? We reinvented jazz improv.

Mimi was an all-star. She went on to conduct the Westchester Symphony.

This is the best a teacher can do.

Late Thursday night, April 7, 2016

Reading these entries now, I find myself wishing I had written more about those years. It's mostly dates and places after this. What have I forgotten?

I jumped ahead in the journal at this point, thinking about how long it had been since I'd heard from Lisa. How did I cope with her absence?

April 1, 1990

A cryptic postcard, postmarked Bangkok, arrives bearing my sister Lisa's handwriting. "I'm sorry" is all it says. Which of a million things could she be talking about? I hope it means she's coming back, but I doubt it.

Lisa doesn't know that our parents' health is beginning to fail in a big way—probably a direct result of their strategy: death by a thousand cuts, from their own medical hypocrisy. They tend to ignore the advice they give to others about getting flu shots, eating and playing well, and getting plenty of rest.

I know everything, don't I?

I know nothing.

Luddy and I continue to slide further apart on the ice of our middle age. Like a pair of books that were used too well, our pages slide open, undoing their perfect bindings, falling apart and to the floor like a score giving up on the music stand.

My father once told me of a professor who wrote equations from both ends of the board into the center, using both hands. This required a lot of planning, but he made it seem easy.

Luddy envied that skill. He told me that he would often try to do it, but he always ran out of space before the middle, hanging the written climax like a stem for a champagne glass, pointing down—unless he ran out of whiteboard, in which case he threw up his hands and said, "You know what I mean."

I knew what he meant. I had plenty of other examples.

The ever-unfixable washing machine leaking into the basement just over my desk.

The hopeless trips back and forth to Home Depot for the wrong part, blaming the store or the directions.

But then there he was, explaining glassblowing to me, speaking about breath like a sculptor, helping me understand his creativity with a microscope.

Bonding was his specialty. In his mind, I was a stable metal while he was a hopping electron of another material, trying to remain in the bond. As a metaphor, it had possibilities. As an intimate technique, it became questionable.

I liked to move; he wanted to hold me still.

Late Thursday night, April 7, 2016

"What makes you good at understanding how software works?" my boss-to-be had asked during my initial interview.

I gave some light answer about being organized. I was cautious about mentioning music and language systems, since I didn't want to blow my cover. I was portraying myself as a business software expert, after all.

In the company's beautiful boardroom, I had tried to seem corporate. Not even a pantsuit. It was still the era of skirts, jackets with shoulder pads, high heels. I was dressed for the job I wanted.

Later, I realized they were looking for PR tidbits, and my ability in music might have made me unique. No matter. I had my pigeonhole as a great explainer, and that was good enough at the time. I was creating something from the organizational and writing skills I'd learned in sixth grade. If I wanted to teach business writing and time management, they would schedule me for that too. *If I wanted to?*

I felt valued at work, and that made up for a lot, for a long time. Twelve years spent training the Fortune 500 here and abroad. Flying everywhere first-class, earning vacation travel for the family. Though exhaustion collapsed my time for composing, I conducted the night skies with an imaginary baton, leading performances of "Lovely Sky

Boat," parsing the air in my ears into beaded curtains of sunstruck sound. The jazz of Alice Coltrane reminded me what it meant to be a harpist floating between the protest of percussion and the wail of the strings when the leader's head tilted left and you plucked your solo. Coltrane reveled in ever-enlarging loops of sound, extending the boundaries of consciousness. These repetitions made her a little freer in each orbit of the song around her grounded center. Nights of circling Newark. Two blinks from my home as the crow flies. Focused. Landing again. Tentative to earth.

And still the old refrain: Luddy could not keep enough money in the checking account because he kept putting most of his paycheck into savings, tying it up so it was awkward to spend.

⧼⧽

Jake once asked me how I dealt with the fear.

"What fear?"

"You know—taking off from the ground, not knowing if you'll come down safe?"

He was on to something. Yet somehow I was never afraid of flying. Perhaps I was tempting fate by doing it so often.

"I have a little poem of thanks I say to myself when I'm flying. But it's a secret. I'm afraid if I tell anyone, it won't work."

"Don't tell me now, then."

"Okay."

"Leave it in a note for me. In case you die."

I never told him about the fragments I borrowed from e. e. cummings and T. S. Eliot. How I would focus on a speck on the seat in front of me in the plane, spotting it like a dancer before pirouetting diagonally across a stage, reciting my mantra.

He seemed content to know I was taking care of business.

I put a sealed note in my top drawer with Jake's name on it. Just in case.

Simon made it clear that he longed for the day I wasn't working anymore.

After a year of working full-time, I cut back to one or two days a week, working only on-site for companies rather than doing public seminars. Although I could still be asked to do a program in California with a one-day turnaround, taking a red-eye home after the workday, I could rest for the next five days. This life was a gift, the best job I ever had. For those dozen years I felt truly valued, and I valued my time in the air, where I caught up with where the music had gone, listening in peace.

Fourth Movement

Grave. Requiem.

Chapter 19

Sforzando. Abruptly.

Thanksgiving Day, November 28, 1996, 3:00 p.m.

"Dead, Grace! She's gone!"

I jerk back from the phone as my eyes flash on Luddy, Jake, and Simon, all crowded around the oven near the phone.

"I'm sorry! I'm sorry!" I shout to everyone, including to the voice on the receiver, which I think is my father's, although it's hard to tell. It could be a woman's voice, it's so high-pitched.

"What happened? Is it Mom?"

"It's me. She's dead!"

"Are you sure?"

"Of course I'm sure—I'm a doctor! What are you talking about?"

Somehow I'm relieved he has enough presence of mind to be insulted.

"Tell me what happened!" I pepper him with questions, mouthing *I'm sorry* to my family.

My father says he'd gone to the kitchen to make her some soup. When he returned, she wasn't breathing.

"Hold on a minute, please, Dad."

"Don't leave me! Don't leave me!"

"I won't. I need to explain to the kids."

"I'm sorry," I say again to my family. "Grandma has died."

As if they couldn't guess.

"Grandpa needs me. I'm going to have to pack a bag and go up there."

Luddy and the boys nod.

"Don't leave me, Grace!" my dad says again. He's a man on the edge, and I will have to function for him. "I don't know what to do, I don't—"

"Dad, is there anyone who can stay with you until I get there?"

"I can't think of anyone."

"Uncle Andy?"

"Who?

"Your neighbor, Andy!"

"Maybe. Can you call him?"

"I don't have another line, but you can go to the other bedroom and use your second line to call Andy. Leave this one off the hook—don't put me on hold!—so it stays connected. I'll stay right here."

"Okay. I'll try."

I am hoping Andy will call the paramedics right away. Maybe Dad is wrong and Mom is still alive. I know this is foolish. He would have tried CPR, even though she was on oxygen because of her emphysema.

I know they haven't made any advance arrangements for a funeral. She told me so last summer. Disorder is mustering in threatening chords.

Triple witching. It's Luddy's birthday today.

December 2, 1996

Despite the Jewish custom of burying quickly, we waited until today to bury Ginger Hayes Feldsher because everyone was away for the holiday.

The winds of a nor'easter kept whipping us down the hill from her grave. We had to fight it to empty our shovels of dirt. In death as in life, my mother seems to push everyone away. People came to the funeral for my father's sake.

Simon and Jake were so brave. I couldn't look at anyone else as I spoke.

Lorelai and Rudy sent their respects by telephone before they left on a cruise with Lena and her husband.

I tried to console Luddy by saying that she had tried to make it through everyone's birthday this year. He said he hoped I wouldn't be thinking about her death on his birthday every year from now on.

December 10, 1996

Still at Dad's house. The strain of our grief and sorting out his finances have worn us both out. My mother always handled everything, keeping her papers in hiding places such as under their bed, or in the warming drawer of the oven in Vermont. In all these weeks, I have not been able to detect a system. I'm resigned to the fact that it was an improvisation around saving every piece of paper that came into the house—and I mean every piece—since 1949.

Lisa cannot be found.

I have been back to my own home only once since our mother died. I'm afraid to leave Dad alone. Depression is too neat a word for what he is feeling. For nearly fifty years he was bound to my mother, a woman he both loved and hated. I could never understand why they stayed together given their different temperaments and the magnitude of complaints they had about each other. They couldn't have been more opposite, or more tigerish in defense of their love.

The last time I saw my mother alive was the day of my dad's eightieth birthday, about a week before Thanksgiving. At her request, I had arranged a family gathering of the Feldshers and the Bergs in a New York City restaurant where there were no stairs to climb, and we could be seated near the door so Mom wouldn't have to walk too far and there would be some movement of air around her. She had been running the air conditioner all winter in a desperate attempt to ease her breathing.

Afterward, while Luddy was getting our car, their limo arrived, and I watched my mother hold up her hand to stop the driver from coming to help her walk half a block to the car in stiletto heels, toting two oxygen tanks for her emphysema.

"Stay back until I'm in!" she had commanded us over her shoulder. "I have more than enough air supply to get home," she told me by way of thanks for my choreography and timing when I leaned in to try to kiss her goodbye.

She had enjoyed a hamburger, a very dry martini, and even the champagne toast I had ordered for everyone. The waiters told my dad how young he looked for his age. He seemed vibrant that day, although he kept repeating himself. They had spent an extra-long time in Vermont, from April to October, and our last visit to see them had been in June. It seemed unusual for them, all that contentment.

Then, the day before Thanksgiving, my mother had contracted the flu. She had refused to go to the hospital, and she wouldn't come to the phone when I called Thanksgiving morning. She would sleep it off, my father told me.

Forever.

I spent yesterday searching for one specific pair of Dad's eyeglasses out of a dozen, the pair that he "absolutely needed so he could do this one thing." None of the eleven others would work. I was growing tired of these spontaneous priorities. When we gave up on the glasses for the day, he launched another search for pictures of his mother, who had died around thirty-five years ago today. We were both too cold in the attic, so I convinced him we would look again tomorrow.

Today the quicksand of his grief is winning. There are more important things to take care of, and both Lena and Lorelai have each called me three times this week to ask why I haven't returned home to Luddy.

"Your dad must be over it by now," they echoed each other.

I shake my head at their emotional mismanagement.

Steven Feldsher will never get over Ginger. Rudy even called Dad to try to convince him. Last night, I too began to wonder why I was staying so long. Should I make a New Year's resolution to go? He doesn't look well, although no one believes me when I say it.

January 1, 1997, 2:00 a.m.

Something happened earlier tonight, and I don't know what I think about it.

After the dishes were done, Dad asked me to help him find something to watch on television. He wasn't about to stay up for the New Year's Eve fireworks, but he needed a distraction. After some searching around the dial, we found *The Glenn Miller Story*. I know my parents love—loved?—his music, so I hoped it would lead him to some pleasant memories of my mother. Moving from the denial phase of grief to nostalgia would be welcome now.

I sat on the bottom edge of my parents' bed toward the middle, and my father stretched out in his spot. It reminded me of how Lisa and I used to perch there with Mom and Dad when we were children. After watching for a while, I felt I'd succeeded, as Dad seemed to be enjoying the movie.

When "Moonlight Serenade" played, I felt the mattress sink and rise. I turned to see Dad getting up, nearly in a trance, brown eyes intense. He came over to me, held out his hand, and asked me to dance. Cheek to cheek, I teared up, remembering how I stood on his feet to dance, how my mother would cut in after a few minutes. I miss her. I wish I could watch them dance together one more time. Dad kissed the top of my head as he used to when we danced. Two lefties, leading.

Suddenly, I was knocked off balance, felt myself falling. I shook myself back into the present, worried that Dad was falling too. Unexpectedly, I was face-to-face with him, lying on the bed, and he was pulling my head toward him, hard. Eyes closed, he was searching my face with his lips, and I heard myself screaming "No!" I pushed him away and stood up quickly.

"This is not happening!" I yelled as I ran to my room, locking myself in. I dragged a chair against the door, adding my weight to it to keep him from pushing the door open. Had he followed me? I had no idea. I just wanted my shaking to stop.

I fell asleep for a while in the chair. I woke up, terrified by a dream of my mother, gesturing at me with a lit cigarette and saying, "This is what you wanted," punctuating her singsong attack with a husky cough.

My mother was jealous of anyone who ever got close to my father. She reserved most of that anger for me. "You're trying to take him away!" she would scream. "How unfair you are," she would shout, "to someone who never had her own father!"

My father and I had gone underground long ago to escape her rage, avoiding any show of affection for each other in her presence, developing our own secret language of winking eyes and slightly moving eyebrows, arms twitching back to avoid hugging. This month of grief had toppled those barriers, but now he was going too far.

He must have mistaken me for her. He's grieving. I should let it go. She was wrong about me. We all paid a price for her love.

I turn on the radio to avoid hearing his weeping downstairs. In my childhood bed, I swaddle myself in the accusatory sounds of *Sonata*

Pathétique. Waiting. Singing. Sighing. I weigh the events of my life against one moment. *I must forgive. Can I forgive?*

January 8, 1997

"Should I come home?"

It's Lisa, calling from Paris. Our neighbor Andy had finally tracked her down through some mutual contacts.

"At this point, why don't you just wait until the spring?" I say, regretting the words as soon as I've said them.

"At this point?"

I am still at Dad's house, but I am going home next Monday. If Lisa comes now, I will have to stay, and it's way past time for me to go home.

"I'm sorry, Lise. I don't mean to sound selfish, but I need to go home. Dad needs to find his new normal."

"Well, I don't want to be there without you."

"It's been nearly two months, Lise."

"Okay. Yes—yes. I'll come in May."

She actually sounds relieved to be off the hook.

"How's he doing?"

"He doesn't look good."

"They were joined at the hip. He's not going to make it, Grace."

"Thanks for the tip, Lise. I'm doing my best here."

"Are you all right?"

"Managing. I've only been home once since Mom . . ."

"You should take care of yourself."

"That's a great idea."

"I mean it!"

"I'll be fine."

"How are the kids?"

"Your nephews are fine. Thanks for asking."

Lisa hasn't seen them since they were toddlers. I'm sure she doesn't even remember their names.

"I'll see you in May, then."

"Staying in Paris for a while?"

"Where the wind blows."

"Let me know?"

"Good night, Gracie."

It was pointless to ask for a phone number. I had long ago resigned myself to the idea that I might never see her again. She's my sister, but I've never been able to depend on her.

Lisa never asks about Luddy. She met him only once after we were married, and she told me he gave her bad chi, so she couldn't be around him. For his part, Luddy imagines that Lisa and her dysfunction will wind up on our doorstep in a basket, like the foundling Moses, and we will have to take care of her as if she were our child.

Part of me agrees with him, but she's my sister, my only connection to what was. I want to stop drinking from that beaker full of ambivalence.

January 13, 1997

"He's going to need a heart transplant, and we don't have the facilities here. When he's stable, we'll move him to Valhalla or New York. You can decide."

Dad had woken up with chest pains that morning. Good thing I hadn't gone home yet.

As I weigh the pros and cons of one city's facilities over another, another physician catches up with me.

"They don't do transplants on people over eighty," he says. "He's not going to make it, and I think it's best that no one tell him."

"But—"

"I have to run to a meeting. We can talk later," he says, and disappears down the hallway.

This goes against everything I know about my father. He believes in telling the truth. I don't know how to lie about this. As part of the ruse, the hospital will keep him in the ICU. Hospice would make him suspicious. The shock might shorten his remaining time.

After I talk to Luddy and the boys, who will come visit tonight, I call Andy to see if he can get another message to Lisa. Now I feel guilty that I told her not to come.

A social worker invites me in for a chat. She wants to know if Dad will sign a DNR.

I doubt it.

Could I use my influence to convince him?

"No. Definitely not!" Dad exclaims when I ask him.

That he wants to live is a poignant surprise after our recent weeks together. I won't ask him again. Every family has its own choreography for loss. He taught me that many years ago.

February 22, 1997

It was 66 degrees and sunny when they lowered Dad's coffin into his grave today. Not your usual February weather, but appropriate for Steven Feldsher, an Aaron Copland kind of American morning.

For me, the world was gleaming all red, white, and blue after the veterans gave me a flag and an old newspaper picture of Dad receiving his purple heart that had hung on the wall at his old post.

One terrible thing. That single hurt. Still my hero.

I'd held his hand as he expired, loaded with morphine and waving to my mother, who summoned him through the ether in his last minutes.

February 22, 1997, later that night

Tonight when I get home, I make love to Luddy like the orphan I've become.

Once upon a time, I conducted Mozart's *Requiem.*

Requiem aeternam dona eis, Domine . . . Grant them eternal rest, Lord.

I am a different person now, and I don't quite know who that is.

Chapter 20

The Siren Song of Sugar

April 6, 1998

It's been more than a year since we buried Dad, and it still feels like a hundred-year flood of paper has swamped me in the never-ending settlement of my parents' affairs.

Lisa calls every month to ask for her money. "Call my Vermont attorney to set it up," she barks into my answering machine.

There's no use pointing out to her that I'm mired in details, figuring out what to do with two houses and a medical practice. I'm only one person. As executor for both my parents' estates, I haven't had a chance to grieve yet. The new person I've become has retreated into a depressive cave so that my inner accountant can take over. It's not a pretty time.

I've needed medication for elevated blood pressure since last year. I'm tired all the time. I've made a resolution this morning, though: I'm turning over a new leaf. Once I've completed the last set of estate taxes, I'm going to find a new life for myself.

During this awful time of "working for Lisa," as she put it so tactlessly after we signed the probate papers, my business has evaporated—not so much because of anything I did or didn't do, but because companies have begun to source their training in-house. Consultants are suddenly too expensive.

Luckily I've had a lot of experience looking for work, so I'm not afraid of reinventing myself yet again. I don't have a strong sense yet of what to do next, but it has to be something different.

If I just weren't so tired all the time.

Luddy has fared better than I have. Shortly after my father died, the university recognized Luddy's research accomplishments and elevated him to a distinguished professorship, accompanied with all the pomp and circumstance of an investiture, and new responsibilities directing a research center for material bonding. There was a beautiful ceremony, including a colorful, full-robed faculty procession in the university's chapel and a reception in the trustees' function room. Rudy even told Luddy he was satisfied. We all hope it's a turning point in Luddy's self-esteem. The university also gave him something he's always needed: an assistant. Some things, at least, have stopped falling through the cracks.

Nevertheless, he still seems overwhelmed, and he's having more arguments than usual with colleagues. I don't have the strength to probe him about why this is happening. Self-satisfaction does not seem to thrive in the Berg clan.

Jake and Simon have taken refuge in sports and school. Simon is halfway through his freshman year at college, and Jake is thriving as a junior in high school. I have missed following the pulse of their daily lives. I try not to grieve their independence, but when did they stop needing me? Did I make that necessary in my frantic searches for work? Or are they happily becoming their own, independent selves? That's what I wanted, wasn't it? I used to tell them: "Parents should raise kids whose parents can take care of themselves."

Can't regret my autonomy now.

April 13, 1998

"I need to schedule a visit with you. Can you come in today?"

In more than twenty years of seeing Dr. Lerman, he's never spoken to me the way he did this morning. Apparently he needs to discuss the bloodwork he ran the other day.

"Can you give me a clue?"

"It's diabetes. Type two. We need to talk about it."

The bottom fell out of my world.

"What time?"

"Five o'clock. Then we won't be disturbed, and I'll be able to answer all your questions. And listen—I know how you are. Take it easy. We'll figure this out together. I need to change your blood pressure meds, and you need to learn a few things about taking care of yourself—especially when it comes to sugar intake."

I have found my new purpose. In one of life's little ironies, drawing blood from my body will again become a routine.

April 13, 1998, later that evening

Luddy is away, giving presentations on bonding in Calcutta. He won't call.

I have less than a week to reinvent the way I cook before he comes home.

I crack open the first of ten books on diabetes to try to understand how I'm going to live now.

Chapter 21

Anniversary Waltz

June 13, 1998

"Why can't we go home?"

We had waited until today to celebrate our wedding anniversary, which was actually yesterday, but that's not why Luddy is trying to get me out of the emergency room at County General Hospital. For the last hour, he's been pacing around my bed and complaining to everyone about the buzzing of the fluorescents and anything else that disturbs him. Periodically, he complains about the fact that we needed to come here in the first place.

Last night I fell and cut my head open on one of Lena's concrete sculptures, which populate our home. I had fallen asleep on the couch watching a movie, and when I got up, I'd felt a force pulling me to the ground. Pain rolled through the back of my head. I lay there for a while because I couldn't get up. Somehow, I dragged myself back onto the couch, where I slept again until morning.

When I awoke I thought my neck was sweaty, until I looked at my hand after touching it and saw fresh blood. I called out to Luddy, but he didn't hear me.

I dragged myself into our bedroom.

"Luddy, wake up! We have to go to the hospital. I'm bleeding."

He never woke easily, and this morning was no exception. Groggy, he looked at me and then ran to the bathroom. I knew it could be a long time before he came back out.

I sat on the floor next to our bed.

When he came out he sat on the bed near me, saying, "Let me see."

I turned my head so he could look at the back of it.

"That's a mess."

"It's still bleeding."

"I'll clean it up for you. I don't think it's very deep."

"It's been bleeding all night, and it hurts. I think I should get it looked at."

"What time does Lerman open up?"

"We have to go to the ER. It's Saturday."

"No need. I can take care of it."

"Luddy, engineering doesn't cover brain surgery. I want to find out why I fell. Something pulled me down. It was the weirdest feeling."

"All right," he growled. "It's useless to argue with you. Let me get dressed."

At least he'd agreed to go. I would have driven myself, but the fall and the blood loss had left me lightheaded.

Almost an hour later, we finally made our way to the hospital. While Luddy parked the car, I started my check-in.

I was relieved to see Jake and Simon's high school friend Ted at the desk.

"Mrs. B! What's going on?"

"I took a little trip," I said, trying to make light of it.

"Looks like you took one for the team!" he answered. He moved me to a wheelchair, just to be safe.

"When did you start working here?"

"I've been a paramedic here for a few years. I just got into med school, starting this fall."

"Congratulations! Your parents must be very proud!" I smiled, thinking about the mountains of pancakes we had cooked together every Sunday for the team.

"Where's the Professor?" he said, using the nickname the kids had always used.

"Parking the car."

Ted took my blood pressure and then looked at my head.

"I'm going to get you a seat in the front row," he said reassuringly, but with a worried look on his face. "Don't worry—I'll make sure the Professor gets right to you when he comes in."

"Thank you. We don't want him to get lost."

He winked at me and wheeled my chair to a spot between two other patients.

Thanks to Ted, I got priority treatment. Blood tests, X-rays, and CAT scan with lightning speed. My vitals were good, but Luddy became agitated when we didn't get immediate results.

The woman next to me had shingles, and she was weeping loudly from the pain. I heard her say she had diabetes, which made me shiver in fear.

Monitor lights were flashing everywhere, and Luddy began to pace. I told him to go home—that I'd call him when I could leave—but he refused. He complained about the cost of parking, the buzzing lights.

I was exhausted. I just wanted to close my eyes while the doctors conferred about my results. Just a little nap, that's all, although a long one would have been good. I had just started to drift off, but in the background I could hear Ted conferring with a doctor about someone, so I listened.

"A head injury on the back of the head. It's classic. He could have pushed her."

"No, no. I know these people. I don't think so."

"Doesn't it worry you, the way he's pacing around, complaining about everything? It's a possible indicator of domestic abuse—that he wants to get her out of here."

"I know. But he's a special case. I've known him since high school. He's always like that. High-strung."

"Just the same, I want to keep her for a while longer. I don't like the way he's acting. I'd feel pretty bad if she came back here tonight with another wound."

It dawned on me that *he* was Luddy, and *she* was me.

The doctor escorted Luddy under protest to the waiting room, and then he returned with Ted to talk to me.

"Tell me again," he said in a kind, concerned voice. "How did this happen?"

I went over my late-night clumsiness, saying I knew it sounded crazy, but I'd felt like I was being dragged to the floor by the weight of my own body.

"You can tell me anything," he said gently.

"No, really, that's what it was."

"No one pushed or pulled you?"

"No."

"It could be a blood pressure drop. Vagus nerve, maybe," he offered. "Your husband didn't hear you fall?"

"He could sleep through a nuclear war."

"Well, your results are normal. We're going to put some staples in your head. I just don't want to see you here again like this."

I was trying to keep it light, so I lied. "That makes three of us. It's our wedding anniversary, and we have plans!"

He stared at me for a moment. I was even less comfortable, so I changed the subject.

"Staples? Will they hurt?"

"Not as much as falling on your head."

"Ha."

"And here's the good news—they don't hurt much going in. Taking them out is another story, but that's not my job; Dr. Lerman gets to do that. Next time, don't get up so fast."

"I'll try to remember that."

Luddy came crashing back into the ER, causing several pairs of eyebrows to go up.

"Can we go now?"

The doctor looked him in the eye and said firmly, "We have to put some staples in to close the wound. Just a little while longer."

A childish whine escaped from Luddy. He wasn't doing much to help our case, but I couldn't catch his eye to reroute him, and he probably wouldn't have understood my cautionary look anyway.

The doctor started to speak, stopped, then left to get his supplies.

Ted patted my arm reassuringly. "It won't take long."

Luddy went into his staring mode.

I shrugged at Ted, and he winked. I knew he was thinking about the stories my sons had told him about their father's fabled concentration, his absentminded-professor moments of focusing on the wrong thing. How he saved a spider once while allowing the dinner he'd cooked for them to run off the stove in a sticky brown river of onions and liver. Ted could see that Luddy often meant well despite his preoccupied demeanor.

I was ashamed of the doctor's suspicions. I'd never thought of myself this way before. Is this the way people see us?

The doctor returned with what looked like a staple gun, and I winced for each one of the six.

"Stay well!" he exclaimed when he'd finished. "See your own doctor next week, and let him have the pleasure of removing these. The nurse will be here shortly with the paperwork, so just a couple more minutes."

"Thank you," I called after him.

"Let's go!" Luddy said.

"I need to wait for the paperwork—why don't you pull the car around?"

"Are you sure?"

"I'll wheel her out to you, Professor."

Luddy smiled for the first time—at Ted, not me.

"All right, then. I'll meet you at the entrance."

"You bet."

Luddy exited the ER and took a fair amount of noise with him. Even the room's buzzing equipment seemed mysteriously quieter; the flashing lights, dimmer.

"You sure you're okay, Mrs. B?"

I wanted to reassure him, though I felt a headache begin to replace my anxiety. I didn't want him to know how awkward I felt about the conversation I'd overheard.

"I'm going to be fine. I'm so glad you were here. Tell your mom and dad how proud I am of you!"

Ted blushed.

My chariot to the exit arrived before we had a chance to say much more, and I was grateful for the end of this saga.

Luddy was calmer in the parking lot, so things went a little smoother.

After we were alone in the car, on the road home, he said, "I told you we didn't need to go to the hospital."

I'm thinking of calling Dr. Friedman. Maybe it's time for a refresher after so much grief. Unlike Marsha, he always got to the point quickly, and I have a feeling Luddy will need to be part of this.

As a favor to Dean Rollins, I'll be teaching a summer school mini-class on the history of music, and suddenly I'm not sure if I can handle the pressure.

September 4, 1998, Dr. Friedman's office

"And your relationship with Luddy—how's that going?"

Dr. Friedman and I have spent much of the summer unpacking the trauma of the last few years following my parents' deaths. He's let me find my own way, listening patiently to my anguish.

Today he's asking about my marriage, saying I haven't mentioned Luddy once. It's possible he tried to bring up Luddy in an earlier session, but I probably ignored him, choosing to perseverate about my grief.

"It's going okay," I tell him. "Luddy tried to help me during all of this, but he's not very good at cleaning up or organizing finances, and those were the major tasks at hand. And that first attorney I hired was—"

"Anything unusual going on between you?"

I start to say "No," because I want this to be about me and not Luddy, but I decide to tell him about something that happened a few weeks ago.

At first I had passed it off as nothing unusual, because it was Luddy, but later I had the same awkward feeling I'd experienced that day in the ER—as if we were being observed—and I couldn't shake the thought that we were sending out loud signals about some abnormality to the world, even though we couldn't recognize them ourselves.

"Well, something happened last month. I don't know if I'd say it's 'unusual.'"

"Tell me about it," Dr. Friedman says, assuming his listening position, balancing his chin on his hand.

"I came home from my class late one evening to find a policeman at our front door, peering through the screen at Luddy. He was sitting, slumped, in his usual position on the couch, and the television was blaring, also as usual. When the officer saw my car pull in, he approached me very carefully.

"He introduced himself as Detective Robert Brinkman, and said he was investigating the report of an intruder attempting to enter the house next door. He'd found no one there, so he had begun interviewing neighbors to see if anyone had seen anything unusual. He had already been standing at our door for twenty minutes, trying to get Luddy's attention. He was seriously concerned that something was wrong, because Luddy wasn't responding. He asked if I would let him come inside to check on him.

"I tried to reassure him, saying that Luddy had proven long ago that he could sleep through a war zone, but the detective wasn't convinced. He said he really wanted to come inside, just to make sure Luddy was okay, and he didn't want me to go in alone, in case he wasn't.

"I hesitated. I knew we had something to hide. I didn't want him to see inside the house. I told the detective it wasn't necessary and called Luddy's name. The detective gestured toward the door.

"'Well, funny thing,' I said, laughing. 'I don't have a key for the screen door because we don't usually use it. I keep it inside, so we'll have to go around the other way.'

"'I'll come with you,' Brinkman offered with concern.

"I really didn't want the detective to come in. The mess in the house was beginning to descend into what I'd call a health hazard, and I didn't want to deal with that issue on top of Luddy's apparently severe episode of narcolepsy. I was running out of excuses for our strangeness. Even if we could walk past the garbage on the floor, I would still have to deal with my husband's confused and sometimes dramatic way of waking up. He was sure to be disoriented and angry, and then the detective might become concerned about something worse than just his lack of consciousness.

"Brinkman persisted, so we walked to the side door of the house and stepped carefully around all the newspapers and mail thrown haphazardly on the floor to make our way past the debris in the living room, where I would have to wake up Luddy, who hadn't heard a thing. I saw the detective look with alert interest at our surroundings as we made our way toward Luddy, and my fear of how this was going to end intensified.

"When I got to the couch, I sat down with Luddy, and I gently pressed his arm until I felt some movement. I said, 'Luddy, there's someone here to see you. Can you wake up?' His eyes fluttered and widened into a familiar confused and annoyed expression, and I dreaded what might happen next.

"Luckily, the officer spoke in a reassuring way, saving the situation. 'Sir, you had us all worried!' he said. I could have kissed him! Luddy looked around to see who was speaking. When he perceived it was safe, he laughed, saying 'I must have dropped off!' as if he were at the beach or something."

Dr. Friedman smiles.

"The officer told Luddy he'd been trying to get his attention for twenty minutes, and was concerned that something might be wrong. 'When your wife came home, I asked her to let me in, and here we are.'

"Luddy laughed a little sheepishly. 'Sometimes it's like that. Narcolepsy!'

"The detective explained about the intruder complaint and asked us to be watchful. I felt like he was the watchful one, eyeing us both carefully throughout and making some mental notes, but he didn't say anything more and politely left our house.

"After my sense of danger had passed, I realized that the detective was one of Simon's old football teammates. 'That was Bobby. Bobby Brinkman!' I said to Luddy.

"Luddy shrugged his shoulders, as if to say, 'I don't know what you're talking about,' and I noticed a slight tremor in his body. Experience told me not to mention it to Luddy, but it worried me.

"'He was ahead of Simon in school. Football?' I added, giving Luddy a clue. His shoulders rose and fell once more. I dropped it.

"I don't remember if Luddy and I said anything else to each other for the remainder of the night. I felt chilled by the fear I had experienced and the conflict within me that would have prevented me from doing the right thing, the sane thing, to save Luddy. It would have been nuts *not* to check on him with Bobby, but I had feared his hostility at being awakened almost as much as I felt the shame of exposing our living situation to an outsider. Fortunately, the detective wasn't going to let me go down that path, but I felt the force of my worst dependent behaviors trying to prevent me from acting that night. I was at war with my lonely coping mechanisms, and I could not let them win. Thank goodness Bobby appealed to my better angel."

"Wow," Dr. Friedman says with characteristic calm. "What do you think is going on with you right now?"

"Stepping out again into the world has made me realize that a separation from Luddy is going to be necessary for my mental health. I don't want to sleepwalk through the rest of my life. My former student Mimi, who's teaching at a college in North Jersey, has contacted me about developing a salsa orchestra there, and I want to grab this unexpected chance to restore my life."

"That's a big leap," Dr. Friedman says.

"Yes! It would be a full-time job, teaching and conducting. I was planning to tell Luddy that I'd like to take an apartment up north so I can avoid driving back and forth during the week. I thought that maybe this way we could experiment with living near New York City on the weekends, which has always seemed financially out of reach, but with my job, we could swing it."

"I have another thought," Dr. Friedman says. "It's about something we didn't know much about years ago, but I'm glad I can tell you about today. The signs are pretty clear to me. It sounds like Luddy has ADHD."

"I thought that was a childhood condition."

"It seems we were wrong about that. It's showing up more often now in adults. And the interesting thing is, it often shows up in high-achieving people. Ask Luddy if he'll come along to your next appointment with me, and we can talk about scheduling an evaluation. I know a good neuropsychiatrist at County General who can help you."

I flinch a little, thinking about my last visit there, but it sounds like there might be an end to this crazy maze we've been navigating for so long. I agree to ask Luddy to come and hear more about Dr. Friedman's theory.

October 1, 1998, County General Hospital, all day

"It isn't the same for everyone," says Dr. Waters, cautioning me about ADHD while Luddy completes some preliminaries with her graduate assistant.

It's disheartening to hear that there are so many unknowns. Luddy has been so excited to learn that there might be an explanation for his behaviors; I hoped he wouldn't be crushed to learn that the treatments and medications were experimental, requiring a lot of tweaking, and that there were side effects, with no guarantees.

During the neuropsychiatrist's exam later, I mull over my concern that there is no actual test for attention deficit hyperactivity disorder, ADHD—in Luddy's case, diagnosed as adult ADHD. Other conditions need to be ruled out before it can be ruled in, but Dr. Waters has given me her gut response. Luddy seems more lethargic than hyperactive, so this leaves me feeling confused.

We had spoken with Luddy's parents about this development, hoping to add some insight to the interviews we would have with Dr. Waters's team. Lorelai had always described Luddy as lethargic as a child. According to Rudy, Luddy was a daydreamer who hyper-focused on the things other people ignored—the worm at your feet, the butterfly or snowflake floating by, the hairline crack in the glass. "Like Ferdinand the Bull in that story," according to Rudy. Luddy's extra focus has always been an asset to him as a student of subatomic structure, but it was also, always, a problem in social relationships that require other attentive skills.

Luddy's annoying childhood habit of pointing out everyone else's errors and imprecision had carried him through a competitive high school into adult life as a scientist—who also happens to be a pain in the ass. No one likes to be wrong, and Luddy himself has a thin skin when it comes to his own mistakes.

There is some discussion of "little professor disorder" as well, otherwise known then as Asperger's syndrome. Dr. Waters acknowledges Luddy's irritating behavior, but explains that Asperger's may or not be another notch on the ADHD spectrum; the jury was still out. She's pretty sure he has a "seriously inattentive" version of ADHD. She tells us the only way we could truly obtain an accurate diagnosis of disorders like these is to do a brain autopsy, so clearly it's not possible to confirm the condition while a person is alive.

"If we hear hoofbeats," she tells me, "we think ADHD." Psychologists use questionnaires, personal narratives, and various concentration tasks to determine whether a patient has ADHD. When they tag it, they offer caveats about the lack of medical precision involved. Nonetheless, this team seems pretty certain about Luddy's diagnosis. We're only an hour into the daylong assessment when they give me this news.

Jake, who has taken a day off from classes to support us, is interviewed with me about our memories of Luddy's behavior and triggering circumstances. The diagnosing doctor explains that one of the testing strategies is to create frustrating challenges for Luddy to experience so that they can try to model the difficulties he experiences in processing and solving problems. I learn that he expressed a great deal of frustration and anger during this episode, and they ask me not to discuss it with him when he comes out for a break.

When Luddy emerges from the testing suite, he is complaining bitterly about not being able to complete things his own way. He seems utterly disheartened, and doubtful about the process.

When he stops venting, I put my hand on his and I break the rule.

"What if they had to create some frustrating circumstances to see how you would respond?"

"That's outrageous!" he exclaims, ready to go back in to protest.

I gently press him back into his seat with my hand.

"Is it?" Drawing on my own experience as a teacher, I suggest, "Since there's no blood test for the condition they're investigating, maybe they have to resort to good old-fashioned challenges to see what you do in response. I remember an IQ test where I couldn't use a pencil to solve a math problem, and I was pretty upset about it. I found out later they were looking to see how I responded to obstacles. P.S. That pencil lowered my score."

"That's different!" he exclaims, but he is calming down. He makes a joke about my deficient math skills to make himself feel better, but I don't take the bait.

"It's just a thought . . . maybe I'm wrong. Only you can decide how you behave in these situations."

He makes intense eye contact with me as a wave of comprehension battles with his adrenaline.

The doctor returns, and it's time for Luddy to return to the other room for further testing.

I am heartsick to see him so humbled. I want to shake him and say *Don't you get it?* But I have said too much already. Who knows; maybe it will help restore his pride for the rest of the test. I didn't mean to derail him with a flood of contrary information, but he is my husband, after all, and I love him—pity him too. I can't just stand by and watch him fail.

In front of Dr. Friedman, Luddy had promised that our marriage would come first from now on. I realized then that I wanted us to make it.

"Just pass!" I say to him as he gets up to leave, smiling at his half-comprehending face.

He smiles back, acknowledging my encouragement as a gift.

My mind flashes warmly to the birthday cards he used to make for me, from the children, patiently tracing their tiny hands and helping them write their names.

Dr. Waters suggests that we might try to forget the last twenty years. I don't know how to do that. What would it mean, to start over from scratch?

At the end of the day, we are told that the test results point conclusively to ADHD as the headline. An alphabet soup of three-letter acronyms—possibly obsessive-compulsive disorder (OCD), oppositional defiant disorder (ODD), and others, such as prosopagnosia (face blindness)—are consequences of the primary disorder, although no one can truly distinguish between the chicken and the egg at this point. Even the narcolepsy can be a consequence of his intense focusing episodes. He needs to regroup by turning off all stimuli in order to get the deep sleep he needs to refresh him. Unfortunately, when he wakes up, he'll work another marathon and then crash yet again. We are told this cycle is detrimental for good relationships and may aggravate some of the other disorders.

We emerge from the clinic with conditions, metaphors, and more confusion. The treatment must resemble an octopus to tame all these things at once. Somehow Luddy has a feeling of relief, all the same. For the first time, he has a name for what is wrong and, more importantly, a belief that he can fix it. Who knows? Maybe now he can become King Engineer in his own personal laboratory kingdom. Maybe this diagnosis explains why the Nobel Prize keeps moving just out of reach.

"I love you," he says as we're leaving, thanking me for bringing him to this place. He could be a four-year-old, thanking me for a new puppy.

As we step into this strange new realm, I am cautiously optimistic that his gigantic appetite for knowledge might carry him—and our marriage—through.

October 8, 1998, Dr. Friedman's office

We are thankful that Dr. Friedman was perceptive about the possible cause of our conflicts, and that he recommended this testing clinic.

"We didn't know about ADHD fifteen, twenty years ago," he said ruefully to Luddy when we went back to discuss the possibilities. "Now, I'm seeing it more and more."

We are confident that this is a challenge we can embrace and succeed at with our mad skills. Gaining new expertise is our shared thrill, we tell Dr. Friedman. We will surround ourselves with books—our favorite stimulants—and try to learn as much as possible about the impediments Luddy is facing. We believe our ability to learn new things will see us through.

As we leave the doctor's office, I feel apprehensively intoxicated by what we've learned, and what lies ahead, though I'm not quite sure how to forget about the past two decades of knowing Luddy. I have managed to live with the quirks of ADHD without understanding it for so long. Now, armed with this new information, I know I'll need to make some radical changes too.

We face each other at this huge moment of truth, which feels like a glacial Alaskan crevasse where feelings and history go to die. The roar of ice calving away from itself is the sound that haunts my waking hours.

It's gonna take a miracle.

Chapter 22

The Right Kind of Wife

October 22, 1998

Following the assessment, I have a wet-blanket moment that I don't share with anyone at the time.

Despite the confidence these professionals feel in their diagnoses, I am concerned that no medical tests have been offered to rule out other problems. Now in his mid-fifties, Luddy seems suddenly unable to work with colleagues or relate well to family or friends. While there have always been difficulties along the way, lately I've noticed a steep surge in his odd behaviors, and I remain convinced that something else is wrong.

I can accept the explanation of a congenital problem that causes Luddy to respond to the world and its stimuli in exceptional ways, but it troubles me that after functioning at a high level all this time, even his peculiar coping mechanisms are now failing him. His life has simply become much harder, and I want to know why. I want to help him. I'm fighting to know what we are in for and what I am supposed to do to help, but his new therapist insists that I need to stay out of his lane while he finds himself.

Personally, I think it's Dr. Allen, the psychologist, who needs the space. When I ask to be let in on the system, to understand the techniques, she shrieks that she is "building a person, after all." This sounds like an overreach to me.

Fight or flight?

I believe I am fighting for our lives, but suddenly "we" are not "us" anymore. Dr. Allen tells Luddy it's normal for a wife to be jealous of her husband's therapist. I feel like an accidental extra beat wrecking their waltz. Although I hate feeling that I can't help, I won't interfere. I'm the wallflower in my own solution.

November 2, 1998, our kitchen

"You might not be the right kind of wife for me."

Luddy delivers this revelation following his session with Dr. Allen today, a few weeks after she has begun to work with him on how to live with ADHD and the myriad other disorders identified during his neurological assessment.

I look around at the small part of the table I have rescued from messy, dusty debris to make space for my coffee cup and cereal. I feel the tabletop curling in on itself like a wave getting ready to grind me into the sand. What kind of wife swims toward this undertow every day? What have I become?

Threat or opportunity? How long do I have to decide?

My tears and the anger I feel tell me I am leaning toward the threat side of the pictogram, and I dig in there.

I search his face. Another ambivalent look. Does he agree with Dr. Allen? I have been informed that I shouldn't try to read his body language anymore because he has no control over it. All these years I have supposedly been responding to the wrong cues because, in the absence of any words, I have relied on his facial expressions. All my inferences are probably wrong. He is going to have to learn how to display appropriate signs, but that will come later.

Would he answer now if I asked him a question about what he just said? Would he hear the question as a wrongheaded rebuke?

Shut up! I tell myself. My questions are useless. No one is going to answer me.

To make matters worse, today is the anniversary of my abortion. Never mind his horrible timing. He's always going to be the bombardier, and I, the unsuspecting villager below. I see no sign that this equation will ever change.

I had sought couples therapy with Dr. Friedman in the past so we could learn how to communicate better. Each time, Luddy had been eager to abandon new skills as soon as the doctor had signaled we were ready to be on our own, and each time, I'd returned to my fallback methods of interpretation. Although we'd somehow raised two children in a collaboration we were proud of, and we'd both held on to challenging jobs, the fact remained: We could not find a way to function together, at home, just the two of us.

Dr. Allen's new therapy proposed to invent a third way—not Luddy's, not mine, but rather a way that would be constructed by her with Luddy, without any input from me.

During the testing, when I'd asked Dr. Waters what I was supposed to do with our more than twenty years of history, she'd said, "Throw it overboard!"

"All of it?" I'd asked.

"Well, maybe not the things that were good!" The doctor had laughed encouragingly.

Who gets to say what was good?

I have conquered a lot of problems in my life, but I don't know where to begin here. This might be an opportunity to end the marriage, but I am stuck in fighting mode, and I simply cannot imagine how to leave.

I want to try to stay. I *have* been trying, but now I understand that the words Dr. Allen relayed through Luddy had been carefully chosen. It would be easier for her without my interference, even if that means ending the relationship that we came to save. I feel like a disaster, interpreting everything: It's my curse. I won't lie about it. I cling to the word *might* as an indication of a possibility, the word *kind* as a fleeting invitation to change. Am I capable of change?

The person who chose me will now become a different person. What would he think of his former choices then? Who is doing the forgetting? How do we recognize each other enough to keep going?

"Is that what you think too?" I manage to say, pulling my breakfast dishes closer to take up less space on the table.

I see a slight twitch and hear a tiny grunt that I would have said was something like a "yes" from Luddy a month ago, but now I try to stay neutral, waiting for a word—any word—that would indicate yes, no, or maybe, or something I haven't even thought of.

Nothing else comes. His silence, like a protective mist, hides him from what he finds intolerable—other people's interpretations. He has found his superpower, and he won't have to suffer my judgment again.

We sit silently for a long time until the mundane business of the day creeps back into our thoughts. After we mumble our separate plans to each other, we take turns at the sink and go about our separate days.

From what I can see, Luddy enjoyed my reaction to his statement. It gave him power.

You can't change anyone but yourself, but you can influence people to behave differently.

For many years I had taught people about the power of change: If you change your behavior, others around you may change theirs even if they cannot say why.

Luddy, the teacher, had come into his own.

Thinking about our conversation, I can see why the psychologist might have doubted my commitment to helping him. Even without other complicating circumstances—and whose life is free of those?—helping someone learn to live with a brain disorder is a large and complex process. I am not ready for all the changes. At this time, I'm barely able to help myself. Exhausted from clearing up the estates of both of my parents during the previous few years, weakened somewhat by diabetes, I am low on resilience. As if two deaths in two months were not enough terror, I've had to start again with my own mortality on the line, and no real consideration from Luddy.

Too much change is stressful.

I have taught that lesson, too, numerous times for corporations throughout America during the last decade. Now I have to figure out how to live when everything around me seems out of control. Our marriage, which imposes all the demands of a helpless infant and offers very little of the mutuality of an adult relationship, is in serious trouble. How can I help Luddy when I cannot help myself?

I'm not sure how much of this Dr. Allen is aware of, but apparently my situation doesn't matter much to her. Luddy is her client; I'm not. She told me she could recommend a neutral third party for marriage counseling. It would have to be someone other than Dr. Friedman, who had helped us to find her. She thought he might be biased from knowing us before.

I don't trust Dr. Allen at all. She has described my feelings to Luddy as a traditional therapeutic conflict. I had not expected this sort of realignment, in which I have to remain ignorant, when I was the one who helped Luddy to find her in the first place. I may be wrong or inept, but I only want to know what Luddy is "trying to do" so I can give him the support he is crying out for.

Some psychologists say that it's typically the healthy one who chooses to get help. I had ten years of psychoanalysis in my rearview mirror, plus several years of shared marriage counseling that I had initiated. I've always been searching for help.

Now Luddy has found an unexpected ally whose diagnosis seems to explain everything. Nothing else matters. The current explanation, however, has led him to the blame game—on steroids. Suddenly, he loves therapy.

Does he love me?

They say you have to find the right one.

Therapist, or wife?

I've never responded very well to "Watch and wait." I have lived in a constant state of triage for several years. As exhausted as I am, I still want to manage the process.

It doesn't help that I have trouble perceiving the small changes for which Luddy seeks the feedback and praise he so desperately needs to carry on.

I need a big change, and I need it now.

Intermezzo

Nocturne. The Nettles.

Thursday evening, April 7, 2016

It's the blue hour now, the time when artists do some of their best work. Composers have pulled a tune or two out of the twilight. My parents treasured a recording of "Deep Purple" by Peggy Lee. There were dozens of recordings of that lyric by Mitchell Parish. He also wrote "Moonlight Serenade." I don't want to think about Glenn Miller right now. Those are not the notes I need.

Semibreve. Rest.

I can't stop thinking about Lisa for some reason.

As little girls, we took to heart a Hans Christian Andersen story that our mother read to us occasionally, "The Wild Swans." We always thought she chose that story because she had a wicked stepmother of her own; we just couldn't understand why she often behaved like one toward us. Lisa and I were determined to stick together like the swans.

We once asked our father if we were adopted. He looked mystified.

To recap, our mother had three mothers: her birth mother, who died; her stepmother, who made her father give her away; and her foster mother (and father), who were kind but poor. She did not meet her biological siblings until she was seven.

"Once upon a time," she would read, and after a few times, we would join in with our own version: "A king marries a wicked woman wizard, who turns her eleven stepsons into swans. They can become human at night, but only in the blue hour. She tries to do likewise to her stepdaughter, Elisa, but the princess is too strong for her magic."

Lisa and I often featured this story in our imaginary play, arguing each time about who would play the sister, and who, the swans. Being the elder, I usually won, even if the princess's name was Elisa. The roles and our struggles over them made sense to us, even as children, although I don't think we could have explained it then. I absorbed the shocks of living with our mother, while Lisa recovered from them under the down quilt on her bed.

I think now of Lisa as my grace note, a quaver, crushed, acciacca-tura, leaning against me while I played rings of distraction around our mother's outbursts.

The important thing about the story for us was that Elisa did not abandon her siblings. Not even when the queen of the fairies suggests a painful remedy for the princes' fate: gathering nettles to make magic sweaters that will break the wizard's spell and restore the brothers to their human form. Not even when a vow of silence goes along with that painful task, leading to a suspicion of witchcraft on Elisa's part.

Racing against a deadly clock that would end with her burning for witchcraft, the princess completes most of the sweaters, but she can't quite complete the second sleeve for the cygnet, her youngest brother.

Just before her fiery punishment, the princess tosses the nettle garments over eleven long necks, and the boys appear miraculously where swans had stood. The brothers explain the spell to their father, the king, the fire transforms into a garden, and in our version, Elisa is saved and forgiven by her brothers.

Lisa always had one wing out the door, and I was nimble with my fingers, so I had the stronger argument to be the princess of nettles. I won so much that I lost my sister, who flew away too soon.

Can it be that I forgot how to forgive? I want her to come home. I am tired of collecting nettles.

Hemidemisemiquaver rest.

I jump when the phone rings.

"Grace? It's Lisa. I'm sorry about Luddy. . . . And I'm coming home."

I'm angry and thrilled. I don't want to lose her again, so I use my superpower: I hold back my feelings.

Until I can't.

"So, you heard? How?"

I didn't know how she would've heard the news, especially as Andy, her main source of updates, had passed away five years ago.

"Remember Mike?"

"You mean the guy we used to call Jean Valjean in high school—the one who carried a copy of *Les Misérables* around after he stole bread from the cafeteria? His younger brother was in my class—"

"That Mike, yes. He's in Paris now. His mom saw something on Facebook."

"About Luddy? How did she know?"

"She always liked you better than Mike's wife."

"So, she was stalking me?"

"Yeah. I guess she thought there was always hope!" Lisa laughs a little. "Anyway, I'm calling because I just heard about Luddy last night. I'm sorry."

Quaver rest.

"How is everyone?"

"*Everyone* is fine." Can't prevent a trace of mockery.

"Really?"

"Why shouldn't they be?"

"Grace—nobody is fine after someone dies."

"Was that on Facebook?"

"Touché. No, I made a few calls."

"Thanks for getting around to me. The last time we talked—what's it been now, twenty years since Mom and Dad died? Oh, wait—you did call to ask for your money . . . many, many times."

"I didn't want to just barge back into your life."

"But sudden moves are your specialty."

Stop doing that, Grace.

"I'm sorry to hear about the divorce too, Gracie. I know you loved Luddy. He was just . . . so complicated . . . so demeaning to you—"

"I wasn't the perfect wife."

"Grace, what does that even mean?"

"Never mind. Forget it. I was just reading my old journal."

"Maybe it's not the best time for you to be doing that."

Semiquaver rest.

"So somebody had to die for you to get back in touch. That must have taken a lot for you. Thank you. Anything else?"

Quaver rest. Lisa will change her tune.

"Grace. I was thinking about how we used to wish we were twins—you know, how we did everything the same, tried to dress alike every morning? Same color, same shirt—"

"Same design. Polka dots. Remember that time?"

Lisa risks another little laugh. "They weren't the same color, and there were different numbers of them, but we showed Ginger—I mean, Mom—we both had polka dots, and they were the same size! When I told her we were twins, she yelled at us—'You are not the same!'—and we fought her on it!"

"I measured them with a ruler to show her!"

"And she grabbed that plastic ruler out of your hand—I can still see it waving! And she broke it—"

"Over her knee!"

We're both laughing now.

"She sent us to our room, so we played silent Go Fish like mimes until we heard her go outside, and then we laughed our butts off! It was hard. Our fish face repertoire was pretty limited."

I want to be wrapped in this old story like a comfortable old sweater you just can't bring yourself to throw away.

"I think she hurt herself and didn't want us to know. She was so fierce!"

The light, plosive sounds of our dissolving laughs are all we can hear for a minute.

When I catch my breath, I say, "The ruler—I always wished she'd just hit me with it, get it over with already."

I am dancing with a dagger, but I cannot stop myself.

Mordent. Subito.

We are into it now.

"Is that why you cut yourself, Grace?"

"You knew?"

"I didn't think you wanted me to . . ."

"So many secrets. They didn't solve anything."

"I used to plan my escape at night, planning what to take with me. Definitely that photo of us in Vermont at Bromley—"

"I still have my copy—that day we both took the Lord's Prayer slope without a fall."

"And half the money from our escape fund, and my Green Mountain T-shirt."

"Half was all you took. I checked. They say the healthy ones know how to leave, Lise. You made it. I'm glad for you."

"Why did you stay?"

"Listen, the funeral is tomorrow, and I have a lot to do, so let's talk another time. Is this your regular number? I don't have one for you—"

"Gracie, I said I'm coming home."

"I heard you. Why now, though?"

"It's time. I want us to be sisters again. I told Rafe I could do it this time."

"This time?"

"We've had offers to work in the States before, but I just couldn't bring myself to come home."

"What about what I want?"

"I hope you'll want the same."

"I don't know, Lisa. I always thought you left because of me."

"I did. In a way."

"What did I do?" I don't need more anguish right now. "Never mind."

"You didn't do anything."

"So, it's something I *didn't* do?"

"In a way—"

"I'm sorry I asked. Look, I'm really not up for this tonight. I appreciate your call, but—"

"You couldn't help it, Grace. You were seventeen, and she was still humiliating you! I was afraid that when you left for college, she would take it out on me."

"What are you talking about?"

"I heard her telling you that you weren't pure, that you weren't clean. I watched you run past my room to the bathroom, and I heard you run the water and cry. I hoped you were just pretending to wash because she was being ridiculous. I couldn't let that happen to me. Gracie, you left your footprint in blood on the green tiles in the bathroom! I couldn't help you, but I had to help myself. I had to run away."

Now Lisa is crying, and I am stunned. In the space of a few seconds, I'm meeting my sister for the first time. She is not the weak one; I am. She got away from our mother. I never did, and when I married Luddy, I kept my weakness going, trying to be pure and perfect for him.

I'm sobbing now. "Lisa, I never knew. Why didn't you say something?"

"I couldn't. . . . I didn't want to hurt you, and then you turned so cold. I thought you would understand."

"I always thought you left because our parents wouldn't let you go to art school."

"Is that what they said?"

"I guess it's what they believed. I begged them to let you have your dream."

Piano. Doloroso.

"I did get my dream, Grace. Rafe and I got our dreams together."

That feeling you get when you lift your foot from the pedal on your instrument, be it a harp or piano, as the last chord fades to a satisfying puff in your ear coupled with the feeling of not having heard this music in years and wishing the song would never end. I want to be happy for Lisa, but I am heartbroken for me.

"I always thought I'd be there with you when you did."

"You can be!"

Lisa doesn't give up. "I'm coming home!"

"To New York?"

"Yes and no. I'll make a stop for a few days in New York, and then we're going to settle in Vermont. Rafe is going to run a jazz program in Burlington. I'm a photographer, Grace, and I'm opening a gallery show in New York. I'm living my dream."

Silenzio.

"I hear you, Gracie. You're doing that quiet crying thing. Mama's not here. You can let it out."

"Oh, Lisa. I want to be happy for you, but I feel so empty right now. I mean, I *am* happy for you, but it's been four days, and I haven't been able to cry for Luddy. I'm so mixed up."

Longa rest.

"Grace, remember that time in Manchester with the wallet? Mom and Dad quarreled over something she wanted to buy—wasn't it that jeweled designer sweater?"

"I don't know. Wait. I do remember he took us for a walk to the train tracks at the depot and then showed us his empty wallet. I remember you got scared—"

"I asked him if he could get more money—"

"He said he hoped so. I felt scared and hollow all the way home. I kept thinking, what if a tire blows out? How will he buy a new one?"

"I wish I could see your face right now."

"I'm that kind of empty now—like the wallet. It wasn't about dollar bills for me and Luddy, even if we argued about it all the time; it was about love, and the wallet always seemed empty. No matter how many things he filled it with."

"Don't say another thing. Put the nettles down. I'm safe. I love you forever, Gracie."

I hoarded my wishes and dreams, and Lisa made hers happen.

I cry for Luddy. I don't remember how I hung up the phone.

No more rests. Fermata. Cyclops.

I have to finish my story myself.

Chapter 23

Minuet among the Sculptures

July 19, 1999, Petrie Court, Metropolitan Museum of Art

Lee is making a visit to New York—a condition of her living in Wyoming with her anthropologist husband.

"Seventy-five two-liter bottles of diet soda, Lee!" I shake my head at the mental image.

"You counted?"

"I was trying to figure out where I could move them because I think the kids had some boxes under the table behind the soda. They might need those things, and if I wait, I won't be able to move—"

"Why so many bottles?"

"Those are just the ones near the stairs in the basement. He has more stashed in several other spots. He said he was afraid he might run out of a flavor, and he couldn't let that happen!"

"Like what kind of flavors?"

"Oh, orange, root beer, cherry cola, then some raspberry ginger ale—that's his current favorite. God forbid we should run out of that!"

"If you don't mind my asking, Grace, does he ever talk about doomsday predictions?"

"You think he's a paranoid conspiracy theorist?"

Lee knows all about Luddy's diagnosis, and she, like many of our friends and relatives, does not believe ADHD is real. Or, if it is, it's not an excuse for bad behavior. Just call me Doña Quixote.

"A lot of scientists are; don't forget Ted Kaczynski—"

"Lee!"

"What? I'm trying to help—"

"Don't go there!"

I remember how terribly frightened my children had been when they learned of Kaczynski bombing technology professors. Luddy had taken the boys' worries seriously, promising not to open any suspicious packages. The kids made a plan to monitor the mailbox at home, just in case. Kaczynski had been sentenced to life without parole a couple years ago.

At least our home with its bizarre collections is not a remote cabin in Montana. Our house may be annoyingly cluttered, but it's at least two thousand miles from crazy.

Lee and I stir our coffee with pretty silver demitasse spoons, and I look at the perfectly white circle that forms our table. We will share a dessert, as always. Lee will want something chocolate. A single beautiful red tulip cupped in a teardrop-shaped vase sits at the center of the table, along with some chrome-corralled sweetener and a delicate silver cylinder of cream. There are twenty identically presented, gracious tables around us, and I am enjoying the serenity of this orderly world. True, they have collections in the museum, but the displays are managed to avoid overwhelming. When does a collection become a hoard?

I want to stay overnight in the sculpture garden and awaken slowly with the sun coaxing benevolent stones to share their merciful warmth with me in the morning.

What would the Medicis do? I tease myself as I enjoy this afternoon of paintings, delicious peekytoe crab salad prepared by someone else, and conversation with my friend. I don't want to go home.

Okay. My house is more than cluttered.

Will the remote finally work so I can get into the garage when I get home? I will probably have to shove open the side door and try not to slip on the glossy direct mail coupons that have undoubtedly flown off the washing machine and slicked the tiles on the floor. I will slowly fight my way past large shoes lurking near the hamper and then hope there isn't too much ground espresso dusting the kitchen floor with grit. The slightly burned odor of a metal sample for the scanning electron microscope might waft into my nostrils when I pass the toaster. Has he forgotten the sample for the experiment, or did it need to bake longer to dry out?

Don't let any water into the 'scope!

Luddy's definition of tragedy. The obvious one in front of our eyes is not large enough.

Maybe there won't be any reference books or hammers on the glass-top stove so I can start dinner without having to relocate them to . . . where? The kitchen table is probably covered again. Perhaps my chair. If he is drying several samples, there is no telling what the condition of the counter will be.

"Do you want to stay in the city for dinner?"

Lee interrupts my thoughts with genuine concern, but the potential cleanup ahead worries me, and there is nothing ready to warm up for dinner. Chaotic clouds are darkening in my head. I cannot let the mess get even a day ahead of me.

"Won't Ray mind?" I deflect Lee.

"He doesn't dare! I won't permit it." Lee laughs.

I try to join her.

"No, thanks—I can't tonight, Lee. There's a stove somewhere under all that crap, and it's my mission to find it."

"Why don't you leave him?"

"I can't."

"Why not?"

"I don't know how I'd take care of myself."

"You can do it. You need to go!"

"I can't do it to the kids."

"The kids are grown up now. They can handle it."

"They're not through with college."

"That's an old excuse. Women don't even say that anymore. If I know you, you'll be saying the same thing when they're in grad school, followed by their weddings, then, grandchildren, then the nursing home!"

"Well, I . . . I'm not sure what will happen if I leave."

"Do you really think he'd stop paying for college?"

"He might not do very well. Then everything will go under."

"He's a big boy. Maybe he'll grow up."

"Maybe he'll take it out on them."

"Maybe he won't."

I set down my cup a little too hard and some coffee splashes on the table, and on my white sweater. I dab at it with my napkin as I feel tears begin to blur my vision.

"You need to get out."

I swat at her certainty. "Why don't you leave Ray?" She often claims he is just like Luddy.

"I limit how much he can collect. The only thing he can buy in bulk is Tide."

"How much do you have?" I'm thinking of the twenty containers we have across from the table near the diet soda. As I visualize a map of the basement, rolls of paper towels begin to crowd my head.

"Ten giant-size containers in the basement."

"So, you count them too!"

"Only to make sure he sticks to the rules. Ten is the max."

"What happens when he shows up with one more?"

"I make him take it back."

I know Ray is no match for Lee if she's angry, but I have never been able to muster the right tone with Luddy to make it clear that doom will follow if one more bottle of anything crosses our threshold. If I stand my ground sharply with him, I hear my father's voice in the back of my head, whispering, "Don't be like your mother." I've always tried to find a quiet way to exist in my own surroundings. To leave without shouting is my goal—if I can ever bring myself to go. At this moment, I feel too angry to be kind, but too worried about the kids to think about it seriously.

"Why don't you go before you lose your looks? You're still young. You could meet someone else!"

Lee is refreshing her lipstick because it's nearly time to leave if she wants to get to her hotel before the traffic picks up.

"I can't."

"You mean you won't."

"Again, Lee, why don't you go? You say you're miserable and there's nothing going on between you and Ray anymore."

"It's too complicated. The money is all tied up in his name. I don't want to spend it on lawyers."

"Aha," I mumbled. "There's that too."

Our quarterly conversations at the Met usually end in these fond stalemates. Lee always whispers, "Go now!" instead of "goodbye," but she never lets me down. She always wants to see me again. After twenty years of marriage and my sad-sack conversations, most of my friendships are withering away from my inertia. Lee is still here with a hug and a giant nudge.

Even though I think about it all the time, my exit ramp has not yet materialized. I don't know what I would have done without her support, these moments she provides where I can think of taking baby steps toward a world without my husband in it. Our mutual loneliness is part of the draw. For our own weak reasons, both of us are going to stay put for now.

Maybe someday we'll be able to empower each other to actually make a move toward a new chapter in our lives.

Chapter 24

Year Thirty-One

April 16, 2008

It takes two people to make a marriage work, and the same two can contribute to its end. I believe we choose every day whether to stay or to go, even if we're not consciously aware of it.

I continue to think about this every day. For a long time my answer has been "stay," despite Luddy's ever-expanding problem of hoarding and the anger that accompanies it. The consequences of his hoarding long ago began to flick their tongues around our home like hungry snakes searching for prey, and now, after thirty years of marriage, no room in the house is safe.

I don't know exactly what was going through my mind yesterday, Tax Day 2008—the day my answer morphed into "Go." Somehow, the last of my optimism dissolved, and I allowed one foot to creep slowly toward the door.

❧

After observing his chaotic process for so many years, I had a pretty good idea of the sequence. This particular Tax Day was not unusual. It began with the annual, avoidable pit of worry for both of us. Would our taxes be filed and postmarked on time? It had become more difficult for my husband to complete them with each passing year, and while

Luddy wanted to control the outcome, he said the forms continued to grow more complex. Although this was probably true, each year he also vociferously refused to hire an accountant.

"People make mistakes if they aren't careful," he asserted.

I couldn't argue with that; however, I also didn't want to see my husband so stressed by the process. Nor did I want to be the collateral damage. What was more important—a perfect tax return, not paying a penny extra, or well-rested, functional, loving spouses?

Actually, Tax Day is always similar in pace and outcome to paper-grading and research proposal episodes I've experienced throughout Luddy's teaching career. He throws himself into teaching his classes and feels truly satisfied by working with students; he likes being recognized for his research. Unlike tax preparation, he's found a way to make teaching work for him, and he's become a highly regarded professor and master teacher at the university. Even the compulsion to keep returning to the house for things he's forgotten does not prevent him from meeting with most of his classes on time, ready to go.

In recent years, however, he's been forced to confront the disabilities that are often part of a hoarder's makeup—ADHD, his primary diagnosis—along with the alphabet soup of behaviors and conditions associated with it: OCD, ODD, perfectionism, procrastination, and depression. Add to this a certain impatience with his colleagues and a generation of students he believes have received a less-effective education, and it often leads to angry outbursts that have begun to contradict his previous level of achievement. Maybe he couldn't help himself, but the explanations he found for his challenges did not smooth the road; instead he argued with colleagues and waved the Americans with Disabilities Act in their frustrated faces.

Yesterday I felt like I'd run out of arguments against his so-called Tax Day "process." I wanted to let him finish, but I planned to put an end to this anguished behavior. To pass the time, I walked nervously among his temporary workstations around the house to see if I could get a feel for how bad it was this year. I knew that each disorganized pile of papers multiplied the possibility of losing a receipt or a train of thought. As the piles proliferated throughout the month before D-day, they had necessitated more frantic trips between them to try to put similar things together. To organize. The breeze created by his running through the house often whirled papers into different piles, amping up the potential crises to follow. That's just the way he rolls.

Throughout the history of our married life, I've always been the cleanup girl who memorized the location of eyeglasses, keys, and important papers. All my labor was beginning to seem pointless as his competence declined further, despite my efforts to prop him up. You might say I'm a martyr, but as we lived these experiences, we never stopped to reflect on our roles in these games. I believed I was helping our family to keep going. Until this particular episode, I hadn't been seeking thanks. Now, however, I did want to see some improvement, and perhaps even some repairs to the broken process.

Luddy had set up his command station in his main "office"—one of many throughout our house. This one used to be Simon's bedroom. I no longer enter this room, partly out of concern for my own safety. The door is usually stuck open because of litter and other obstacles, so I can only peek in at the desk and partially around the corner.

This was the room where Luddy had gently bathed our firstborn with a miniature washcloth, gently avoiding the umbilical cord stump that had so terrorized me. As Simon grew older, it was Luddy who talked him through his imaginative fears about the *E.T.* poster attached to the bottom of the bunk bed above him. Luddy refused to let his son give up on himself. Instead, he shared his ingenious way of coping with fears, guiding Simon to move the cherished poster to the basement doorway as a warning to all monsters: *Do not come upstairs!* The poster has stood sentinel over the basement for twenty years, and Simon's room became a safe space where we'd once taken turns sleeping on the floor to scare away the bad dreams.

Now the room itself has become the bad dream.

When I finally peeked in yesterday, I could see our son's old hockey sticks rising from a precarious pile of boxes blocking the side window. A three-inch-deep river of loose papers covered the floor around his desk, where I had slipped and fallen more than once. I did not know if this moat was accidental or protective, but I was putting off wading in there to check on the status of our tax return. I couldn't bear to sit in Jake's old room next door—my office, neat as a pin—even if it was my only refuge from Luddy's clutter. I didn't want to listen to the thrashing around.

All morning I kept hoping Luddy would emerge, triumphant, rising like Neptune from the depths of his sea kingdom, but as the clock approached his promised update hour of noon, I became less convinced that anything good was happening in there. It had been too quiet, particularly during the past hour. I wanted to remain calm, but I was close to panic, considering an intervention, fearing the consequences of dancing in the paper sea.

From his muttering, I imagined what was going down in his mind as he looked at the piles surrounding him:

I guess it's true; I'm "Luddite Luddy," as my fellow nerds from Bronx Science call me at our Washington Heights reunions.

Then, after some meaningless shuffling:

What name should I paint on the prow of the beautiful new kayak staring up at me from my screen? It's mine for the taking if I can just finish the damn 1040. I know I can ace it this year if I can just get started. I've planned for this moment for a month—even read the instructions early this year.

It's all in my head; now, if I can just get it down on paper.

Christ, I have about twelve hours to do it and get it to the post office. Piece of cake!

The new kayak!

The new kayak is waiting. It's almost mine!

I can feel myself gliding through the water in peace. Even if Grace won't go with me on the river, I want this kayak—this peace.

That neuropsychologist told me to de-stress ten years ago. This kayak is overdue.

I need a break from work, taxes, family. Everyone wants something from me. I never want anything for myself. Isn't it time? Don't I deserve it? I'm making the lion's share of the money, after all.

Where's the pen? Only pencil stubs on the floor.

Have to look for a pencil . . .

There's a bird out there—cardinal? They always came back.

Pencil.

Everything always works out in the end.

This year, I'm going to clean up the floor once I finish the taxes . . .

And so, it must have gone as Luddy distractedly toured the room for a pencil or something else he meant to find until the kayak would reappear on the screen and engage him once again, taking him far away from thoughts of itemized deductions, alternative minimums, or the predicament he was inadvertently creating.

While I'm certain he didn't want to disappoint anyone, I knew there would come a moment when he couldn't sit still any longer. He might storm around the house, hand raised to warn me against talking about it, find something he might have been looking for, or something else altogether, eventually returning to the desk and its tortures, where the mental struggle with distractions would begin again.

Some researchers have hypothesized that Holocaust survivors were altered in such a way as to lead their children to become hoarders. Anxiety about losing everything figures large in some of these arguments. I wondered if the shadow of the Holocaust—which Luddy's parents had narrowly escaped by coming to America—played into his development at all. Sadly, the many theories explaining hoarding behavior have not led to any clear solutions to the problem.

We know that hoarders generally cannot stop collecting on their own. Even with a great deal of assistance and compassion, recidivism is more common than not. In addition, the other disorders that often accompany hoarding make finding a treatment or a cure even more complex. The multifaceted solutions must be hoisted together like circus tent poles while taking care not to let a single rope slip, or a week's progress could vaporize in a blink.

Hoarding, once considered a Midas-like condition, is not the province of wealthy people who can afford to collect many golden goods. My own mother was an orphan who grew up with "nothing but the kindness of her foster mother" after the death of her foster father, and she kept anything that came into her hands. Even when my father began to succeed in his medical practice, my mother continued to express her fear that we could "lose everything" nearly every day of my life. Her fear of returning to the Yonkers street corner where she once sold flowers to support her mother overshadowed much of the comfort she might have felt in the beautiful home she created for our family.

After my mom died, around twelve years before this Tax Day of 2008, I was tasked with cleaning her cluttered home. I laughed—and cried—when I discovered more than two hundred perfectly folded shopping bags in her attic. I used them to carry numerous piles of paper from her bedroom and spare room down to the shredder.

∞

I figured that when Luddy finally returned to his chair after storming around, he might be thinking he deserved a reward. He had been randomly mentioning kayaks during the week.

He often chose random strategies to keep himself on task, like setting a timer, which he could easily ignore. When it would chime from where it had sunk in the clutter at his feet, he usually couldn't find it to silence the alarm. He'd eventually give up after scratching fruitlessly through the fallen papers, and the sound would simply become part of the white noise of the house. He would counter the ineffectual sound with his fantasy of the moment—on this day, perhaps, paddling on a smooth river. He wasn't good at meditation because his mind always wandered, so this dream of floating was as close as he could come to relaxing.

On this Tax Day morning, apart from the timer, the house was as quiet as the river behind it. No swimming, and no motors allowed—a paddler's paradise. It was so quiet that Luddy might have imagined I had stepped out. This thought would have provided some relief. I imagine he considered taking a peek out the living room windows at the beckoning river but probably restrained himself, fearing I might be out there, looking to check on his progress.

Digital images of the kayak on the Eastern Mountain Sports website would have to suffice for the time being. He clicked slowly from one model to another. There was his dream boat—and it was in stock!

His hand shook against the mouse as he moved awkwardly around the page, reviewing the details over and over in the same careful way he parsed data from his scanning electron microscope. Mistakes were unacceptable, especially now. This day was going to have a perfect ending. He would find the right model and the right price. The kayak would finally replace the canoe that had somehow slipped its chain and floated away. Although he believed our neighbor had simply forgotten to tie it up properly, he had punished himself for three years for letting it happen. "Neither a borrower nor a lender be," his father Rudy had always quoted. His dad had been gone for five years now, and it was up to Luddy to make his own decisions, but he still wanted to satisfy his father's standards—even if Luddy had made them twice as strict.

I imagine that these thoughts of his father probably led Luddy to experience a pang of guilt about the task at hand. He was, down deep, a good boy—a good person. He would set a goal to prove it; he would work on the taxes for ten minutes before continuing to research his kayak. He could finish in an hour if he just kept his mind on the job. He could live with ten minutes at a time.

Luddy reached for the tax forms he had placed carefully under the laptop. There was not enough space for him to put things. He had run out of closets even after I'd yielded the coat closet and a storage closet in the hallway. The basement floor was covered. The living room was starting to fill. Why couldn't I see that he needed the other spare bedroom now too? I'd moved into it with my filing cabinets and writing projects when Jake had moved out.

He probably didn't believe we were any different when it came to saving papers; he claimed that I just stashed my huge collection in a filing cabinet. It was easier for him to have everything out and visible. Folders just hid things. Plus, he meant to clean it up. Someday.

I imagine he thought the kayak was going to be different from the canoe. It would have its own place of honor, down the hill, near the narrow path along the river. He would not lose it. He would protect it, hold on to it for dear life. He would cherish his reward for getting the taxes done. He was going to allow himself to have it, and no one was going to stand in his way.

He would also buy a rack for the top of the car. Perhaps it would be safer up there than on the riverbank? Or maybe he'd put up a new rack in the garage. Someone might steal it in the parking lot at work. He was going to think this through and do it right. In any case, he was going to keep this kayak close forever. He hadn't even seen it yet, but he'd already fallen in love with the photo on the screen. I heard him talking to himself about his plan.

I was standing in the hallway near the office, observing his struggle. When Luddy started to get up from the desk to stretch, his foot slid on some papers which caused the timer to start chiming again. This time he found it, embedded between two ridges of junk near a toppled trash can. He picked it up, shut off the alarm, and returned to the taxes.

I watched him stare at the Form 1040 instructions for a full ten minutes. It was not clear if he was actually *seeing* anything. He certainly didn't notice me waiting in the hallway.

When he gave up trying to focus, he turned back to the computer, clicking off the screensaver to gaze at his dream boat again. Something about the digitally sparkling water around the kayak coupled with the blue sky outside the window must have broken his resolve. He jumped out of his chair and rushed past me into the kitchen, grabbing his car keys from the table—right where he'd put them, for a change!—and thundered out of the house to his car.

Somehow I made it to the garage before he could drive off.

"Wait! Where are you going?" I shouted to Luddy over the engine. "We still have time to finish the taxes!"

"To buy a kayak!" my husband shouted triumphantly, pulling the car rapidly out of the garage.

He narrowly missed my car, parked outside because he hadn't had time to fix my garage door, which had broken six months ago. (He hadn't wanted me to call a repairman for something he could easily fix himself.)

Luddy ignored the disappointed look on my face, shouting, "It's my reward! Don't thwart me!" as he sped off.

I knew he would feel bad about it later, but he couldn't think that far ahead. He would bump against my resentment until it faded into the back of my mind, where I collected all the other episodes. To him, it was a risk worth taking.

I walked to the living room couch and sat down. I wasn't going to check the papers on his desk to monitor his progress; I'd wait until he returned. Lately, I had found that festering about the unknown was a lot easier to live with than seething about the known.

I did not know how this episode was going to end, but after more than thirty years of treading water, I believed our marriage was finally about to drown. I was in no rush to confirm what I feared. I was exhausted.

Nearly an hour passed before I decided to venture into his office after all.

I found some scribbles on a legal pad and the blank forms on the floor, near the computer.

The witching hour for filing was just eleven hours away. Cue up the organ for "A Whiter Shade of Pale."

Chapter 25

The Valkyries Meet Mastercard

April 16, 2008, continued

Luddy was gone for two hours yesterday, shopping for the kayak. I knew I'd have to wait even longer for him to return to the project at hand. His endorphins would be flowing with joy from the purchase, his hand raised in the air to render me invisible as he ran past me again, not wanting to discuss what had just happened. He would be eager to put an oar in the water, to enjoy possessing the item he'd wanted so fiercely, for as long as the euphoria lasted.

I'd have to wait until he was ready to talk about it. How long would it be until he faced the crisis he had created?

Death and taxes.

I was nearly exhausted from waiting and sorting through plans in my head. "What might work?" was a question borne not of optimism but of quiet desperation. My executive skills were fine; it's just that his problems were overwhelming unless they involved serious adhesive or duct tape. There was no adhesive for the current situation, because he could not define the larger, broken context in a way that would yield to his beloved epoxy.

The broken vessel between us was neither metal nor ceramic; it was our love. Procrastination on our yearly taxes was just one fracture among many in our relationship. It had become difficult for me to identify the separate strands of our problems, many of which originated in a crisis of self-esteem from which Luddy could not recover. He could have chosen to perceive of himself as successful. He had achieved a rank of distinction, holding an endowed chair for a term—an honor many professors only dream about. For some reason, however, his failures loomed larger than his successes because he had always aimed higher—as in Nobel Prize higher.

Learning about ADHD may have liberated Luddy from his past confusion about himself, but the diagnosis could not help him find a way forward that accommodated his true self, his professional life, and his family. He always chose the work first. The resultant misunderstandings generated more feelings of failure. For some reason, he clung to these despite his anger about them, trashing himself and his home as he railed against the world for not recognizing his brilliance.

Yesterday I realized once and for all that we have come to an impasse in the house.

He keeps everything, even yanking back discards from the trash when I try to put them there and preventing me from giving anything away.

I will concede that I have a lot of books and files of writing. The Japanese have a lovely word for book hoarder: *tsundoku*, which consists of the words *tsunde*, or "pile up things ready for later," and *dokusho*, "reading books." We both proudly embrace this title, and as academics, neither of us can bear to part with any of our well-thumbed volumes. But when our shelves become too full and I begin to weed out my collection, he rescues every single one of my discards from the Goodwill pile, despite the overflowing house, stacking them in the basement and creating a labyrinth that becomes moldy from occasional floods.

I'm not sure how we go about digging ourselves out of this.

∽❧

When Luddy finally got home yesterday, he ran right down to the river with his beloved kayak without a word to me.

At this point I was sure there was no way we'd make the tax deadline, so I decided to make a survey of the house instead. I was too upset to just sit there and do nothing.

What caught my eye first were the cracks. Broken windows, damaged artwork, a hole in the porch roof through which I could see the sky. Luddy had taped a poster of the Periodic Table of Elements over the hole so it wouldn't show, but that was hanging by a thread of masking tape, as if taunting him. There was water damage everywhere. There was no place in our house that did not smell of mildew or overripe food. I wanted to make it whole again. I wanted to make our family whole again.

We'd shared happier times together. We were good co-conspirators when it came to fostering our children's imaginative lives. Paper-bag robots, tooth fairies, sleepy songs. Parenting was our strongest bond. But after the children left to pursue their own lives, we seemed to make the wreck larger rather than digging in to clean it up.

I believed we needed something better than mere restoration—a stronger bond, to put it in his engineering terms—and I did not know how to achieve it. Whatever we had been trying to be up until this point was no longer strong enough to carry us into the future. Luddy had given up on counseling after finding the answers he wanted. I'd never been able to tempt him into wanting anything more for the two of us.

He had intense focus when he was interested in something. When he was at Oxford before we met, during time borrowed from his post-doc work, Luddy had created some beautiful art by completing seventy-five or so rubbings of famous brass tombs. He used shoemaker's wax, painstakingly rubbing black inside the outlines of the figures to produce the more-dramatic images. A rubbing of a couple hung in the front hallway of our home; dozens of monumental floor-to-ceiling examples papered the walls of much of the house. These were becoming damaged by the stacks of books and papers lapping at the bottom edges of the frames.

The image of the couple, John Ailemer and wife, Margery (AD 1435), was a smaller one, perfectly sized to fit above a small floor cabinet near the front door. They seemed to have been happy in life, and death, hands folded on their tomb in pious prayer. Because he had begun to stack books, bags, and papers on the cabinet, and they occasionally grazed the bottom of the rubbing, the couple's perfect wax composure now seemed threatened by the curls of torn paper below. Several dozen others were packed in tubes, dormant in our basement since his time in England during the 1970s. Someday, he said, he would do something with them. Or not.

Our home had become the capital of a wasteland.

As sunset approached, John and Margery contemplated our living room with their usual pink calm, unaware of how much was about to be disturbed in the room where such happiness and strife had occurred beneath their unchanging gaze.

❧

The loud ring of the telephone suddenly broke through my regrets.

Credit card company, calling about a missed payment.

Couldn't be, I mumbled, defending the one agreement we had made when it came to paying bills. He always paid the full balance on time, no matter what we had to juggle to free up the cash.

"We've always paid on time!" I said, triumphantly parroting the party line.

Did I want to make a payment now? the voice persisted.

I was somewhere closer to denial than submission; still, I was worried that Luddy would be angry if "we" had already paid and I created a problem by paying twice. I said I would check and call back. We hung up.

The phone rang again. Same number. A robocaller making the same request.

We'd had only one debt (that I knew of) in all the years of our marriage—our mortgage. We were both proud of living within our means, even if that meant doing without or postponing things we needed, or wanted. Had he given that up and just not bothered to tell me?

Agitated, I sat on the small section of couch I vigorously defended against his advancing hoard. He had said everything was under control whenever I asked if he needed help.

Facing the fireplace, I looked above the mantel to the spot where we had once happily hung a reproduction of *The Garden of Earthly*

Delights during our first overnight at the house. It was where some people would have lovingly placed a family portrait. Maybe that was our version of paradise, gluttony and all. The image had long ago given way to a big-screen television, always on when Luddy was present, belching forth loud shoot-'em-up Westerns and other black-and-white cinema treats through the long nights of his twilight sleeps and narcolepsy in the living room, occasionally blamed on my snoring. When it was silent, the TV dared reinterpretation: a shiny black orb offering knowledge of the future, if only Luddy could find the remote control.

I thought about the few times he would light a fire and tell me he wanted to hold hands. The first part, from offering to kindle it to actually lighting it, might take two or three hours of distracted searching, meaning the second part was often derailed. But he'd wanted to do it, and I had wanted to, too. At least, I always had before.

I looked over at the two large picture windows that formed most of the back wall of the living room—the breathtaking view that had sold us on the house before we'd even toured the rest of it. We had agreed that the view of the woods overlooking the river was our heart's desire, and nothing else mattered. This house would be a perfect place to retire; we would never move again, even after the children were grown. That was our fantasy then.

Now it seemed like the only way to clean the house so we could live in it would be to hire a crew and throw everything away.

My eyes wandered back to the pile of papers and random stuff near my feet. I saw the envelope with the name of the credit card company. I opened it. Past due. Interest charge.

So, it was true.

I began to wonder what else had escaped his notice or been tossed to the floor. My trust was breaking as I started peeling back the cushions, boxes, and tarps that he had tossed in a casual-looking way over the tide of mail that had overwhelmed us in recent years. My marriage-long pattern of ultimatums followed by tacit forgiveness was being exposed for the desperate, dysfunctional kindness that it was. We were both guilty, but I would have to be the one to clear up the problems.

I started sorting and opening. The horror had only just begun.

❧

Much of the mail on the floor had been ignored for a long time. Bills. Had they been paid? Luddy had avoided putting accounts online because he hadn't wanted me to interfere with his "system," and we'd struggled and failed with a joint checking account. An uncashed reimbursement check was near the middle of the pile—a patch of sky in this grim expedition. I'm not a divide-big-tasks-into-smaller-pieces kind of girl, so I made myself look at everything, sorting and occasionally opening as fast as I could. I wanted to be done before he returned so I could speak to him in large terms about what I saw as the scope of the problem.

I thought about Jake's frequent attempts to organize the hoard; he so wants to help his dad be functional. During the most recent attempt, Jake had arrived with see-through sorting boxes to clean up the living room, thinking this would make it possible to go through all the duplicates and make some decisions about throwing out or giving away some of the items that surrounded Luddy's recliner. When we'd completed the sort into the boxes, Luddy had looked at them and shaken his head.

"I don't know what any of these things are!" he moaned. "None of it looks like my stuff!"

The placement of objects that seemed so chaotic to us was more important than we'd realized. The hoard was not an aide-mémoire for finding his belongings or papers; it was the relief map of his comfort. The sorting boxes would stay on the porch from then on, to be joined by new piles of things covered by tarps.

As I continued I found more envelopes from health insurance plans, from organizations he worked for, and miscellaneous places I did not recognize. I stacked them in piles, postponing further investigation at that point. Next I found multiple letters from our bank about our mortgage—past due—certified letters he hadn't opened, the green receipts still stuck to the envelopes in an act of faith by our letter carrier.

And then I found the foreclosure notice. After nearly thirty years of good payments, he had missed a few, and the bank had threatened to take the house. The same letters, addressed to me, had been shoved further under the hoard.

A big lie. Why hadn't he asked me for help? He had mostly stopped communicating with me about anything important—financial decisions, feelings—surely he felt some enormous guilt here that might have been too big for him to handle alone? How humiliated did he want to be?

By the time I'd torn through this first round of sorting, I had discovered nearly $10,000 worth of uncashed reimbursement checks for business expenses and for health care from the last five years. I had barely scratched the surface of the piles in the house.

I was angry, thinking about the times he had complained that I was spending too much money, and that was why we had so little cash available. I was sad, thinking how painful it must have been to conceal all of this from me—if he even knew it was there.

When we were younger, he had found bill-paying excruciating. I sometimes thought it was because he disliked spending money, but I was beginning to comprehend, finally, what *lack of executive skills* really meant. For years, while I'd been begging him to simplify so we could manage together, he had been slowly falling apart. I had given up trying to talk to him about it on the weekends, ignoring the mess, because he would angrily refuse to do anything about it. He had taken to carrying all of our bills and papers in a knapsack wherever he went, pretending when we were together that everything was under control, up to date.

What else didn't I know?

Lightning shots of rage and grief alternated in my head as I blamed myself for closing my eyes when I couldn't stand to look at the hoard anymore.

❧

I didn't know what to do first. I wanted to run shrieking to the river to summon him back from his fantasy world, to make it clear that all would be lost if he did not reverse course right now. How could he do this to us? Why wouldn't he seek help? How much lower could he sink? Would I give up myself and melt into the hoard with him?

No.

I put away the unopened registered letters to me. I would need those if I decided to leave, I thought. I copied a few of the larger checks to show him. Tomorrow, I would begin to call all the places that had issued those checks to see if they would cut new ones. How many more could there be? I'd begin there and work my way up to the credit cards and the mortgage.

We had almost lost our house!

I was going to make it clear that he had one year to show some progress with his hoarding. I would help him get our finances back in order, but he would have to take care of himself. *Set a deadline*, people told me. *Be ready to leave.*

I'm too old to stay, too old to go.

How did we get here? I have to make this work.

It won't, a therapist had said some years ago.

I felt I had no other choice but to try.

❦

Japanese ceramicists have a custom of repairing damaged ceramics with gold to make an object more valuable than it was before it was broken. This art is known as kintsugi. Luddy was fascinated by it, and that's what I wanted for us. I wanted him to listen to reason and try to repair our relationship and our home in a way we could both treasure.

But on this day in April of 2008, I had to admit to myself that there wasn't enough gold in the world to handle the damage that was spreading like overflowing water through a widening crack in the vessel of our marriage.

Interlude

Floating with the Water Music

April 16, 2008, in a daydream

Luddy tosses a pebble into the water. Ripples form and separate from the center in rings. Fluids return to their shapelessness. All is calm above. The pebble beneath the surface does not disturb for long. I may find it again, worrying the floor of my lake, redirecting my unsuspecting feet. Or maybe I won't. I have ignored a great many pebbles over the years.

I watch Luddy toss an item into the hoard—another pebble.

The relief is instantly reconfigured in my eyes. It is jagged in a new way. I know where the used yogurt container sits. I can tell you where a copy of a poem I wrote for him ten years ago scrapes the floor near the sagging couch whenever he rises from this throne. Where three pairs of scissors lurk between two cushions. It all worries me while I am in the house.

When I leave, it may be hours before I recover my lake from his pebbles. His calm comes from hoarding. If I clean up to calm myself, I am the enemy, dissipating his fugue.

My broken heart and I leave home more frequently as this continues.

A physicist. An engineer. A student of why things break. In pursuit of strong bonds, he has had a long run of doing things his own way, trying to create fusions of ceramics and metals. Our home is a testament to these experiments. Heaps of unrelated, unprioritized ceramics and metals. Whole things. Parts of things. Tchotchkes. The good watch. Wind-up toys. A ceramic plate. Metal parts of a broken engine. Rivulets of pieces. Layers of soothing discards charting the seasons of depression and fear. Struggling for a verb. A completed action. Not finishing. Always starting. Over and over. Creative inspiration. Stuck. The absence of pronouns. The dislocation from other people. An occasional *you*. Unconscious of the tossing witnessed by me, his wife, ever-evolving enemy. He told me he could not stand an empty table. I did not listen to what he was really saying.

I need my space.

He collects. Another pebble, and another.

How many more can I ignore?

Fifth Movement

Largo gives way to triple meter. Giddy fragments of a waltz.

Chapter 26

Solfège. Do Re Mi.

August 10, 2009, sunrise, at home

Today I write to express my thanks to tenth-century musician Guido d'Arezzo. Do re mi . . . So sang the Broadway and Hollywood von Trapps, thanks to Richard Rodgers, as they practiced their pitch using this solfège, always on key—at home, in the city, in flight, always melodious. I play the scales in my head for comfort against the storm. No matter where I begin the ascent, they end a predictable octave higher, Do to Do. In the turbulence we call home, I often tap the "One Note Samba" against the fugue of our day. This has been my way for decades.

Today will be different. I'm going to introduce a giddy "Tico-Tico no fubá" counter-rhythm of my own. I won't hop on the convenient engine of major scales this morning; all my sharps and flats will be on display like a cuckoo clock. I have an announcement to make.

After the day of the kayak, I watched Luddy squander the time as if he could suspend it like sand stuck in the narrow waist of an hourglass. He started and abandoned tasks as if measures and scales did not exist, as if patience could be infinite. They do, and it is not. I gave him a year to make significant efforts in home repair and cleanup. I let him define what that would look like. He plodded. I found contractors. He angered. I made a notebook with the plans. He stopped. My resolve evaporated.

We have continued to live in a sea of discontentment. It doesn't matter why anymore.

The only person I can change, I know, is myself. I cannot wait any longer. Today I will formally give up on the idea of transforming my marriage and turn my attention to how I can create my successful elder self. I know I will have to keep certain plates spinning in my household system, but if Luddy needs to settle into the cracks, I will not interfere.

Yes, this means that I have given up yet again, but this time, unlike the others, I have been looking for a project that will take me away from my toxic house. I have reconnected with friends and family I haven't seen in years. My conversations with them have revealed that I am not alone. I have pulled an opportunity from the ashes of my burnout. I'm going to make a documentary about deferred dreams, incorporating my Clean House Concerto. It will be a multimedia film, incorporating my music and featuring puppets, a dancer, and her dance.

August 12, 2009, Dr. Lerman's office

"How are things at home?"

Dr. Lerman was wrapping up my exam with his customary quest for information about Luddy. This was never a comfortable moment for me because my husband valued his privacy, and he didn't want Dr. Lerman to know any more than what he told him.

"About the same!" I had chirped with as much fake cheeriness as I could.

"Seriously. What's been going on with Luddy?"

The loud organ of my mental carousel piped up, and I couldn't stop it.

"Well, I picked up a voice message from a fire marshal at the university. He was very kind, but he was urging Luddy to clear the debris from his office by the deadline. He offered to come help Luddy on the weekend if he was having trouble getting started."

Dr. Lerman's eyebrows shot high above his glasses. "What else?"

"Last weekend he got out of his car at a tollbooth to yell at people who were trying to move out of the exact-change lane. I heard him threaten to take an ice pick to their tires."

"Have you ever seen him do anything like that before?"

"There's been a lot of New York tough-guy behavior, but lately it's taken on a new edge."

"How so?"

"A few days ago, we took the bus to New York to go to a play. On the way there, a woman in the seat in front of us was making a lot of cell phone calls. After a few, he said 'Shut off your phone!' When she didn't, he started talking about rude people who ignore the rules about cell phones. I asked him to let it go. Since we couldn't exactly hear what she was saying, I suggested she might be handling an emergency. 'Five emergencies? Nobody has five emergencies!' His voice was getting louder—his usual MO when confronting other people's rule breaking.

"The woman clearly got annoyed by his remarks and started talking louder and referencing the rude guy behind her. He lost it, and started shaking her seatback and shoving her forward with it. I begged him to stop, but he wouldn't. She screamed that she was going to call the police, but he kept yelling and shaking her seat. I was terrified, and felt helpless. I begged him to stop. The bus driver just kept driving, even though we were just two seats behind him."

Dr. Lerman looked concerned.

"I covered my head with my arms like we used to in civil defense drills. She was almost daring him to do something, but it seemed like she was only pretending to call the police. Luddy was loving the adrenaline rush and, taking a risk that this driver didn't want to get involved, he kept it up for a good fifteen minutes while we were stuck in traffic."

"What's the name of his psych?"

"He isn't seeing one anymore."

"Why not?"

"The reason varies. Sometimes he admits it's because he couldn't stop obsessing about suing the university for ignoring his disability. In the beginning, his therapist kept egging him on about it—she referred him to a lawyer, and she said he had a case! Other times, he says it's because I wouldn't help him get well."

Dr. Lerman noted grimly that there had to be a psych if he was taking meds for the ADHD. He asked when the situation had changed.

"A long time ago."

Dr. Lerman took a breath. "Please ask him to come see me."

"I doubt he'll listen to me."

"And tell him there's got to be a psychologist."

෪ﾟ

I didn't relish the thought of having this conversation with Luddy.

I had decided not to tell Dr. Lerman about the night Luddy locked me in the attic with a mouse for a caretaker.

The attic in our dream house was accessed through a pull-down door with a staircase attached, and the light switch was downstairs. Entrances and exits needed to be planned and weights manipulated to raise and lower the stairs. The mechanism terrified me. The stairs had functioned well enough as long as we'd lived there, so most of my fears of being locked in were allayed over time.

I kept my off-season clothes in the attic due to my acute closet shortage, so twice a year I made the pilgrimage to exchange warm for cold and cold for warm before the elements overwhelmed the micro-climate where our heating and air-conditioning did not reach. I was up there, retrieving sweaters due to a chill in the August air, when I saw and heard the stairway slam up right next to me.

"Luddy!" I shouted, hoping to catch him before he left the area. I knew he might not hear me in the better-insulated areas of the house.

Nothing. No response.

The lights clicked off.

I screamed his name again. Nothing. I made as much noise as I could, searching for the flashlight that I thought we had up there, but no luck, and still no response.

I cursed the darkness. More screams.

I was afraid to move too far—say, over the living room, where I was sure he'd head next to turn on the television and begin his nightly doze to the loud soundtrack of Western films. Once he had succumbed to the rifle bursts, I knew he wouldn't hear me.

I started screaming even louder and banging suitcases and boxes against the floor, but to no avail. My voice was becoming hoarse. Could he truly not hear me?

As my eyes adjusted to the darkness, I saw something scuttle by. The next sound I made was loud crying and shrieking. I was afraid of mice, spiders, and any creature that might prefer the dark. For a half hour, I pleaded with the unresponsive darkness, trying to get Luddy's attention.

I was due for fifteen grams of carbohydrates on my tightly controlled diet for diabetes, and I was deeply distressed, which was using up whatever energy I had left. I thought about dropping something through the insulation over the living room, but I didn't want to hurt him. I couldn't stop crying.

Something finally woke him, and the television was silenced. I heard his footsteps in the hallway near the door, and I began shrieking again. The lights came on, the staircase descended, and I came face-to-face with my smirking husband.

I nearly fell down the stairs in my haste to get out. I started to complain, but when he said, "It couldn't have been that bad," I realized I was wasting my breath.

Law of the jungle, honey. Only the strong survive.

What kind of person treats his wife this way?

I swallowed my terror and ran past him to lock myself in another room. My sympathies to Bertha Mason. Luddy, you may have bested Mr. Rochester.

August 13, 2009, 10:30 p.m., Jake's old room

"He said no such thing! You're lying!"

Luddy had not handled the question about the psychologist with any kind of cool.

"I suggest you ask Dr. Lerman about it," I said, trying to stay calm. "You have an appointment tomorrow. You can tell him the name of your shrink then."

"That's not going to happen."

"You need to clear it up with him. I'm not going to be in the middle."

Those glaring blue eyes.

I stared back.

He waited until I looked down and then stomped away.

❧◦❧

Luddy never mentioned Dr. Lerman again. I'm not sure what happened between them, but the bottles of pills continued to accumulate. I surmised he might be storing up for Armageddon.

So Desafinado, off-key. Our wedding song, a prophecy.

Chapter 27

"In Search of the Lost Chord"

Don't only practice your art, but force your way into its secrets,
for it and knowledge can raise men to the divine.
—Ludwig von Beethoven

Thursday, April 7, 2016, late at night

The next twenty pages of my journal chronicle the development of my documentary in 2011. They resemble nothing so much as a hated photo album from which one estranged spouse has cut out the heads of the other, only it was my words that were obliterated.

Luddy had taken one of his beloved permanent markers, the fat ones that cover a lot of ground at once, and drawn solid rectangles over large sections of my words on every page. These black placards resemble the explanatory embellishments of a silent movie, except they have effectively removed most of the text.

A closer look at the writing around the edges shows that he also squiggled out the names of my artistic collaborators on the documentary, as if to cancel out the existence of the film—of Dave, the cinematographer; Malcolm, a puppeteer and Tasha, the dancer. Like an angry child, he had blacked out what he hated, drawing a circle around and crossing out the words "jazz harp," which referred to my music.

I'd had to resist my own feeling of rage when I first saw his mocking destruction of my thoughts. It had taken a lot of work to draw these black holes on twenty pages, but I knew his strength of will. A man

237

who created brass rubbings of more than a hundred tombs in England would find this destructive project mere child's play.

Why these pages?

Because they represented the history of my art, a project that was close to completion.

I imagine the feeling of satisfaction for him was epic. The fumes from the marker may have fueled his furious violence. He clearly wanted to obliterate me for leaving him. I did not follow his script for our lives, and he was embittered by mine.

I still have my notes from the original script for that film:

FADE IN:

1 INT. SUBURBAN HOME. LIVING ROOM. NIGHT.

Lights up slowly on rear stage comprising a large black panel (lining Rear Stage Right) next to a large white panel (Lining Rear Stage Left), filling the distance between the wings. TITLE projected on to the white panel in red neon letters: "The Clean House Concerto." These fade slowly as "Music by Grace Berg" appears in red neon letters on the black panel.

Music up: "Salsa Fusión" played on jazz harp. "Grace Berg" fades. CAMERA takes in the entire stage.

Enter DANCER as MIME (DANCER-MIME), wearing yin-yang mask. The panels represent a division in her mind, which she illustrates with a tight salsa flirting with the boundary between the panels. Film with quick cuts to different poses around that border; keep the mime's body aligned with the line. As the music fades, the mime uses her hands to beckon two marionettes from the ceiling—one is black; one, white. These puppets should descend slowly to their matching color panels. They are stick figures, made of what appear to be loops of shiny material at first, eventually revealed to be word clouds when pulled apart by the DANCER-MIME. The BLACK PUPPET comprises words about knowledge and science; the WHITE PUPPET, words about love and feeling.

CUT TO:

2 CLOSE-UP: DANCER-MIME's face without mask, now each side painted white and black to match the panels.

Music up: First five measures of Bach's "Toccata Fugue in D Minor," played on an organ followed by a fugue improvised on a harp as CAMERA pulls back to show entire stage.

INT. The panels are now covered with curtains of iridescent, vertical strips in black and white, with the marionettes standing in front of their opposite-colored panel. BLACK(Knowledge) joins WHITE (Love) on the black side, and the DANCER-MIME assists BLACK in drawing all of WHITE's word cloud into BLACK's arms. DANCER-MIME improvises a panic dance as WHITE melts to the floor in the sea of words that is rising around BLACK.

CUT TO:

3 INT. SUBURBAN HOME. LIVING ROOM. NIGHT

MUSIC crossfades to a march as WHITE puppet weakens and BLACK won't let go. Project words about bonding from science and love poetry falling into a heap in close, disorienting patterns in white on the black panel.

CROSSFADE TO:

4 EXT. A RIVER. BLUE HOUR TWILIGHT

BLUE LIGHT UP on DANCER-MIME, back to camera, looking into the house. DANCER-MIME improvises a dangerous waltz with wild arabesques, punctuated by different harp sounds. BLACK and WHITE remain huddled on the black panel side.

MUSIC UP: Dangerous Waltz on harp.

THE HOARDER'S WIFE

Watery word trails about love, knowledge, and bonding should be projected onto the stage. DANCER-MIME appears to be engulfed by word-trails; strobe lights on rear curtains. The white strips move behind the black strips, reemerging alternately to suggest a piano keyboard.

CUT TO:

5 INT. SUBURBAN HOUSE. DAWN

White light up on huddling marionettes. Piano curtain is opened to expose panels again. DANCER-MIME enters and picks up the tango, with a broom for a partner. WHITE tangos away with DANCER-MIME from BLACK toward the white panel side. DANCER-MIME gives WHITE a rose. BLACK is hopelessly entangled in and drowning in words. BLACK sinks into the pile. STAGE RIGHT goes dark. DANCER-MIME sweeps the rest of the words from the white panel side and exits. STAGE LEFT is illuminated brightly, spotting WHITE holding a rose.

MUSIC UP: Salsa Lullaby on harp. "LOVE" appears in red neon letters, which fade to "FIN."

FADE TO BLACK

❧

There's a diagonal slash through the page that follows the script notes, as if the marker had plotted the path of a pirouette from the upper left corner to the opposite lower right one, plus another short diagonal on the other side. It seems Luddy had started to form an X here, but then thought better of it. The entry he was attempting to cancel out describes the last gasp of our marriage. It was the only explanation he'd ever gotten, because he never asked me why it ended.

October 17, 2011, evening, Jake's bedroom

On the morning after the documentary film debut, we could have woken up and laughed about the frustrations of the day before. We could have taken a break from crazy. I might have helped him tone down a response to someone else so he wouldn't point a flamethrower at his enemy du jour. Maybe he still would have, but it wouldn't have been as noxious as his first draft.

But on this particular morning I was neither his editor nor his friend. Instead, it marked the beginning of our nuclear winter—the day I finally saw my surroundings as filthy and unredeemable.

Medications had made Luddy a funhouse version of his peculiar self. His language had deteriorated from the British affectations of long-ago Oxford to that of a man without human pronouns and an even more stilted academic syntax. I have read that language may be a cue to oncoming dementia. Luddy had no way to say "I" but had recently rediscovered "you." This morning he'd wielded it with the force of an assault rifle. Until this moment, I had been the last one standing in his path, the one his anger mostly stopped short of—but not today.

I suppose I could have listened when he announced he had something to say. After years of Luddy declining to share his feelings, I simply wasn't ready to hear about any, so I cut him off with my own wish to just relax and enjoy the achievement of my film screening the day before.

Yes, I said, some things may have gone wrong yesterday, but the project meant so much to me, nonetheless.

It didn't matter. His locomotive mind jumped the track and mowed down the formerly flexible woman in its path.

"You bitch! You fucking bitch!"

Shocked into silence by this verbal assault over morning coffee with Luddy, I did not respond. His attack rondo was certain, fast, and furious.

Again. "You bitch! You fucking bitch!" He was screaming now.

I felt bees. The bees from the earliest days of our marriage were stinging my breasts.

He shouted those same words at me again, and we both saw his hand rise over my head as if to hit me, but he slammed the table instead.

The bees stopped, and I felt naked, numb. My nightgown of shame and worry had slid to the floor and pooled around my feet at the kitchen table. I was never going to be the same.

Luddy stood up and fled to the living room, still shouting his refrain, adding, "And if you're unhappy, it's your own damn fault!"

❧

Where did this begin?

The day before, to celebrate my upcoming sixtieth birthday, I had invited about fifty of my friends to attend a screening of the first cut of my film. We had a long way to go to complete the film—a blend of my *Clean House Concerto* and a dance performance by Tasha—but I wanted to begin to tell our story to the people I held dear.

Luddy had wanted to share in the event by doing a specific task. I tried to put him off, fearing unintended consequences, but he insisted on helping. He would run the projector, he declared.

I should have known better. I should have insisted he be a spectator. I think he meant to try to be part of my world again, but his bullying intrusions into the project repeatedly sank what I had managed to float. He was jealous of my time away and the friends I made. I came to understand that he was fighting to save his relationship with me in the worst way possible.

This was an old pattern—whenever I started to achieve a goal, he would try to insert himself in the process, to share in the achievement and express negative views of the people he thought were in the way.

He'd been dismissive about my film project from the start.

"My camera would do a better job . . ."

"They're trying to take advantage of you . . ."

"It's costing too much money . . ."

There was a time when I would have wanted him to say, "I want to make this happen for you. What can I do to help?" But now I just

242

wanted him to sit back and enjoy the performance without inter-fering—even if he thought I needed help. I wasn't thinking about failure; I was thinking about learning. I was thinking about sharing our beautiful concert creation. I was thinking how much I wanted this day to be mine.

Apart from appropriating first right of refusal for any of the event's arrangements, Luddy had one job—running the projector. I figured he was an engineering professor—how hard could it be? I had run digital projectors often as a teacher, and so had he. They weren't diffi-cult to operate, so I didn't foresee any complications. I had created a PC-compatible version of the film so he could use his own laptop to connect and wouldn't have to worry about different buttons on the Mac computer I preferred. I tried to anticipate every issue he might raise and respond to every complaint he made, as if he were the director.

He had two weeks to practice with the equipment, to learn to click a couple of icons and adjust the volume as needed. He would not let me watch him, so I'm not sure if he simply procrastinated about prac-ticing or if he decided he'd be able to wing it on the day. In any case, I underestimated the lapses in his skill set. He used all the code-red words to hint at his flammable worries, like "control" and "perfect," but I ignored them. He wanted to help. I could be gracious. What could possibly go wrong?

As it turned out, everything.

Actually, it was only a small thing, and it could have been easily fixed, but pride and perfection swung at him like twin axes slashing through a forest.

The projector's bulb was failing, and there was no spare in the case. He didn't want to admit it might be the bulb. *Never accept the easy answer.* There was an AV store a few blocks away. *No.* We could buy or rent a new projector, even. *No.* Minutes were slipping away in my setup schedule. An hour evaporated.

We only had the event room at the Gershwin Hotel for a certain amount of time, and would have to follow a strict schedule or risk not having enough time for the screening and reception. With its focus on the arts, the Gershwin, in a beguiling location near the Museum of Sex, was the perfect venue for my multimedia collaboration. The hotel offered residencies to artists, and I was looking forward to applying to the board for a future project, using my film as a springboard for a larger work.

I felt myself succumbing to panic, but knew that expressing this would only incite a worse resistance in Luddy.

Too late.

"Leave me alone!" he raged, blue eyes flaring as I tried to step in.

I went outside and chatted about nothing with Tasha and Dave, who had noticed Luddy's odd behavior whenever he'd sat in on our filming. Tasha performed some stretching exercises, and Dave blew smoke rings to relax. I paced. We killed a half hour that way before I couldn't stand it anymore. We went back in.

"Where were you?" he hissed.

I was sweating, nervous.

Three hours of prep time hadn't been enough for him to complete the setup I usually accomplished in fifteen minutes before a class.

Part of his dilemma was stubbornness. He kept running through the same steps and wondering why the image was not in color, running the steps again, probably consuming the last working moments of the bulb, insanely trying to achieve a different result.

Perhaps the other part was pride. I truly believe he did not want to disappoint me.

I didn't know what to do.

"Leave it," I suggested, trying to sound nonchalant. "The color isn't such a big issue. "Let's try the speakers." Although they were small and emitted an uneven sound, the speakers worked, even if they did block the aisle the way he'd set them up. People were likely to trip on the cords and knock over the equipment, but my fingers were crossed. After all, the sound was most important to me—the sound of my music.

The guests arrived and were soon munching on hors d'oeuvres. At last, the show went on.

Everyone was nice about the faulty sound and the absence of color. "You couldn't even notice" was claimed sweetly more than once. At least they had seen the beginnings of our story and heard my *Clean House Concerto*, and that made me feel good.

After the screening, I was ready to collapse, exhausted. I chided myself for losing my head. I knew I would have to keep Luddy away from future projects, but felt good about accomplishing a first draft— and a month before I was sixty! You know that saying, "Bad dress rehearsal; wonderful opening"?

Onward. I believed in my life project. I believed in me.

We had traveled home in silence, saying nothing to each other that night.

I didn't know that the usual rift between us would enlarge to the size of the Grand Canyon while we slept, and would erupt over coffee the next morning.

❧

As he continued to rage, I sat at the table in an unfamiliar neutral mode. He delivered his charge in the first two words. After that, all the angry blood within me transformed into a new calm I didn't quite understand. I knew only that I was finished with the wounds of our relationship.

I cannot live this way any longer.

Although I believed I had achieved something good the day before, I was ashamed of my life. Even if I'd "brought it on myself," as Luddy said, *it* had to stop. We were toxic to each other.

My choice now was to ignore and accept our problems yet again or to leave and start over. I had tried the first approach for most of my life, but our life together didn't work anymore. This relationship was no longer about love. My side screamed for survival—beyond "hate the sin; love the sinner" reasoning.

Our house was no longer survivable, in my opinion. The smell of abandoned food containers assaulted my nose. Its hazards taunted me—piles of knickknacks mixed with junk and sharp knives—steak knives, pocketknives, paring knives. Empty boxes leered at my suddenly empty heart.

I no longer cared about trying to explain why the hoard had come to stay. That shift was the most liberating feeling of all. As long as I had been able to place another piece of the puzzle, I was hooked into analyzing it. Not in an effort to solve it, mind you, but simply to understand how it worked.

The irony was that there was no solution.

Today's outburst had dumped thirty-five connected years off the table, and I could neither pick them up nor go near the heap. I *would*, however, set the wheels in motion for a divorce. I would take my time, but I was going to take care of *my* needs. Luddy could call them wishes, or wants, or desires, but I knew it was more than that. I *needed* to flee. I could not live with him anymore. I had run out of rationalizations.

When he left the kitchen, still shrieking about how badly I had treated him the day before, I stepped into the living room.

This dream home—the place I'd wanted to connect with—wasn't mine anymore. It wasn't home. It was hell. Even the tableau of leaves falling into the beautiful river outside wasn't worth the torment. I was paying too big a price for the view.

Looking back, I realize I should have let him speak when he said he wanted to talk about what had happened the day before. I was selfish. I'd wanted to focus on the moment of fulfillment I was feeling. For just this one day, I'd wanted to savor my project, what I was creating. I was astounded by what happened when I'd shut him down. Clearly, he had been holding this in for a long time. In my attempt to save myself from drowning in the chaos of our marriage, I had shifted the balance away from the drowning man.

I knew I had to make a plan.

I stopped talking to him from that morning on so I could use every moment to figure my way out. I only had enough energy for myself, and I wouldn't sacrifice any of it—not even to try to preserve what little was left of us.

❧

During the next few weeks, Luddy stomped around the house and slammed every door he touched. I think he interpreted my silence as my being cowed. Despite my decision to leave, a small part of my heart waited for an apology, for some word of reconciliation that might have persuaded me to stay. Nothing came.

I continued my lonely but liberating research into divorce and became more and more convinced to go through with it. If I had understood more about the rigors of dissolving a marriage, I might not have come to this conclusion, so I guess it was fortunate I learned only so much about the procedures ahead of time.

The one part you cannot plan for is your spouse's response. While I could admit to myself that I no longer loved Luddy, I didn't want to be unkind. *Civil* is a word with a great many ironic burrs.

Chapter 28

"As Tears Go By"—Mick Jagger, as sung by Marianne Faithfull

February 16, 2012, morning, in the kitchen

"I have something I want to talk about."

As I spoke, I saw Luddy's body shift angrily into his resistant listening mode. He had finished unloading twenty minutes of complaints about work, and he wanted to move into his day. I had to finish what I had been rehearsing for several weeks. I hoped the recorder in my open purse was working. There was not going to be a do-over.

"Luddy, I love our family, and especially the children we've raised. I'm grateful we could accomplish this in partnership, and hope that one day we'll come to a better understanding of each other so that we can enjoy our grandchildren together. However, at this time I find myself unable to continue living with the hoard, and especially with your anger around it. I am going to begin divorce proceedings."

Luddy's eyes widened with shock. I felt my nerve starting to fade.

"Are you leaving now?" His voice quavered with a small child's fear.

"I'm going away for a few days." My lawyer had suggested this, to allow Luddy's anticipated anger to diminish a little before we talked further about details.

"I don't suppose you will try counseling."

I hadn't expected this. I wavered a little.

"Well, it hasn't worked before. But if you arrange it, I'll go with you."

"No. It's not worth it. You always get what you want. You always win!"

This was the self-defeating Luddy I knew.

"Well, I'll be back on Monday. You can let me know then if you'd like to make an appointment. In the meantime, I'll continue to pursue the divorce."

"Where are you going?"

"Not far from here." The attorney had cautioned me not to say where. "My cell phone will be on if you need to talk."

"Who are you going with?"

"No one."

He snorted his doubt.

I thought about whether to respond to this.

"Is that what you think—that this is about someone else?" I sputtered. "Well, if that makes you feel better, I'm sure you'll continue to believe it, so you won't have to look at yourself."

I bent down and picked up my purse from the floor, having packed and loaded a suitcase into my car during the night while he slept. I hadn't wanted too many things to juggle in case he tried to prevent my departure.

My annoyance probably helped as I moved quickly to where he wouldn't be able to block my exit from our one relatively clear doorway.

He remained rooted to the chair at the kitchen table, protected by the mess of junk he insisted on keeping there, some of which I had pushed aside earlier before sitting down to our point of no return. He looked like a little boy in a collapsed blanket fort.

I pushed against this sadness and walked out.

I didn't know if I'd ever see the house again. Might he change the locks? Would he call a therapist?

I had taken a lot of pictures of the hoard in recent months, but I knew it might look worse after the weekend. I doubted that he would try to make it better, but because I had disturbed his equilibrium, anything could happen.

I walked to my car and drove off to a coffee shop before I took a real breath, simultaneously defeated and victorious. I was ready to begin this adventure, for once not knowing the outcome. All I knew was that I needed to be free. I was acting for myself at last. There was no more asking, "If not now, when?" I had launched.

I called my children to confirm that I had talked with Luddy and that I'd left so they could prepare themselves to answer his questions.

I hadn't told Luddy that the boys already knew my plans. They had argued against it at first, but eventually offered their support. They were patient and kind; they didn't want me to lose my head now.

I hadn't thought about it being the week of the anniversary of my father's death, but when I drank my first sip of coffee as an estranged spouse, this was the first thought that entered my mind. I was sure my father wouldn't have wanted me to continue my unhealthy marriage. I think even my mother might have agreed it was time to leave.

I spent the weekend at a small hotel just across the highway from our home. I had dinner with a friend and prepared for the next intense round of what would prove to be an overly long and hostile goodbye.

Luddy didn't say a word to me when I returned on Monday. He ran to our bedroom and shut the door, making it clear he was keeping the room—and the bed—to himself. It was the bed he had purchased when he started graduate school in the 1960s. I had no interest in sleeping in it again.

May 16, 2012, writing in my car

Luddy made it very clear how he intended to behave during the months preceding our divorce. My lawyer and the judge anticipated that he would resist moving out of the house. I was granted power of attorney to take out a loan in order to make repairs and clean the house so it could be sold for our mutual benefit. Unfortunately, they did not anticipate the extent of his territorial attitude, or how permanently he would encamp himself within.

I realized that it would be an expensive proposition to try to evict him, as the divorce papers required, so I formulated a backup plan. I offered him the option of buying out my share of the house so he could stay. He accepted.

After his classes ended for the semester, Luddy barely left the house. He spent his time accusing me of stealing and glaring at me like a hawk as he plodded between various perches in the kitchen and the living room.

I tried to maintain a semblance of normal life because I had nowhere else to go in the short term. Because Luddy had accepted my backup plan—allowing him to keep the house—I needed to find another place to live. Unfortunately, it was easier said than done. Alimony was delayed, so rental companies didn't want to know me. Even after I found a condo I could afford, mortgage companies were looking for a biweekly check, rejecting my assets as proof that I could make the payments.

It was a temporary situation but one I hadn't prepared for, and Luddy made it as difficult as he could, simultaneously refusing to handle his part of the paperwork and yelling at me about leaving every chance he got.

Knowing that the turmoil would end one day made it easier to ignore some of his anger, but it was awful, nonetheless. I often found it intimidating to be in the same room with him and his menacing expressions. I was counting the minutes until I'd be able to leave, feeling increasing relief as the clock wound down.

Luddy refused to respond to my lawyer, so the divorce proceeded without him. He represented himself pro se by not appearing, so it was accomplished without even a word from him, only the bitterness and rage he felt at being left.

July 12, 2012, County Court

People get divorced for far less significant reasons than I presented. The clerk moved our case to the last spot on the docket because of its complexity: elder divorce, a long marriage, assets, mental illness. Luddy's unpredictable behavior might have made for an unruly courtroom scene if he had decided to come. I had begged him to get an attorney during each round of the process, after he had declined to respond to the offer of mediation. I was not certain he understood the divorce complaint. He expressed occasional bursts of anger about particular items, but he did not acknowledge that his participation was required. The judge would have granted him a voice and possible leeway in the settlement if he had put in some effort, but he had not engaged in the process as of yesterday's hearing.

As I waited throughout the morning for our hearing to begin, I heard sad tales of abandoned young mothers; young men who couldn't hold jobs to pay child support; marital violence; incompatibility. The legal cookie cutter assigned custody to the young women in most cases and made villains of their former mates; the men hanging their heads sheepishly in the front rows would soon be best friends with their probation officers, who would supervise alimony and child support. These sorrows would be cut short by Family Court before they had time to disable another generation. New Jersey had streamlined the process of disrupting dysfunction. It was cutthroat and simple, yet it gave these tiny families a chance to move forward.

My story was different because I had waited so long, and we had so much to divide. And then there was the cleanup of the hoard. I was grateful my children had launched their adult lives from an intact family. I hoped that the illusion I had accepted and promoted would help them thrive in spite of this break with the past, but the literature did not bode well, suggesting they might not. I had taken this leap with no guarantees.

I remember the judge's perplexed face as I tried to explain why I'd decided that now was the time for me to leave. I had sent more than one hundred photos to illustrate the problem. She asked me logical questions about the hoard: How long was it? How high? Why? This familiar exercise in the five *W*'s really does not convey the truth about hoarding, but people ask these questions anyway, trying to create a logical container for scenes of irrational behavior. The mind wants a song with a beginning, middle, and end, but it was the atonality of contemporary music that shaped our marriage. I shared disturbing photos of unruly stacks, but these did not convey the depth of horror and shame I felt about the mess and the filth.

Not knowing how much, in her opinion, would be too much, I told her the dimensions of the pile of shoes in our bedroom.

"Four to five feet tall, about three feet wide at its base."

"Were they old shoes?"

"Some—but some were new, with tags. Other piles of clothing and other items are maybe a foot and a half high."

"When did the hoarding begin?"

"Well, there was always a problem with clutter, but we were teachers. We both had a lot of books and papers. In the beginning, I found all the little trinkets annoying, but not impossible to live with. It crept up on me over time. I would say that it started to feel unmanageable about fifteen years ago, when Ludwig first learned that he had ADHD."

"Fifteen years from his diagnosis?" the judge mused.

I could hear her unspoken *What took you so long?*—although I think we both knew that the uncertain fate to which she had consigned the young women at the beginning of the day would have been unthinkable to me that long ago.

The judge asked me how I thought I was going to live, because the alimony she was going to award (*phew*) might not cover everything.

When I told her that I planned to work again, she looked over her glasses at me, worried about my age of sixty. I did not have my whole, healthy life ahead of me; did I understand that?

I talked about having reinvented myself several times, and that I believed the assets I would receive in the settlement would see me through the rocky beginning of my efforts.

Pity laced with respect allowed her to accept my plea. My lawyer had suggested that I not go back to work until after the divorce, and I was anxious to start again.

I had worried at first that my answers might not be convincing—that some optimal height of the piles might be required in order to release me from the hoarder's den. But that wasn't the problem at all. At a certain point I realized that the dimensions of the collection really had no bearing on her decision; the judge simply had to understand it all in a way that made sense to her. My tolerance for the hoard was possibly as nutty as Luddy's creation of it. She must have wondered whether either of us was rational anymore. Who could blame her?

Hoarding does not respond to logic, and it makes no sense.

Some experts think there might be a neurological trigger, and various behavioral routines can possibly manage some of the hoarding tendency. But we also know that recidivism is more than likely.

Others believe that a childhood trauma may activate the behavior at any time in life. I have read that part of the slow, uncertain "cure" for hoarders is to learn to tell a different story about the items they try to embrace. While not every item is useful, hoarders feel they must keep it all because the things *might be useful someday*. A hoarder needs to stop claiming that possibility if he or she is to quit saving.

I have watched with sadness as my husband clutched an object to his chest like a child, pleading in a childish voice, "Don't spoil my life!" or "I might need it!" The habit of hoarding gradually interferes with a family's quality of life as it insidiously penetrates and controls every open space, every thought and dream. But in some cases, like mine, the family member fights back with an involuntary survival reflex.

After that angry encounter in the kitchen with Luddy, my once-for-giving self finally fought back: "Get out! It's now or never—sink or swim!" I knew I had to leave. Hoarding was a symptom of the problems we shared, but I no longer believed it had to be a life sentence. Luddy was my security until I felt threatened, and then there was no turning back. In too deep after thirty-five years, I had to resurface.

Luddy did not come to our hearing, though a gasp ran through the courtroom when a supportive friend of mine arrived to sit with me late in the morning. False alarm. Luddy had never responded to any of the court papers or lawyer's letters, and this time was no different. The judge asked me if I thought he had received them. I told her about the sea of summonses and requests splayed around his recliner in the living-room hoard. I could not vouch for the amount he read or understood, because he refused to talk about them. On one occasion when I tried to reach him, he had yelled at me that I was a "quitter." Even though he couldn't change my mind, he could still try to make me miserable. He said I had "never made a contribution to our marriage." I disagreed, then stopped talking. The only useful thing for me to do was to leave as peacefully as I could.

I believe Luddy was too terrified and heartbroken to face the end of our marriage—but not enough to take any action to disrupt his way of life in the recliner. I had seen other evidence that Luddy preferred revenge over reconciliation. I knew he enjoyed the angry adrenaline rush of fighting a political battle at work or protesting an "unjustified" speeding ticket.

The judge really wanted to understand our divorce. I knew she was wondering about me as well. Why had I stayed so long? How was

I going to live now? She asked more of those journalistic questions about me, and her thoughts were fair. "The world," she pointed out, "is not kind to sixty-year-old women." The look of pity she gave me when I said I was going back to work was hard to accept. I didn't want to contradict her, but she was going down a well-worn yet useless path. The world was not the problem. I had run out of the common excuses—the happily-ever-after, the kids, the financial security—to ride it out anymore.

I explained my previous attempts to change our situation—the apartment on the Hudson I had rented; the house-hunting I had attempted with Luddy, traipsing through larger and larger homes throughout three surrounding counties. Nothing made him as happy as our current house, which was overpopulated with his things. He would not move.

Our quarrels had become hurtful long ago but had recently plummeted down a rabbit hole to the screaming verbal abuse of that fateful morning, his hand raised high in the air, about to strike me. All my hopes had evaporated then. *Fucking bitch* was not going to be my epitaph.

Hoarding is not logical—no matter whether it is the emotional or compulsive kind. The height of a pile of never-worn shoes is irrelevant to the hoarder. Hoarding is as illogical as love and anger, as relentless and vast. To try to disrupt it is to feel the force of a hurricane. Our home was the beach where the gale force had landed, and there was no turning it back. Repeated counseling had created only temporary solutions to our problems. Luddy's emotions would always find a way to overwhelm his promises, like the mistress another man couldn't leave.

If you are going to understand the problem, you need to understand how vital the hoard is to the hoarder's life. "Don't answer unasked questions," my lawyer had advised me. Nonetheless, I wanted to tell the judge that hoarding is like water for humans. We need water, but not all water is benign. Water has natural cycles and causes; water builds, and it destroys with its flow, and logic has nothing to do with it. Just as water finds its way around and through the stones in a stream, crushing some and merely tickling others, the hoard ebbs and flows according to the chemistry and feelings of the hoarder.

Criticism is also pointless. While water feels no shame, the hoarder collects it and won't discuss it. Oh, we can set up charts and records, maybe sandbags to try to control it, but neither our need for water nor its sudden epic floods are controlled by numbers or predictions. Likewise, the hoarder.

The personal hoard collects elements, washing them out in unpredictable waves, yielding beautiful shells along with used, corroding aluminum cans without prejudice. Humans project their feelings onto water, searching for meaning where the sea joins the horizon. As quietly as it shows us peace, it can turn to destruction when a riptide gathers its unseen might. In the asynchronous hoarder pair, one hoards while the other must yield space, even after the house is endangered by the flood. In the battle for control that is your marriage, you could be ground to sand by this sea. If there is another way, my years of searching could not find it.

I would have explained to the judge that the hoard is a similar tangle of comfort and mayhem for the hoarder. We try to determine the reasons, but I think we are on the wrong track. Many of us love dualities: Logical—Illogical. Black—White. Old—Young. Useful— Not useful. In the case of the hoarder, these do not apply. At some point the once-delineating fjords and ice floes of stuff fill in, and the amorphous chaos of the hoard floods what was formerly a home that had discernible lines and rooms. There is nowhere to sit that the cache is not present.

But these conditions evolve into worse scenes. The mind floods too. Dysfunction develops insidiously through years of angry collecting. A man who studies how things break, as my husband did, has a lot of repair tricks up his sleeve. Luddy was always more interested in explanations than solutions. *Why?* and *How?* he could tunnel through. The hoarder may be inventive with duct tape, epoxy, and wires to keep survival systems functioning, and the frustration levels can be epic. Luddy asked "Why?" instead of "What to do about it?" When confronted with the ruins of a hypothesis, he could not answer for himself.

Earlier in our marriage, all the visible evidence of new hoarding did not stop me from trying to keep the walls from closing in. Each long day was spent fighting the tide.

Example:

Me: Don't you want to live in a clean place?
Him: Yes.
Me: Then let's clean this up!
Him: *Silence.* Or: Not right now. Or: I don't know where to start.
Me: I'll help you.
Him: I'll take care of it. Everything is under control.

Of course, it wasn't.

I didn't realize we weren't really talking to each other during these conversations. Each of us had a phantom spouse who we imagined was listening.

For many years, I woke myself in the middle of the night to disturb the stacks so I could mop floors, wash dishes, and put things away, hoping he wouldn't notice. I was trying to make the house habitable for our children, using the tactics of a teenager filching from the liquor cabinet.

For the latter half of our marriage, the growing hoard was topic number one, in ever-louder iterations. While I had many good reasons for cleaning up the hoard, Luddy had just as many reasons to leave things as they were.

It baffled me. As an engineer, he could be brutally logical about, say, the subatomic structure of alumina, angry about a speck on the surface of a microscopic sample. But as a life partner of thirty-five years, the hoard had replaced me as his primary love. If I wasn't going to dive into that ocean with him and love the swim as much as he did, he was going to save it, not us. Didn't I see that the hoard had everything we might need? It wasn't just our home; it was a gold mine. There was similar chaos in his office, a similar argument with a fire marshal there. When we traveled, he made short work of re-creating our "homelike" atmosphere in a hotel room, covering every surface with trinkets that he carried in overweight suitcases he had to pay for. An empty table was like a vacuum; he abhorred it, so he covered it.

I am ashamed to admit that even as I saw the hoard accumulating everything from car keys to ketchup packets to broken metal shards, food, and uncashed checks, I could not leave. I loved him, but I think I also loved my anger, which kept me blinded. Coming into my own house meant steeling myself to dive into a shipwreck. "Might as well try to stop lava flowing from Kilauea," said an attorney after looking at the photos.

For professionals whose career depends on researching and diagnosing mental illness, Luddy made an interesting study. He would sit down on a chair, and when he got up there would be a ring of tchotchkes, nutshells, junk, and food wrappers that appeared as if out of thin air. Could all of that have been in his pockets? There was quiet kidding about reverse locusts. If I tried to intercept his trash before it landed on the pile at home—be it spoiled cheese or a broken keychain—he would follow me to the garbage can and rescue whatever I was throwing out. He routinely checked the trash to see if I had betrayed him. Medication lowered the volume on his anxieties intermittently, but the loudness always returned.

I am forever asking myself why I stayed for so long, but in the end, all the data I gathered helped no one when it came to the divorce proceedings. I didn't want to hurt him despite the contempt that grew within me as he ignored the hearings and refused to take care of his part of the financial work, costing us much more money than it should have. At one point he had said he wanted to use a mediator and keep it amicable, but he didn't seem to understand that he would have had to participate in order to make it work. Lacking his participation, I had to find another way, and since he refused to change, we were forced to repeat the same steps over and over.

July 31, 2012, in my car

I remember the look of confusion on the bank employees' faces as I brought Luddy in to take my name off our joint account and safety deposit box. "This never happens," they murmured. He said nothing—I imagine they might have been wondering about his mental capacity—but somehow we did what was necessary to separate our accounts.

When we went outside, Luddy opened the trunk of his car and handed me the mail he had withheld from me for six months, along with the coffeemaker I'd mistakenly had shipped to his house instead of my new one. Sheepishly, he offered to carry it to my car. I let him.

Later, at his employer's human resources office, things went about the same way as I removed myself from his benefits and waited while he heard explanations of what would happen next. He ignored it all and apparently did not sign up for the golden health-care plan he was entitled to use. "We've never seen something like this," the counselors said to me when they returned him to the waiting room. "No divorced spouse ever comes."

Again, I saw their confusion; how could he be so negligent about his own interests? We were inscrutable to everyone but ourselves, united in dependency even after the breakup.

I prayed for an end to the list of things I needed to accomplish for him so that I could be free. There is no logical explanation, but even in these separating activities, my feelings held way too much power over me. I unwittingly hoarded the damaging effects of love, anger, pity, frustration, guilt, and, finally, fear, even as our marriage entered its last days.

～✖✑⌘

"Thief!"

"Whore!"

Most people would stay away from this sort of venom. I gave up trying to move anything out of the house beyond my clothing, personal possessions, and a small selection of my books. My encounters with Luddy had become so rude and upsetting that I believed it was easier to simply write off the rest of our shared household than to prolong these toxic encounters. I could eliminate his ability to withhold and set myself free. His punishments finally ceased to have their old power.

Some months later, I returned at his request, as we were settling the matter of our house. I agreed to take a couple of wedding gifts from the broken cabinet. I also took a crystal paperweight Luddy had given me years ago.

"At least you're taking something I gave you!" he muttered inexplicably.

I understood that he felt personally rejected by my renouncing of things that held value for him, and I started to rethink my decision. I reached for an additional item. When he began to curse again, I let it go.

260

I left behind a small garden table held up by a frog. He had given it to me impulsively when I'd asked for it a few years earlier, and there was a lot of symbolism for both of us there.

Luddy chased outside after my departing car, grasping the table and shouting, "I thought you wanted this!"

No one calls me a thief.

Why did I stay so long? And what finally made me leave?

These memories are my answer.

October 31, 2012, Jake's house

My departure from the house was accomplished in stages, with my sons' help and moral support. I went to live with Jake, who was readying his own house for sale. He would have space for me for a couple of months before the house would go on the market.

Luddy scolded Jake for helping me, but he and Simon had both decided to handle their parents in an honorable way and to stay out of the middle. Neither would listen to criticism. For young men in their thirties, they mustered a remarkable degree of evenhandedness.

I know they believed I would survive.

They were not so sure about Luddy.

I moved to Jake's house shortly before Superstorm Sandy roared up the coast to New Jersey, delivering devastation throughout the state and felling a tree in his neighborhood so the power went out. Jake was on the road most nights, so he escaped some of the worst of it. When it became too cold to stay in the house, I found a hotel room every couple of nights to relieve the desperation. I attended a conference to present programs I had become licensed to sell.

Luddy had suffered similarly in the storm, so Jake visited him a couple of times to check on him. The first time he found Luddy shivering under a blanket next to a fire he was feeding with Jake's old desk, which he'd broken into pieces for kindling. He refused to leave the house when his son offered to help him. His anger with me was still keeping him warm.

THE HOARDER'S WIFE

❧❧

My journal picks up in electronic form around this time, as I'd left the handwritten notebook in the kitchen when I moved out.

Our marriage ended in a silent movie. I gave up reading the placards and concentrated on scoring the plot, as if I were creating a piano roll for the music in our scenes together. As Nietzsche would have put it in his aphorisms: "The end of a melody is not its goal: but nonetheless, had the melody not reached its end it would not have reached its goal either. A parable."

April 1, 2016, evening, flying over Boston

Dave Brubeck improvised one of my favorite pieces of music—a radical rescoring of the song "Someday My Prince Will Come." Stripped of its elegant waltz dressing, he opens it with the bare, almost-ruined crashing chords that structure its brilliance. The result is jarring. He arranges several different iterations before the familiar Frank Churchill tune seeps into our ears, teasing us into a glorious waltz.

This piece was the lovely paradox I played over and over in the car when the busy workday gave way to my loneliness. While driving at night, I dissected my fantasy of the marriage. I wanted to build a better prince. He lived somewhere in the future, and if I could just travel far enough from our breakup, I would someday see the outline of a new life.

I ran away. But I listened. In those dissonant sounds, I re-crafted myself.

For four years following the divorce, I worked my way around the country, sharing communication tips, crying in my rental car when "Let Her Go" played on the radio. My lingering regret that I had failed Luddy left me with doubts about my own expertise, but the miles I covered began to put some distance between me and that counterproductive thinking. I finally released the hoard from my head.

My last piece of music, the *Clean House Concerto*, was actually a collection of the flotsam from my marriage. I felt it was simultaneously an attack on and a tribute to our life situation. Luddy, despite his own lifelong fascination with bonding, hadn't understood the duality, couldn't see the electrons flickering in and out, back and forth, trying to connect.

I never found out what set him off the morning after the projector fiasco—my song or his problem with the equipment coupled with his fear of failure. Nonetheless, after the fallout, I knew I was done with hanging on.

You cannot hoard the sound of music. Unlike light, sound cannot travel through empty space. Each tick away from the moment of a sound redefines it until the pleasing tone of a remembered arpeggio or the dissonance of a minor chord is no more than an audible shadow of the original—a fierce and fleeting silhouette, an encrypted snapshot that flickers like a candle, then goes out.

Luddy could turn out the lights, but his shadow was no match for the echo.

Sixth Movement: Finale

Allegro non molto. Allegro maestoso.

Chapter 29

"The Rest Is Noise"

Monday, April 6, 2016

"Gone! He's gone! Dead!"

Caller ID had taken some of the mystery out of the call I picked up on my cell shortly after I checked in at Newark Liberty Airport on my way to work in Washington, DC, that afternoon. It couldn't be good. I heard Simon's voice telling me the terrible news that Luddy had died, and that he had found him.

I turned around and ran back past Security and outside. I cut into the taxi line, shrieking, "My husband is dead! He took his own life! Please let me go first! I need to get to my family—"

I thought I might have to argue with people and was prepared for the battle, but a river of shocked faces stepped away from my partial truth, and the dispatcher grabbed my suitcase and handed me into the first car. I yelled "Thank you!" to the crowd, my face a perfect model for Munch as the car sped toward the Jersey Turnpike.

I called Simon from the road. He cried out the details of his father's suicide by drowning. The story broke my heart.

After I divorced Luddy, both sons had tried to take on the withering task of making sure he was all right. They coaxed him, pleaded with him, and laid down conditions for him, and he continued to evade the promises he tried to make. They faced the daunting task of trying to take care of their father while juggling marriage and young families.

A man found Luddy after he had fainted and was revived on a New York City street, waiting with him until Simon and Jake arrived. Simon made a plan to take Luddy to a doctor, hoping that he could be hospitalized for an evaluation—that some physical cause might compel him to get help. Luddy had lost so much weight that he was half his former size. He didn't seem to be eating despite evidence of shopping at the house—soup cans all over the kitchen floor, which was covered with slippery supermarket circulars. The house looked worse each time they picked him up to take him out to a restaurant, to ensure that he actually ate something. Both sons were considering an intervention.

Simon's plan sounded reasonable, but it had failed the Friday before, when Luddy could not bring himself to get dressed and go to the appointment. Luddy had pleaded for one more weekend, to spend time in his house with his things. He agreed to go on Monday if Simon could come back for him after noon. Afraid to negotiate and ruin it again, our son accepted his father's disingenuous deal.

Call it the morning of the unanswered phone call.

When I arrived at my former home, the cab driver expressed his condolences and apologized for listening in on my phone call. I might have been screaming at the beginning. There were police cars parked in front of the house, and some investigators were inside. It was raining. A soaking drizzle.

I left my suitcase at the edge of the driveway and hugged Simon as we cried. The coroner was on the way. The police couldn't let us go inside. Apologies were offered. New Jersey had rules for situations like this. Did we want to sit in their car? "We think he took his own life, but we have to ask you some questions . . ."

Finally, we moved back under the eaves of the garage.

Simon had already been talking with them for an hour by the time I got there. They wanted to know the last time I had been to the house. They explained that they had first suspected a crime had taken place because the house appeared to be ransacked. I explained the long-term hoarding problem. The divorce. Where I lived now. They had to rule us in or out as suspects, even though their instincts were leading them to the terrible, sad conclusion of suicide.

I saw that Simon's clothes were soaked through. It finally hit me that it was more than just rain. He was shivering, covered with water from his father's last moments. It was he who had bent over his childhood bathtub where he and Jake had played and splashed, searching for signs of life, calling 9-1-1, begging for help. Luddy had made sure to drown himself before help could arrive. Nothing more to do. He was a morbid medical mystery now.

The coroner told us that most people who try to drown themselves do not succeed, and the hunt for drugs in his system began. In the end, they determined he'd made some inconsequential cuts on his hands to aid the process, but no traces of substances were found.

We talked about how stubborn Luddy could be once he'd made a decision. The police took his computer and a note he'd left. They thought perhaps they might find a clue as to how he had done it. The coroner asked to run some extra tests. Hoping to finally understand this man and looking for an explanation for his behavior, his son said, "Yes."

Nothing more was found. The police tape would remain loosely fastened until we could go in again, but they would subdue the barriers to prevent the house from being disturbed by others. Apologies, again. But death by one's own hand was still a crime in New Jersey.

Chapter 30

Simon's Song: "Marche Funèbre"

April 9, 2016, day after the funeral, at my home

The children have returned to their own homes. The sounds of Chopin's "Funeral March" have finally left our ears.

Word of the funeral had spread among the small group of friends, relatives, and colleagues who remained attached to us. Most people were kind to me. I was there for my children. The funeral director advised us against taking one last look because the autopsy had been severe. No one disagreed.

In the gathering room before the service, Luddy's sister, Lena, made the rounds of all the mourners. As usual, she took command of the room like a "modern major general," even if no one felt obliged to follow her leadership. In a stage whisper, Lena forbade everyone from explaining how Luddy had died so their mother, Lorelai, would not learn the truth.

When Lorelai stepped out of the room for some air, Lena made it her business to say to me: "This is your fault—because you left him." Although this cut me to the quick, I allowed her this interpretation without saying a word. While I knew it contained a partial truth, I also knew that if I had stayed with Luddy, it might have been two of us being buried yesterday.

Bumped rudely out of the first row by Lena, Lorelai, and Joel, who sat with Simon and Jake, Angelica and Gia both took my hands as we sat in the second row of the chapel. The Bergs took suggestions from no one.

From her first gathering words, Rabbi Jada Goldsmith washed away the unkindness of our situation. She delivered a gentle eulogy based on the information we gave her, the stories we could tell, and she helped us find the strength to move through the customary motions of the day. A murmur of satisfaction was heard in the chapel when Jada described, as promised, the Japanese custom of ceramics repair, *kintsugi*, and encouraged us all to repair the earth, *tikkun olam*, to honor the memory of Ludwig Berg, ceramist and metallurgist, father, and friend.

But not for me. The Gershwins' lyrics enveloped my heart.

Last, it was Simon's turn to speak. I'm sure he was conflicted over his aunt's prohibition against revealing the true circumstances of Luddy's death, opposing his father's usual insistence on clarity and truth. I am proud of how my son reconciled his need to inform the mourners about his father without hurting his grandmother. I can't remember the exact words he used to expose the wounding gray area, but he found a way when he said something like this:

"One of the things I remember about my father was his strength. There used to be this watermelon competition at the faculty pool. He would always win because he could hold his breath longer than anyone we knew. I will always picture my dad rising from the water with a melon over his head, roaring, 'I won! I won!'"

This story broke the tension in the room as people could laugh about their various memories of Luddy's different strengths, the good and the difficult. Simon did not need to say more to close the loop for those of us who knew how Luddy had died. He chose to focus on a celebration of Luddy's positive powers—a time when Luddy was able to conquer the power of water. In so doing, Simon found the golden repair.

Because we had always cheered his underwater exploits, those of us who knew what happened on his last day understood we could also smile through the tears of our mourning. Well played.

Coda

Pastoral. Elegy.

March 31, 2018, evening, in the garden

Passover. This morning I went with my two sons, their wives, and my grandchildren to plant a tree in a garden at the university. Luddy would have liked the gesture. Our pain had been so great that it took us a long time to come up with a fitting memorial.

The tree is located across the river and not far from our former family home. We each turned a symbolic shovel of dirt over the roots in our quest for closure, recognizing that our grief might have no end. I brought the rocks and seedpod we had taken from the house the last time we were all there together. Jake placed the blue one; Simon, the red one. The seeds came from me.

We stood there for a while, talking about Luddy and, finally, reading the Kaddish with phonetics, repeating our rarely used Hebrew names: *Shimon ben Lotan, Yaqob ben Lotan*, and *Chaniel bat Shmuel*—Simon, son of Ludwig; Jacob, son of Ludwig; Grace, daughter of Steven.

We came from somewhere.

We hummed "Sunrise, Sunset," Sheldon Harnick's anthem of American Jewry. Then we walked around the garden with the children, awkwardly at first, like the puppets in my film. I could hear Alfred Hitchcock's familiar theme song, Gounod's "Funeral March of a Marionette," in my head.

Tacitly, we agreed not to sink into sadness. The shroud of pain was beginning to slip from our shoulders, to mix with the memories we cherished as Emma and Gabe told funny stories of their Grandpa Luddy to little Dante, Jake and Gia's son.

When Emma could no longer contain herself, she began to sing "Can't Stop the Feeling," and we all followed her, dancing conga-style, hands pulled up in the air by invisible strings.

❧

Luddy's ashes remain in my spare bedroom because no one is ready to let them go to a permanent place. The old house has been leveled by someone who built a bigger one on the site. Each of us drives by as often as we can bear, to let a thought of how we loved fly off in the wind.

Perhaps that thought lights on a stone or a speck of dust that might have been part of our house in the time before. One remembrance at a time is all we can stand.

❧

Simon still asks me occasionally if I can remember anything good from our life together as a family. Luddy and I must have been happy, at least in the early years? He is searching for ordinary and normal. I'm seeking that same reassurance about my own parents too, so I understand.

To help him, I scroll through my memories and find some that make me smile—how we all loved vacations at Disney World, how we cheered for each other at sports competitions, academic honors, trips to the zoo, museums—the things families do. They are not unique to us, but they're the ordinary events that all families remember. At least we have those.

I think he wants to know if it was all just a fraud, and he's afraid to ask.

For a long time, I was so angry with Luddy that I would have agreed with this assessment. Something was always wrong, but in the beginning, there was also a healthy dose of right.

I understand my story better now.

Luddy was probably not the right kind of husband for me, but I kept on waiting for my dream to come true. I, too, maintained a hoard. Mine consisted of emotions unexpressed—a stubborn refusal to accept what was right in front of me. I kept faith with a discredited fairy tale and scars that never healed. The things I could not release were always looping and knotting, constant strands like accidentals canceled in the wrong damned key.

I cherished my husband, and I felt for him, until he stopped feeling for me.

I would have to move on while I still had my heart.

It's hard to describe now, but way back in my own personal cache of memories, I know there's an image from when we desired each other. I have sorted through most of the jagged, angry ones to find this scene.

I see our two hungry-for-each-other faces rippling in the smoky mirrored tiles on the bedroom ceiling of his apartment. I remember how his eyes would overflow with love and desire as we looked up at each other. He liked to watch how I let go.

But the prince departs Elsa in Wagner's *Lohengrin*. "In fernem land . . . far and away," mourns the aria.

In our first days, I felt pure, never dirty. I gave Luddy nearly everything of mine to keep, and he obliged. What was "ours" became no longer mine. When his conflicted feelings about his life became too painful and deep, what he'd kept of me no longer filled his void.

We all try to answer the question: "Do you have what you want, or do you want what you have?" Even if Luddy wasn't able to answer this for himself, he gave me a beautiful gift when he provided me with *my* answer.

Although I didn't understand it at the time, I now want what I have.

Caesura.

Improvisation. Freedom. Structure.

Ceteris silentium est. All the rest is silence.

Come clean. So clean.

Acknowledgments

As I complete the work on this book, it's July, about three years after I began in earnest, and I'm allowing myself to enjoy happy music and feel sincere gratitude to the many people who listened to me and helped me on this journey, some of whom are listed here.

I offer my heartfelt thanks to the following people for making this book a reality:

First, to David LeGere, of Woodhall Press, for expressing his faith in my book and my decisions about the writing and for publishing *The Hoarder's Wife*; and to David's colleagues, Melissa Hayes, for her excellent and empathetic developmental editing to bring this book together, and to Paulette Baker, also of Woodhall, for bringing her sensitive, sharp eyes to the final draft. Any errors that escaped them belong to me;

To the committed folks at When Words Count in Vermont, who want to create a better way for authors to survive the publishing process: founder, Steve Eisner; and Amber Griffith and Trish Lewis, who nurture and cheer on all writers in countless ways, always above and beyond the call.

To my Pitch Week Masters, Steve Rohr, Marilyn Atlas, and Dede Cummings, who crafted a better compass for me by asking the tough questions; to Sharyn Skeeter for her strategic guidance; to Charles Johnson for so many gracious words of encouragement; to Peggy Moran, my first editor for this book; and to Asha Hossain for her intuitive, inspired cover design, which contributed so much to my own understanding of this narrative;

To Scott Barhold, my thanks for a special consultation on mentalist effects and for being a great colleague, always.

I would have given up many times were it not for the love and support of WWC colleagues, including Barbara Newman and pitch week gangs of writers, who got up early and stayed up late in solidarity, including Wanda Ambroziak, Elise Von Holten, Roselyn Obrien Markowitz, Leah Moore, Jane Hardin, Micah Brown, and Lauren Sevier; and to Nancie Laird Young, whom I met later, but whose candor about the process kept me engaged and asking questions. Look for their names on the Internet—many books will bear their names in the coming years. It's wonderful to have a hive mind.

I especially thank musician and songstress Maritri Garrett for making the pandemic disappear from my head for one beautiful hour each weekday evening during my year of rewriting.

I thank my friends and beta readers Erin Woodward, Lynn Thiesmeyer, Philip Vassallo, Audrey Fisch, Donna Walker-Nixon, Alexa Kelly, Lezley Steele, Brian Richardson, Tucker Dyer, and Kelvin Ortega, who have cheerfully, thoughtfully, and for many years done the hard work of reading, listening, acting, lighting, and filming through so many iterations of my stories.

To Corey Rabin and Stephanie Furgang, I offer my heartfelt thanks for their clarity and supportive legal advice.

I remain grateful to Rabbi Eric Eisenkramer, who gave my family a lifeline when we were caught in the undertow.

Although they cannot hear me, I offer my gratitude to Marcie, Kathryn, Bea, and Jackie, four friends who passed on before the novel was born but asked me regularly: "Why don't you write a book?" I hope you know somehow that I have, and I'm grateful for your nudging.

To my sister in life, Wendi, and her parents, Barbara and Mitty, who stepped up for me when mine were gone: your kindness was epic and appreciated;

Frank Rubin: I thank you for coming along "Just in Time;"

To my children, their spouses, and my grandhildren, who have supported my writing even when they had to take a back seat to my projects; thank you for listening.

About the Author

Deborah Greenhut earned her B.A. in English from Middlebury College then a PhD from Rutgers University. Her poems and cultural reviews have appeared in print and online at www.oobr.com, medium. com, and Red Booth Review. Her way-off Broadway production of "Difficult Subjects," was selected for the Best Plays of the Strawberry Festival, Volume 2. In 2017, she received the Princemere Poetry Prize. *The Hoarder's Wife* is her debut novel. Deborah lives in New Jersey.